Introduction to Computer Science
WITH ANDROID™

-{ THE LEARNING-BY-DOING SERIES }-

First Edition

Hamzeh Roumani

Department of Electrical Engineering and Computer Science
York University, Toronto, Ontario, Canada

Contents at a Glance

Table of Contents

CHAPTER 1	THE LANDSCAPE	LEARNING

CHAPTER 2	DECLARE, SET, GO!	DOING

CHAPTER 2	DECLARE, SET, GO!	LEARNING

CHAPTER 3	A SYMPHONY OF APIs	DOING

CHAPTER 3	A SYMPHONY OF APIs	LEARNING

CHAPTER 5	COLLECTIONS	LEARNING

APPENDIX A	OPERATORS

APPENDIX B	REGULAR EXPRESSIONS

APPENDIX C	CHARACTER CODES

APPENDIX D   THE I2C API

PREFACE

In addition to self-learning, this book can be used for a first-year computing course themed around object-oriented programming, Java, and Android. No prior exposure to any of these topics is assumed.

What makes this book different is that it:

1. **Uses Android to teach Computer Science.**
   As such, while it does teach you how to write maintainable and scalable Java programs and Android apps, its focus is not on the technologies. It uses them as a catalyst to elicit fundamental computing concepts, ones that will endure long after the platform and the programming language fall out of fashion.

2. **Adopts Experiential Learning throughout.**
   All chapters come in pairs: a *Doing* part that focuses on building an app, and a *Learning* part that exposes the underlying concepts. This choreography—a concrete experience followed by just-in-time conceptualization with reflection in between—lies at the heart of experiential pedagogy.

The book has *six* chapters, and since each has a Doing and a Learning part, there are *twelve* parts in total. The chapters are numbered **0** to **5** to stress the fact that indexing in Computing starts at **0** rather than 1. The Doing/Learning parts are distinguished by a **D/L** prefix, so D3 is the Doing part of Chapter 3.

The exercises at the end of the Doing part ask the student to refactor the app or augment it with new features. The exercises at the end of the Learning part involve the implementation of methods (not related to the app) in a self-contained setting.

It is recommended that two weeks be spent per chapter. This allows the student to build the Doing app (on their own or with minimal assistance), reflect, and start abstracting (guided by the Learning part). Biweekly assessment patterned after the exercises is also recommended.

The website of this book has the URL shown below. It contains the book's errata and links to relevant resources and APIs. In particular, it has a link that allows you to download the **i2c** library associated with this book.

> `http://book.roumani.ca/`

ACKNOWLEDGMENT

I would like to thank my wife *Souad* for reviewing the manuscript and building the apps. She has provided insightful critique and refreshing suggestions, including the juxtaposition of the doing/learning parts.

Hamzeh Roumani,
Toronto, Ontario, Canada
June 2018

CHAPTER 0 – DOING

Preliminaries

D0.1 – THE TOOLBOX

D0.1.a – The IDE

Android Studio is the official Integrated Development Environment (IDE) for the Android platform. It includes all the tools needed to create, edit, build, test, and deploy Android apps. You will therefore need to install it on your development machine before attempting any of the projects in the "Doing" parts of this book.

The IDE is available on all the major platforms and can be download for free from:

    https://developer.android.com/studio/

This single download has all the needed components, including Java, so no other download is needed. Follow the installation process and accept all the defaults.

There are a multitude of tools bundled within this IDE. In particular:

- **Java Tools**
  To develop the Java components of the app.

- **User Interface Tools**
  To develop the user interface components of the app.

- **Build Tools**
  To translate Java code to Dalvik (the code that Android devices can execute) and then to package all components and resources in one **APK** (Android Package).

You will learn how to use the IDE in the remainder of this chapter.

D0.1.b – The Device

The IDE has tools that test each and every component of your app. For example, there are tools that check your Java code as you type, and ones that verify your user interface as you build it. But even though each component is tested thoroughly on its own, you still need to ensure that the components work together when combined into one app. This type of integration testing is done by **deploying** the app on an Android device.

App deployment can be done on a real device or a virtual device. In the former, you connect the device to the computer and transfer the APK to it (a process known as **sideloading**). In the latter, you use the **AVD** (Android Virtual Device) tool bundled in the IDE to select any emulating device you want and run your app on it.

D0.2 – A Quick Tour of the IDE

D0.2.a – Creating a Project

Follow these steps in order to create your very first project:

1. Launch Android Studio.
2. Start a new project.
3. Name the new project *Zero* and accept the other defaults then click Next.
4. Accept the Phone/Tablet platform and the default minimum SDK then click Next.
5. Select the "Empty Activity" option then click Next.
6. Name the activity *ZeroActivity* and the layout *zero_layout*. Keep the default checkbox.
7. Click Finish.

When Studio completes its project setup, it displays its main screen.

D0.2.b – The Main Screen

Spend some time to become comfortable with the content of this screen. Yes, it can be overwhelming at first but by focusing only on a few aspects, you will gradually overcome the initial jolt. These aspects are highlighted in the remainder of this section.

The screen contains two key panes:

1. The **Project Pane** on the left, and
2. The bigger **Editor Pane** on the right.

Note that the Project tab (on the left margin of the project pane) is selected by default. If you accidently de-selected it or if you find the project pane empty, simply click on the Project tab.

The project pane shows the components of your project and it does so in a number of views. By default, the **Android view** is selected (as shown in a drop-down tab that appears just above the project pane). In this view, the components appear in a tree outline that you can expand or collapse by clicking the arrow of each component. Two aspects in this view are key:

- The subtree under **app**, **java** contains three so-called **packages**. The first package contains our activity, *ZeroActivity*. Verify this.

- The subtree under **app**, **res** contains several so-called **resources**. One of the resources is called **layout** and in it, you should find our layout, *zero_layout*, with an *xml* extension added to its name. Verify this.

In addition to the Android view, the project components can be viewed via the **Project view**. Drop down the list of views (the tab above the project pane) and select Project. The resulting tree outline contains two aspects that are of concern to us:

- The subtree under **Zero**, **app**, **src**, **main**, **java** contains the java package that holds our *ZeroActivity*. Verify this.

- The subtree under **Zero**, **app**, **src**, **main**, **res**, **layout** contains our *zero_layout.xml* layout. Verify this.

Hence, you can reach these two key components of our project via either view. We will find later that the Android view (the default) is best suited for development work while the Project view is best suited for file-based operations, such as backup and restore, because it mirrors the directory structure in which the component files are stored on disk.

The Editor Pane to the right of the Project Pane is where we enter our code and do our user interface design. Note that our activity and layout names appear *in tabs* above the pane. Click the two tabs and verify.

D0.2.c – User Interface Tools

Click on the *zero_layout.xml* tab of the editor pane to bring the design editor to the front. By default, the editor shows two design surfaces: *Design* and *Blueprint* but we only need the former. Hence, the first configuration to be made is to select the design-only surface using the toolbar above the design editor as shown in Fig. D0.1 (click the box marked ❶ and select *Design*).

Figure D0.1 Configuring the design editor: ❶ choose the design surface, ❷ choose the device orientation.

The design surface shows the app as it will appear on the device. You can pick the device to be used (replacing *Nexus 4* on the toolbar of Fig. D0.1 with another device) but there is no need to change the default. More importantly, the box marked ❷ in Fig. D0.1 enables you to change the device **orientation** from *Portrait* to *Landscape*. Try it out. This feature is extremely useful as it allows us to verify the correctness of our design. Good user interface design should tolerate orientation changes and this button helps us test this.

The *user interface* (UI) of an app involves a number of widgets that allow the app and its user to communicate with each other. The three most-used widgets are:

- **Label**
  This is a box in which the app can display text for the user to see. The user cannot write into this box (i.e. it cannot receive the focus). In Android lingo, it is known as a **TextView** because this is the name of its Java class.

- **Textbox**
  This is a box in which the user can type text in; i.e. make an input. In Android lingo, it is known as an **EditText** because this is the name of its Java class.

- **Button**
  This is a button that the user can tap in order to ask the app to perform some action. The button has a *caption* written on it to let the user know the action it performs. In Android lingo, it is known as a **Button** because this is the name of its Java class.

Each widget has a unique **id** that identifies it and a large number of **attributes** (aka properties) that you can control during the design and programmatically while the app is running. One of these attributes is called **text** and, for a label, it holds the message displayed in it; for a textbox, it holds the text entered by the user; and for a button, it holds its caption.

The Android library comes with a large number of ready-made widgets that allow you to create almost any required UI. These widgets appear in the **Palette** window that appears to the left of the design editor. Click *All* in the palette window to see all the available widgets. Note that the EditText widget (i.e. the textbox) is listed under the name **Plain Text**, so whenever you are asked to insert a textbox in this book, pick the Plain Text from the palette.

Our Zero app comes with a default label with "*Hello World*" as its text. Click on it to see its attributes displayed in the **attributes pane** that appears to the right of the design editor. The pane lists the most-often used attributes such as the id, layout, text, and text format (font, colour, style, etc.). You would normally set the attributes specified in the requirement document and leave the rest at their default values.

Note that the displayed attributes are only a subset of the widget's attributes. To see the remaining ones, click on the box with two arrows (see Fig. D0.2) in the toolbar above the attributes window. Every time you click this box, it toggles the display between a full and a partial list of attributes.

Figure D0.2

We now turn our attention to how widgets are laid out relative to each other and relative to the borders of the device. This task is rather challenging because we don't know the size of the device on which our app will be deployed or how the user will hold it.

Note that the default *Hello World* label appears in the centre of the screen. Flip the orientation to landscape (as was explained in Fig. D0.1) and note that it is still in the centre. You can also change the emulated device from Nexus 4 to a watch and the label will remain in the centre.

The placement of widgets should not be done via absolute dimensions but rather through **layout managers** that reposition the widgets dynamically (i.e. when the app is running) based on device size and orientation.

Android comes with several layout managers such as:

- **ConstraintLayout** which is explained below.
- **LinearLayout** which arranges the widgets vertically or horizontally.
- **RelativeLayout** which arranges the widgets relative to each other.
- **Grid** and **Table** layouts which place widgets in rows and columns.

The **constraint layout** is the default—the IDE auto-selects it when an activity is created. We will use this layout for all the apps of this textbook because it is very versatile. One of its key advantages is that it can accommodate most UI requirements with a *flat* hierarchy; i.e. all widgets would reside inside it without having to put a layout inside another layout.

In order to familiarize ourselves with the key features of the ConstraintLayout, let us build the UI shown in Fig. D0.3. This UI has the following features:

- The first row has two buttons, with captions 0 and 1, residing in the upper-left and upper-right corners of the screen.

- The second row has a button with caption 2 centered horizontally in the screen.

- The third row has two buttons, with captions 3 and 4, with equal distances between them and the screen edges.

- The fourth row has two buttons, with captions 5 and 6, stretched across the screen.

- Finally, there are two buttons, with captions 7 and 8, residing in the lower-left and lower-right corners of the screen.

Note that adding a button to the design surface is easy: you simply drag the button widget from the palette to the device and then set its *text* attribute (in the attributes pane) based on the required caption. Laying out the button to match Fig. D0.3, however, is not as easy. If you do it manually, by visually placing the button where it belongs, it may look fine at first, but once you switch the orientation to landscape, you will immediately realize that it is not. Instead, we should let the constraint layout place the buttons as explained below.

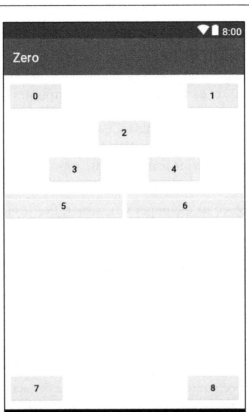

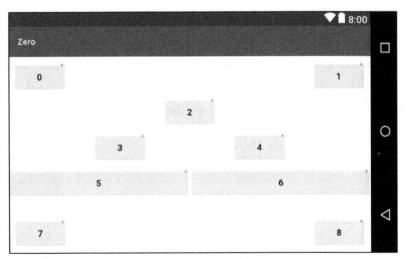

Figure D0.3 UI of the Zero app in portrait (top) and landscape (bottom).

Follow these steps:

1. Delete the Hello World label which was added by default.
2. Drag a button from the palette and place it somewhere in the middle of the screen.
3. Click the button and set its text attribute in the attributes pane.
4. Note that the button has **circular constraint handles** on each side.
5. Click and hold the constraint handle on the left side and drag it to the left edge of the screen. This forces the button to hug the left edge (in any orientation).
6. Click and hold the constraint handle on the top side and drag it to the top edge of the screen. This forces the button to hug the upper edge (in any orientation).

The 0-button is now anchored to the upper left corner. Perform similar steps to anchor the 1-button to the upper right corner.

7. Drag another button to the middle for the 2-button.
8. Click and hold the constraint handle on the top side and drag it to the bottom handle of the 0-button. This forces the button to be under the first row.
9. Click and hold the constraint handle on the left side and drag it to the left edge of the screen. This forces the button to hug the left edge. Then, click and hold the constraint handle on the right side and drag it to the right edge of the screen.

The 2-button has to satisfy two horizontal constraints, one pulling it to the left edge of the screen and one to the right edge, so it centres itself across the screen.

10. Drag two more button widgets to create the 3 and 4 button.
11. Select both buttons (use shift-click) and right-click the selection. Choose **Chain** and then *Create Horizontal Chain*.

The 3 and 4 buttons are now properly laid out horizontally. To anchor them vertically, simply drag the top handle of each and drag it to the bottom handle of the 2-button.

12. For the 5 and 6 buttons, do the same thing (i.e. chain them) but change their **layout_width** attributes from **wrap_content** to **match_constraint**.

Finally, add the 7 and 8 buttons and constrain them to the bottom left and right corners. Verify your design (ideally after every placement) by switching the device orientation. The constraints of the top four rows are shown in Fig. D0.4.

It should be noted that we have covered only a small subset of the capabilities of this layout manager. In particular, the attributes pane allows you to control the margins and the horizontal bias of every widget.

As you add widgets, the IDE keeps track of their types and id's and depicts these in a pane known as the **component tree**. This is shown in Fig. D0.5 for our app.

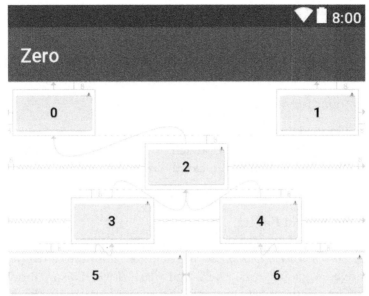

Figure D0.4 The top components of the Zero app with constraints shown.

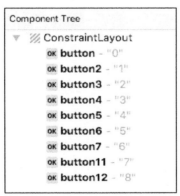

Figure D0.5 The component tree of the Zero app.

D0.2.d – Saving Your Work

Whenever you work on a project, it is important that you save your work frequently so that it can be recovered should your development environment become unusable (perhaps due to a software bug or a hardware malfunction).

There are several options for saving your work:

- **Use a Version Control System**
  This is by far the most professional approach. A system such as *git* allows you not only to save your work both locally and to the cloud, but also to keep track of changes made by you or by others in your team. Moreover, it integrates seamlessly with our IDE.

- **Zip and Save the Project Folder**
  This quick-and-dirty method uses the operating system's zip utility to compress the project folder (e.g. *AndroidStudioProjects/Zero* for our Zero app) into a file (e.g. *Zero.zip*) which can then be moved to cloud storage or a USB flash drive. This method has a high overhead as it is not automatic and the zipped file is rather large (~30MB). Moreover, it has a dependency on the particular version of the IDE.

- **Save Only Your Work**
  For most projects, your work is captured in very few files, typically one XML file and a couple of Java files. You can find these files in these folders:

  AndroidStudioProjects/[app]/app/src/main/java/[package]

  AndroidStudioProjects/[app]/app/src/main/res/layout

  where [app] is your app name (e.g. *Zero*). These *text* files are tiny (~kilobytes) and can easily be saved; in fact, you can simply copy-and-paste their contents directly from the editor. Most beginners like this method because it allows them to actually see and study the copied files, and easily reuse them in future projects.

D0.3 – EXERCISES

1. Modify the layout of the *Zero* app so that Button 3 becomes as in Fig. D0.6 below.

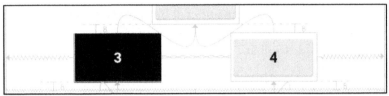

Figure D0.6 The modified look of Button 3 in the Zero app.

As you can see, the button's background has become black and its caption's colour has become white.
Hint: Click on the three-dot ellipsis to the right of the attribute to access the available colours.

2. Add a ninth button to the Zero app with layout and caption as shown in Fig. D0.7. Its location must be such that:

    • It divides the screen horizontally by three quarters to one (75% of the screen width to its left and 25% to its right).

    • It divides the distance between the fourth row (i.e. Buttons 5 and 6) and the bottom edge of the screen by one quarter to three; i.e. 25% of that distance above it and 75% below it.

    Verify your design by changing the orientation of the emulated device from portrait to landscape and by changing the device type.

    Hint:
    The attribute window shows an outline of the button widget above the partial attribute list. That outline has two so-called bias slider that allow you to adjust the left-right and top-bottom ratios. The default is 50-50 but you slide the bias to any desired percentage.

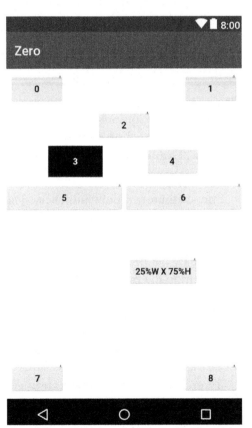

Figure D0.7 The Zero app with an added button.

3. We viewed our design on the screen but have not yet deployed our *Zero* app on a device. Let us do that now. Click the *Run* menu of the IDE and select Run… and then app. To run on an emulator, pick any emulator you like (or create a new virtual device). After a delay, the emulated device should appear in a window of its own (separate from the IDE). It will boot up like a real device and your app will be downloaded on it (i.e. it will be stored in its *Downloads* folder). The app will be launched automatically and you will be able to interact with the app using your mouse. You can even rotate the device or trigger its sensors by using its side toolbar.

4. We will now deploy the *Zero* app on a *real* device rather than an emulated one. You will need an actual Android device for this. By default, Android allows only signed apps to be installed on the device (for security reasons) so you need to change the settings of your device to allow our *unsigned* app to be installed. Once done, connect your device to your computer's USB port and re-run the app. The IDE will now ask you to select the device to run the app on and it should show the emulated device and the real device just connected. Select the real device. After a brief delay, the app will be side-loaded and it will appear on your device screen.

❖ ❖ ❖ ❖

5. Change the captions of the eight buttons of the Zero app from digits to names of digits; i.e. ZERO instead of 0, ONE instead of 1, and so on. But rather than hard-coding the names, we will learn a more professional, best-practice approach.

    To change the text attribute of Button 0, click the ellipsis to the right of the attribute in the attribute window and click *Add new resources* in the upper right corner of the window and then add a *New string Value*. Enter s0 as the *Resource name* and ZERO as its *value*. Click ok and note that the text attribute of this button has become: **@string/s0**.

    Repeat this process for the remaining buttons to make the final layout is in Fig. D0.8 (ignoring the button added in Exercise 2).

    Referring to the values ZERO, ONE, … EIGHT via names (such as s0, s1, … s8) creates a level of indirection between the attribute and its value. For example, the text attribute of Button 5 is now @string/s5 rather than a fixed value. The advantage of this indirection is that it makes our app scalable and easier to maintain. A case in point is shown in Exercise 6 where the indirection enables the app to become sensitive to the device locale thereby changing the caption from FIVE to CINQ to خمسة automatically depending on the device's language.

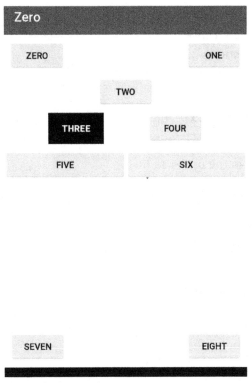

Figure D0.8 Digits replaced with digit names.

As you will discover, indirection is a recurring theme in Computer Science. By separating the concerns and creating intermediate abstraction levels, we can confront complexity and architect robust and scalable solutions.

Note: The name-value pairs that you have just created are now recorded in `strings.xml` *(a file that resides in app/res/values in the Project Pane) as shown below. In fact, you could have created these resources yourself by editing the file directly. Go ahead and double click this file to see it.*

```
<resources>
    <string name="app_name">Zero</string>
    <string name="s0">ZERO</string>
    <string name="s1">ONE</string>
    <string name="s2">TWO</string>
    ...
    <string name="s7">SEVEN</string>
    <string name="s8">EIGHT</string>
</resources>
```

6. Let us make our Zero app English/French bilingual by making the captions locale sensitive; i.e. they automatically switch language based on the language of the device the app is running on. Follow these steps:

- Double-click the `strings.xml` file that was built in the previous exercise.

- Click on *Open editor* in the upper right.

- Click the globe in the upper left and select French (Canada).

- For each of our eight resources, click the English name and then enter its corresponding French translation in the bottom. You can see the translations in Fig. D0.9.

To test our work, go back to the layout tab (or double-click zero_layout if the tab is closed). The toolbar above the device has a **globe** that allows you to select the language. Switch to French and observe.

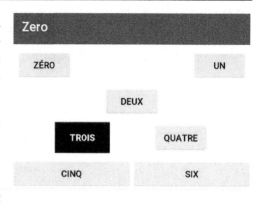

Figure D0.9 The Zero app in a French locale.

Notes:

- *To test your work on an emulator, run the app as usual and when the emulator window boots up, go to the emulated device settings and change the default language to French. You may have to add the language if it is not already present.*

- *Similarly, you can test your work on a real device by deploying the app on it and then changing its default language.*

- *Go back to the resource editor and click the globe again. Select a new language that you know and enter the translations. Verify that your app is now tri-lingual.*

- *The translations that you have entered get stored in a file that is also named* `strings.xml` *and you can find it also under* app/res/values *in the Project Pane. On disk, it resides under res in a folder parallel to values named* `values-fr-rCA`.

- *As before, you could have created the translations by editing this file directly. In general, anything that the IDE does can also be done manually by creating files.*

7. In Exercise 1 you were asked to change a couple of attributes for one of the buttons. In this exercise, you are asked to make the same change to *all eight* buttons, but rather than doing so one button at a time, you need to style all buttons in one shot. Specifically:

- Double click the `styles.xml` file under app/res/values.

- The file already contains a default style. Add a new style named "i2c" by appending the file (but before the closing </resoueces> tag) with the following:

```
<style name="i2c">

    <item name="android:textColor">#ff0000</item>

    <item name="android:background">#0000ff</item>

</style>
```

- This style sets the text colour to #ff0000. This hex number specifies the red-green-blue components of the colour, with each component's intensity ranging between 00 and ff. Hence, the text colour is set to maximum red, no green, and no blue.

- The style also sets the background colour to #0000ff or blue.

- Change the style of all eight buttons to this new custom style. For each button, click it and type i2c in its `style` attribute in the attribute window.

Did all buttons change as expected? If so, modify the i2c style so that the background colour becomes black and the text colour becomes white. Again, you should see the change immediately taking effect in the layout tab.

Finally, elaborate on the following statements by arguing for or against them:

- This styling methodology introduces a level of indirection between a widget and its attributes.

- This styling methodology makes our app easier to maintain.

- This styling methodology enables us to give our app a consistent look and feel.

- This styling methodology separates presentation from the formatting.

- If you are familiar with *html* (hyper-text markup language) and *css* (cascading style sheets), then compare and contrast this styling methodology with css.

8. In Exercise 7, we created a custom style for all our buttons. In this exercise, we create a second style as follows:

   • Double click the styles.xml file under app/res/values.

   • Add a new style named "i2c.big" after the first and before the closing </resoueces> tag as follows:

```
<style name="i2c.big">

    <item name="android:textSize">20sp</item>

</style>
```

   • The name of the new style is prefixed (with a dot separator) by the name of the first style. This means the new style inherits all the items in the first style but it can add or override some items.

   • ~~The new style adds an item relating to the size of the text font. It sets it to 20sp.~~

   • The unit **sp** (scalable pixel) allows device independence because it is converted to actual screen pixels based on the resolution of the device. It is similar to **dp** (which is used for widget size and layout) but is intended specifically for font size.

   • Change the style of some of the buttons (e.g. the even ones) to the new custom style.

   Did the captions change as expected? If so, modify the i2c.big style so that it overrides the background colour so it becomes different from the one set in the parent i2c style.

CHAPTER 0 – LEARNING

Preliminaries

L0.1 – COMPUTER SCIENCE

L0.1.a – A Broad Definition

As a relatively young discipline, Computer Science (CS) does not have a formal, universally accepted definition. And given its ubiquitous nature, you will likely get a different definition depending on the research area of the person you ask. The following is the author's take on the subject. Drawing on the definitions of more mature sciences:

- *Physics is about matter and forces and it studies their interaction.*
- *Biology is about living things and it studies their evolution.*

we posit:

- *Computer Science is about information and it studies its transformation.*

As a simple example, when you store a piece of information, such as a number or a name, in your phone, the CS in the phone must transform the sequence of key presses that you make to a form that can be represented in memory. Sending a text message, compressing a picture, encrypting a file, and performing a computation are all examples of CS transformations.

A central problem in CS is to transform information from one form to another. For some problems, such a transformation does not exist (the problem is called *undecidable*) or it does exist but it is not efficient (the problem is *intractable*). For others, a process can be found to efficiently carry out the desired transformation. The process is known as the *algorithm* and it, together with a description of the information being transformed, is known as the *program*.

It should be noted that a profound difference exists between transformations studied in all natural sciences (the division of a living cell, the melting of ice, or the fission of a uranium nucleus) and those studied in CS. The formers are governed by the laws of nature, so they cannot be changed, whereas the latter can be changed at will—after all, it is us who write the programs that perform the transformations. This difference is key to the pervasiveness of CS and the proliferation of its applications in disparate areas.

Another difference is that natural sciences describe transformations using mathematics (such as formulae, differential equations, or matrices) whereas CS describes them via a step-by-step algorithm. And although the two formalisms are related at a deeper level, the CS description promotes *process-based* thinking which is a hallmark of CS.

L0.1.b – Programming

We found that a program consists of a description of information (such as two integers of a given range) and an algorithm to transform the information (such as finding their sum). The task of *programming* thus involves finding a data structure to represent the information and devising an algorithm to carry out the transformation.

But even after the program is designed, we still need to cast it in a form that can be executed by a computer, and this is no small feat because computers can only execute a very small set of operations. These operations, collectively known as the elements of *machine language*, are so primitive that it would be extremely protracted and unwieldy to use them directly to write programs. CS confronts this challenge through a sequence of intermediate translators that allow us to write programs in a high-level language. For example, when you write a program in *Java*, the first layer of translators will turn your program to an equivalent one written in a lower-level language known as *bytecode*. Next, the second layer of translators, known as *just-in-time compilers*, will translate bytecode into machine language plus a few *system calls*. Next, a third translation layer within the operating system (the *linker*) replaces the system calls with machine code, so the program would finally be expressed in the language of the machine.

Using intermediate layers like this is a recurring theme in CS, and although it pops up under different names such as indirection, abstraction, and separation of concerns, the essence of it is always the same. We will encounter this theme repeatedly in this book so it is important that you take some time to think it through and be comfortable with how it works. To that end, here is a second example: to make something bold in HTML, you would write:

```
<b>some text</b>
```

The <b> tag is not a machine language instruction, so what happens here is that the browser will replace it with several instructions to be sent to the rendering engine, which in turn, will replace them with other instructions that will ultimately be replaced with machine language.

There are many *general-purpose* high-level programming languages in use today (C, C++, Java, Python, JavaScript to mention a few) and each has its advantages and disadvantages. (There is no best or worst language but there are bad and good programmers!). In addition, there are many *special-purpose* languages that are suited for specific applications or environments, such as HTML, XML, CSS, SQL, and MATLAB to mention a few.

We will be using **Java** in this textbook to write Android apps and **XML** to represent the user interface and the various resources of our apps.

L0.2 – A BRIEF ENCOUNTER WITH JAVA

L0.2.a – Creating a Class

The smallest executable building block in Java is the **class**. To get acquainted with classes, let us add a class named *Hello* to Project *Zero* that we created in Section D0.2.a.

Follow these steps:

1. Right-click the first package under app/java in the Project Pane.

2. Select *New* and then *Java Class*.

3. Enter Hello for the class name.

The Project Pane should now show a new class in this package (in addition to the already present class named *ZeroActivity*), and the Editor Pane should now have a new tab named Hello open and showing the content of the new class.

We see that the IDE has already set up the new class for us:

- It placed a package statement at the top.
- It inserted the class header.
- It followed the header by an open brace and a close brace.

We are now ready to write the code of the class (aka the *class body*) in between the two braces. All classes in Java must have these elements: a package statement and a class header followed by two braces.

Note that the placement of the braces is a matter of style. One approach is to place the open brace on a line by itself after the header line as shown below on the left. Another is to place it on the same line as the header (as shown below on the right):

```
public class Hello              |    public class Hello {
{                               |        ... (class body)
    ... (class body)            |    }
}                               |
```

Both placements are in common use and it is up to you to use one or the other, and you can configure the IDE to use either. We adopt the former (shown on the left) throughout this book when we write code fragments because the open/close braces are vertically aligned in it which makes it easy to spot a missing brace.

L0.2.b – Running a main Method

We will insert a so-called `main` method in the body of our class (between the braces). The header of that method is rather lengthy:

```
public static void main(String[] args)
```

but there is luckily a shortcut (an acronym) that the IDE recognizes for this header:

Type **psvm** *and then press* **ENTER**

This will automatically insert the method header in place of the shortcut.

Enter one line for the class body as shown:

```
public static void main(String[] args)
{
    System.out.println(Math.max(3, 5));
}
```

If you make a typing mistake, the IDE will detect the problem as you type, and in that case, it will highlight the mistake in red and suggest a fix. The suggestion appears when you make the mouse pointer hover on top of the red highlight.

Spend some time looking at the code and try to figure out what it does. Here are some highlights of what are trying to achieve in this method:

- We are using the services of the **Math** class.
- The **Math** class is in the **Standard Java library** that comes built into the IDE.
- We are invoking the **max** method of the **Math** class.
- We are sending the two integers 3 and 5 to the **max** method.
- The **max** method determines which of the two integers is bigger.
- We print the result returned to us by **max**.

To test this we run the class as follows:

1. Right-click the `Hello` class name (in the project pane).
2. Select **run** *Hello.main()*.

The output should appear (after a delay) in a new pane at the bottom.

Did you get the correct output?

Explore changing the two values and running the class again.

L0.2.c – Installing a Library

The standard Java library is bundled with the IDE so you don't need to install it in order to use it. The same applies to the Android platform library. For other, third-party libraries, however, you must first fetch the library and store it on your development machine, and then incorporate it (as a dependency) into your app.

Most Java libraries come in the form of a **JAR** (Java Archive) file. This is just one file that contains all the classes of the library. After downloading this file from its maker, you must store it the subfolder named **app/libs** under the app's folder in AndroidStudioProjects and then link it with your project.

As a concrete, step-by-step example, let us install the **i2c** library associated with this book into our *Zero* project:

1. Visit the book's website at: **http://book.roumani.ca/**

2. Download the book's library file: **i2c.jar**

3. Save the downloaded file in **AndroidStudioProjects/Zero/app/libs**

4. Select **Project Structure** in the **File** menu of the IDE

5. Select **app** in the left sidebar and the **Dependencies** tab at the top

6. Click the **+** symbol at the bottom and add a **Jar dependency**

7. **Navigate** to the jar file you have just downloaded and click **open** then **ok**

The first three steps install the library while the last four link it to your project. This way, when it is time to translate your code to machine language, the translator (aka **gradle**) will look inside the jar file to complete the build process.

The i2c library was designed as a pedagogic scaffolding tool that sheds light on the more intricate aspects of object oriented programming. It is therefore strongly recommended that you add this library, as a dependency, to all the projects that you build.

L0.2.d – Using an API

The services provided by any library are known as its Application Programming Interface (**API**). The API of the i2c library is listed in Appendix-D as well as on the book's website. The API of the Java Standard Library and that of the Android Platform are built into our IDE and are also available online.

In order to test the correct installation of i2c, let us use its API. Add one more line to the main method of the Hello class so it becomes as shown below:

```
public static void main(String[] args)
{
    System.out.println(Math.max(3, 5));
    System.out.println(Utility.gcd(24, 18));
}
```

The IDE flags the word **Utility** in red and suggests that you import this class by pressing Alt-Enter. Do that.

Let us compare the added line to the original:

- The original uses the **max** method of the **Math** class (of the standard Java library).
- The added code uses the **gcd** method of the **Utility** class (of the i2c library).

Look up the **Utility** class in Appendix-D and read the API of its **gcd** method. As you will find, it determines the *Greatest Common Divisor* (hence the gcd name) of the two integers. In the above example, it looks for integers that evenly divide both 24 and 18 and returns the largest one.

Re-run this class and observe the output. You should now see a second line appearing. Did you get 6 in the second line? Explore changing the two values and re-running.

Using APIs to solve problems (rather than developing everything from scratch) has become the hallmark of modern software construction. Indeed, a typical software system today is nothing but an assembly of a large number of components, some from libraries, some from the platform, and some built from scratch specifically for the system at hand. For example, a typical, medium-size mobile app would contain tens of thousands of methods, but of these, only a hundred or so are written from scratch (by the app developer). This miniscule ratio (of custom-built to ready-made components) enables us to tackle problems that would be formidable were we to build everything from scratch.

The success of component-based software construction relies on the components being able to "talk to each other". Hence, being able to understand APIs; convert data types; validate incoming and outgoing parameters; detect component defects and handle exceptions, has become as important a skill as that of developing code from scratch.

L0.3 – EXERCISES

1. Computer Science is rooted in Math so it is not surprising that all its terms have precise meanings. The following two phrases, for example, are synonymous in everyday language but they have distinct meanings in CS:

   - *A list of integers.*
   - *A set of integers.*

   What is the difference between the two?

2. We use the word "bracket" often in everyday life but different people associate different meanings to it. The rigour in CS does not tolerate such ambiguity. Consider the three-column table shown below

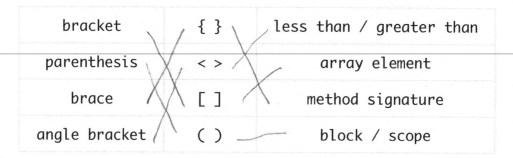

   The first column shows four terms, the second four pairs of symbols, and the third contains four Java element names. Associate each term with its corresponding symbol and corresponding Java element.

3. Provide an everyday life example in which abstraction layers (Section L0.1.b) are used to make a task easier.

4. Consider the task of following a recipe to make a cake. In one recipe, we use eggs, flour, sugar, baking powder, baking soda, and vanilla plus frosting. In a second recipe, we use a ready-made cake mix plus frosting.

   a) Which recipe is easier to follow?
   b) Is abstraction involved here?

5. Add a line to body of the main method of the Hello class as shown below:

```
public static void main(String[] args)
{
    System.out.println(Math.max(3, 5));
    System.out.println(Utility.gcd(24, 18));

    System.out.println(Math.pow(2, 3));
}
```

The pow method computes powers. Its two arguments are the base and the exponent of the power to be computed. Hence, the above invocation computes $2^3 = 2*2*2$ which is 8. Run the class and verify that the output is as expected. If all is well, modify the class so it computes 2^{10} and then test your work using a calculator as oracle.

6. Complete the fragment below which appends a line to the body of the main method of the Hello class whose job is to output the square root of 2:

```
public static void main(String[] args)
{
    System.out.println(Math.max(3, 5));
    System.out.println(Utility.gcd(24, 18));
    System.out.println(Math.pow(2, 3));
    System.out.println( ?? );
}
```

Replace the two question marks with code that uses the sqrt method of the Math class. Make sure you test your work by running the class. Could you have used the pow method instead of sqrt? Verify.

7. The fragment below adds two lines to the body of the main method of the Hello class:

```
public static void main(String[] args)
{

    . . .

    System.out.println(Utility.factorial(3));
    System.out.println(Utility.gf(104));

}
```

The added lines use the factorial and the gf methods of the Utility class (of the i2c library). Here is a partial API of the e Utility class:

Utility API *(partial)*
Methods
`public static double factorial(int n)` Determine the factorial n! of the passed integer. The factorial of a positive integer n is the product of all integers in [1,n].
`public static int gf(int x)` Determine the Greatest Factor (GF) of the passed integer. A factor of a positive integer x is an integer in [1,x) that divides x evenly.

We will see later that the API of a class describes the services that it offers. The above API is incomplete (e.g. it does not specify what happens if n is negative) but it is good enough for now (the complete API is in Appendix-D). Run the class and test your work by using your calculator as oracle.

8. Read the API of the uses the **m2FtInch** method of the **Utility** class (of the i2c library). Do you understand what it does? To verify, add lines to the `main` method of the `Hello` class to use this method and display the result. Does it return what you predicted?

CHAPTER 1 – DOING

The Landscape

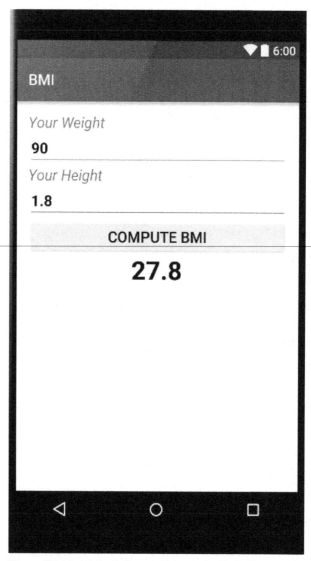

Figure D1.1 App launched, two entries made, the button tapped.

D1.1 – REQUIREMENT

D1.1.a – The BMI Calculator App

The objective of this project is to build an Android app that computes the BMI (Body Mass Index) given the weight w and height h of a person. If w is measured in kilograms and h in meters then the index can be computed using the formula: $BMI = w/h^2$. The architecture of the app must adhere to the **MVC** design pattern (see the Design section for details).

D1.1.b – UI and Behaviour

As shown in Fig. D1.1, the UI (user interface) of the sought app consists of *six* vertically aligned elements (aka widgets):

1. A label that says "*Your Weight*".
2. A textbox for entering the weight.
3. A label that says "*Your Height*".
4. A textbox for entering the height.
5. A button with caption "*COMPUTE BMI*".
6. A label for displaying the answer.

Each of the six widgets must extend across the entire width of the device (phone or tablet) regardless of device dimensions and whether held in portrait or landscape. Text must be left-aligned except for the button caption and the computed index which must be centred.

In terms of behaviour, the app must display the computed index whenever the button is tapped. The index (which is a real number) should be rounded to one decimal, and must appear in large blue text.

It should be noted that no requirement specification would be complete if it did not clearly define the validity condition of the input and how the app is to behave should the input be invalid. Failing that, the app will have bugs and vulnerabilities that can be exploited. For our app, we consider the input to be valid if w and h are positive real numbers. And in this first release, we will assume this validity *as a precondition*. This means the app should *not* attempt to validate the entries. If the user made a non-numeric entry, or a non-positive one, then it is the user who bears the responsibility for the consequences (a wrong answer or the app crashing). We will see in later releases how to validate, and thus, remove this precondition.

D1.2 – DESIGN

D1.2.a – The MVC Architecture

We will adopt the Model-View-Controller (MVC) design pattern for structuring our app. In MVC, an app must have three components: the *model* (an abstract component that encapsulates the data and the computation), the *view* (a component responsible for interacting with the user), and finally the *controller* (a component that liaises between M and V, thereby embodying the app's behaviour).

In Android lingo:

- The **model** is represented by a *POJO*, a Plain-Old Java Object that is Android agnostic. As such, it can be tested on its own and can be ported as-is to other platforms such as a desktop application or a web service. We will call our model *"BMIModel.java"*.

- The **view** is known as a *layout* and is represented by an XML document. We will call our layout *"bmi_layout.xml"*.

- The **controller** is known as an *activity*. It is also represented by a Java class, but unlike the model, its class extends the Android platform. We will call our activity *"BMIActivity.java"*.

D1.2.b – The Model's API

The model class is responsible for holding the data of the app (the weight and the height) and for performing the BMI computation. Hence, its API (Application Programming Interface) must explain how we can transfer data to it and how it can transfer the result back to us. The API document looks like this:

Constructor
`public BMIModel(String w, String h)` Construct an instance of the class having the given weight and height.
Method
`public String getBMI()` Return the BMI of this instance rounded to 1 decimal as a string.

The API of a class can be thought of as a boundary that surrounds it (thereby hiding its internal implementation) and defines how outsiders can interact with it. It specifies *what* the class can do without revealing *how* it does it.

D1.3 – IMPLEMENTATION

We will now turn our design plans into a concrete implementation. Follow these steps:

1. Launch your Android Studio. If it prompts you to update anything (whether in this screen or in any other), reject the update by closing these prompts.

2. Start a new project.

3. Name the new project *BMI* and accept the other defaults then click Next.

4. Accept the Phone/Tablet platform and the default minimum SDK then click Next.

5. Select the *Empty Activity* choice then click Next.

6. Name the activity *BMIActivity* (the *java* extension is implied) and the layout *bmi_layout* (the *xml* extension is implied). Keep the default checkbox.

7. Click Finish.

When the IDE main screen appears, you will see two panes. The bigger one on the right is the editor pane. Note that the created activity and layout are available as tabs in it. The pane on the left is the project pane and it outlines the components in your project. Note that the **java** components (where the model and controller will eventually reside) appear in it under **app**, and so does the **res** components (where the layout, values, and other resources will eventually reside). If you are not comfortable with these two panes, review Section D0.2.

D1.3.a – Building the View

Click on the layout tab (i.e. the one entitled *bmi_layout.xml*) in the editor pane. Note that the view comes with a default label that says *"Hello World"*. Right-click it and delete it. We now need to add the six UI widgets specified in the requirement document.

To create the view, simply drag the six needed widgets from the widget palette to the left of the emulated device screen onto the screen. For labels (i.e. a box in which you display text for the user and the user cannot edit it), look for a *TextView*. For textboxes (i.e. a box in which the user writes), look for a *Plain Text* (aka *EditText*). For buttons, look for a *Button*.

As you build the view, the *Component Tree* pane below the palette gets updated.

Lay out the six widgets as you learned in Chapter 0. In particular, make sure the top label is anchored to the upper left corner of the screen and that each of the remaining widgets is anchored to the one above it. The result label should be centered across the screen with its layout_width wrapping its content.

When you click on a widget, you can set its *attributes* (aka *properties*) in the attribute window that appears to the right. You will become familiar with these attributes as needed. Keep all the default as-is except for the following ones, which must be set:

1. Set the *id* of the weight label to *weightLabel* and that of the weight box to *weightBox*. Do the same for the height (*heightLabel* and *heightBox*). Set the id of the button to *button* and that of the label of the computed BMI to *answer*.

2. Set the *text* attribute of all six widgets as per the requirement document. In particular, set it to blank for the two textboxes and for the computed index.

3. Set the *textColor* and *textSize* of the answer label to match the requirement. You can experiment by temporarily setting the *text* attribute of answer to some number (so you can see the effect) and then reset it back to blank.

You have implemented the view!

The IDE keeps track of your created view through an XML document and keeps updating it as you drag or set attributes. To view this document, click the *Text* tab just under the editor. This switches you out of the *Design* tab and allows you to see the generated XML. Take a few moments to familiarize yourself with the XML contents and try to connect it to our six widgets. Note that any change you make in the XML will be reflected in the Design tab. In fact, it is sometimes easier to tweak the UI using XML rather than through the IDE.

D1.3.b – Building the Model

Unlike the view and the controller, Studio does not automatically create a model in the app. Instead, we create the model ourselves as follows:

1. Open the *app* tree in the project pane to the left.
2. Open the *java* tree within it.
3. Three packages appear under Java: the main package of the app and two test packages.
4. Right-click the main package and select *New* then *Java Class*.
5. When prompted for a name, enter *BMIModel* and press Enter.

You can think of a class as a factory that manufactures *objects* each of which holds a state (such as w=90 and h=1.8) and is capable of computing the BMI. In order to use the services of a class, you would need to first request an object from it by calling its constructor and specifying the desired state. The obtained object (aka *instance* of the class) can then be used for computation. This two-step process is implemented using two Java statements:

```
BMIModel myModel = new BMIModel("90", "1.8");
String myBMI = myModel.getBMI();
```

The first statement creates an instance of the class customised to 90 kg weight and 1.8 m height. It names the object reference that points at this instance *myModel*. The second statement uses the obtained instance to find the BMI. We say that the second statement *invokes* the getBMI method *on the instance*. The returned index is then stored in a variable named *myBMI*. The value of this variable at this point should be 27.777… .

As you can see, the API of the class (as shown in the Design section) contains all the information you need to use the class. It enables you to specify any weight and height you want and obtain their BMI without knowing how it was computed. This is how our activity, which lives outside the model, can use the model.

But how about the internals of the model? The internal implementation is shown below and you need to enter it as-is in the editor pane:

```
public class BMIModel
{
    private double weight;
    private double height;

    public BMIModel(String w, String h)
    {
        this.weight = Double.parseDouble(w);
        this.height = Double.parseDouble(h);
    }

    public String getBMI()
    {
        double index = this.weight / (this.height * this.height);
        String result = String.format("%.1f", index);
        return result;
    }
}
```

Since this is your first encounter with a Java class, you are not expected to fully understand it. You are, however, expected to recognize the pieces that make up its structure and map them to the API. You are also expected to be able to get the gist of what the code is doing. To that end, take some time to think through the following observations:

- The class is made up of three *blocks* each of which has a *header*, followed by an opening *brace*, the block *body*, and then a closing *brace*. Note that a brace "{" is different from a bracket "[" and different from a parenthesis "(".

- The outermost block has the header *public class BMIModel* and its body encompasses the entire class. The braces that surround the body are vertically aligned.

- The second and third blocks are nested within the outer class block. They have the headers *public BMIModel(...)* and *public String getBMI()*.

- The first thing we see within the class block are two *attribute* declarations, one for the weight and one for the height. This is where the model holds the data. The attributes are declared as *double*, which means they can hold real numbers (as opposed to integers or something else). They are also *private* and that is why the API does not mention them.

- The *constructor* block is easy to recognise because its name is the same as the name of the class. It receives the weight and height as strings; converts them to double; and then uses them to set the state of the instance by initializing the attributes.

- The last block designates a *method* (aka function in other programming languages). This method performs the computation and returns the result after converting it to string.

- Note that since the UI can only deal with strings, the model interacts with the outside world through strings. Internally, however, the model stores the data and performs the computation using double. That is why the constructor converted its string parameters to numbers and the method converted its return to string.

D1.3.c – Testing the Model

Since the model is a standalone class that is not derived from the Android hierarchy, it can easily be tested as a unit on its own independently of the view and the controller. There are two well-known approaches for unit testing in Java:

1. The JUnit Framework
2. The PSVM Approach

We will use the latter in our first project because it is direct and easier to understand. Simply add a new block to the class containing a special kind of method, known as the *main* method. Unlike other methods, the main method can be launched (executed) as if it is external to the class, and hence, it allows you to test it. This method has the header:

```
public static void main(String[] args)
```

and hence the **psvm** acronym.

Let us add this method to our model. It can be added as a separate block anywhere but it is customary placed last. Insert a new line just before the closing brace of the class and type in it *psvm* and press Enter. Studio recognizes this acronym and will expand it to the complete header.

Here is the full block that you should add:

```
public static void main(String[] args)
{
    BMIModel myModel = new BMIModel("100", "1.8");
    System.out.println(myModel.getBMI());

    myModel = new BMIModel("45", "1.35");
    System.out.println(myModel.getBMI());

    myModel = new BMIModel("80", "1.2");
    System.out.println(myModel.getBMI());

}
```

As you can roughly figure out by looking at the code, the method creates three instances of the class and outputs the computed index in each, thereby providing three test cases.

To run this test, simply right-click the model class name (in the project pane) and select to run its main(). The output appears after a delay in a new pane at the bottom. In general, you should pick test cases that sample the input range and include its boundaries. And to verify the correctness of the model, you need an *oracle*, a reliable source that provides the correct answer for each test case. For this app, use your calculator as oracle. Feel free to change the body of the main method in order to add additional test cases, perhaps to compute your own BMI.

Do not delete the main method after testing is done. You will re-use it whenever additional features are added and the model needs to be re-tested. Its presence in the model class does not have any effect on what the user sees in the final app on the device.

D1.3.d – The Controller-View Interaction

When the button is clicked, the view must inform the controller. We therefore need **V2C**: a mechanism that allows the view V to talk to the controller C. To do that, add the following method to the activity class (place it under the *onCreate* method):

```
public void buttonClicked(View v)
{
}
```

As you enter these lines, you will notice that Studio has coloured the *View* word red. This implies something is wrong and needs to be fixed. In this case, simply click on the red word and press Alt+Enter. What is happening here is that the View class needs to be imported; i.e. added to the *import* list at the top of the class.

Note that the added method has an empty body for now, but nevertheless, it is sufficient to create the needed V2C glue. Click on the layout tab in the editor, switch to the design tab, and click on the button. One of its attributes is **onClick**. Setting this attribute will present you with a drop-down list, and one of the options in the list is the above method that we have just added (this option was not there before adding the method). Select it.

You have now linked the V to C! In technical terms, we say that clicking the button *triggers* an *event* and the above method is a *listener* to (or a *handler* of) that event.

Once the controller knows that the button is clicked, it needs to find out the entered weight and height. Hence, we also need **C2V**: a mechanism that allows the controller to talk to the view. This is achieved via the *findViewById* method. This method takes the id of any widget in the view and return a reference to the object that represents that widget. This method can be used as shown below to grab the weight textbox from the view and extract the text string that the user has entered in it:

```
EditText weightView = (EditText) findViewById(R.id.weightBox);
String weight = weightView.getText().toString();
```

D1.3.e – The Controller-Model Interaction

To perform the computation, the controller needs to talk to the model in order to compute. Hence, we need a **C2M** mechanism. We already know how to do that! The controller can simply instantiate the model and then invoke the getBMI method on the instance:

```
BMIModel myModel = new BMIModel(weight, height);
String myBMI = myModel.getBMI();
```

Hence, no new features are needed to implement this mechanism.

Similarly **M2C,** a mechanism for the model to talk back to the controller, does not need any new feature thanks to the *return* statement in Java which does just that.

Enter the complete implementation of the *buttonClicked* method as shown below.

```
public void buttonClicked(View v)
{
    EditText weightView = (EditText) findViewById(R.id.weightBox);
    String weight = weightView.getText().toString();
    EditText heightView = (EditText) findViewById(R.id.heightBox);
    String height = heightView.getText().toString();

    BMIModel myModel = new BMIModel(weight, height);
    String myBMI = myModel.getBMI();

    ((TextView) findViewById(R.id.answer)).setText(myBMI);

}
```

As mentioned earlier, a class name in red (EditText and TextView in the above) implies that the class must be imported. You will need to click on the red name and press Alt and Enter so that Studio would add the class to the import list.

Take some time to examine this code. It is not expected that you understand every aspect of it but you should be able to get the gist of its functionality.

One particularly subtle point is the *cast* that appears in the first, third, and last statement of the method's body. A cast refers to putting a class between two parethesis as in (EditText). The following paragraph sheds some light on why these casts are present (but you can just skim through it):

The *findViewById* method allows us to fish out any widget from the view as long as we know its id. These widgets could be labels, textboxes, or buttons, amongst other things, and hence, the type of the method's return is a generic View. In order to work with it, we need to cast it to its proper specific type and we do that by writing the type's name between parentheses. In the first statement, for example, we know that the returned object is *EditText* so we casted it as such. Had we not done that (i.e. had we kept it as a generic View object), we wouldn't have been able to use the *getText* method in the following statement

D1.4 – DEPLOYMENT

The last step in the development process involves deploying the app on a real device. Follow these steps:

1. Turn the device on.

2. Connect the device to your computer's USB port.

3. Grab the device from the host O/S if you are operating in a virtual environment.

4. Run the whole app (not the Model's main method). To do that, use the *Run* menu and select the *Run…* and then select *app*.

Tap OK on the device when prompted to allow USB debugging and click OK in Studio. The app will be installed on the device.

Test your app. This is known as *integration testing* (because you are testing all its MVC components and verifying that they work together) as opposed to *unit* testing.

Ensure that the view adheres to the requirement and verify that it remains so after rotating the device. Run some test cases and verify the correctness of the app's behaviour and output formatting. Run also the following two test cases::

- Enter zero for the height.
- Make a non-numeric entry for either the weight or the height.

Since these cases violate the precondition, we are not responsible for whatever the app does when they are executed. This is the essence of input validity as a precondition: it assigns responsibility on the user (or client) of a piece of software rather than the implementer. Put differently, the app is supposed to behave as required (aka meet its post-condition) if and only if the pre-condition is met.

Note that your app is now downloaded on the device and it will remain on it after you disconnect it from your machine. Verify by going to the apps screen on the device and locate your app by looking for its name (BMI). It will have a default green Android badge.

Note: if you prefer to deploy your app from the command line rather than from the IDE, go the project's directory and issue the command: gradlew installDebug.

D1.5 – EXERCISES

In order to practice your skills, augment your app by implementing these new requirements:

1. The **keyboard** that pops when the weight and height boxes are focused contains letters by default. Since these are numeric entries, modify the app so that this soft keyboard becomes numeric only. Moreover, we like the computed index to appear in **italics**. Deploy the modified app and test it.

    Hint: Look for a textbox attribute that controls the input type, and look for a label attribute that controls the text style appearance

2. When the app is deployed, it appears in the home screen with a default **badge** (an icon). Change this badge to a picture of your own choosing. To do that:

    a) Pick any png image you like to be used for the badge.

    b) Download this image to your desktop.

    c) In the project pane, right-click the res folder, select *New*, and then select *Image Asset*.

    d) Select "image" as the Asset Type and then navigate to the downloaded png file.

    Deploy the modified app on a real or virtual device and then go to the home screen and verify that its badge has changed.

3. Add a **new method** to your model:

    public String toPound()

    The method should return the weight in pounds (rather than kilograms) rounded to the nearest pound. Note that:

    *   The weight in kilograms is already stored in the model's state.

    *   To convert from kilogram to pound, divide by 0.454.

    *   The method's return should be a String, not a double.

    For example, if the stored weight is 77 then the return should be "170".

    To test your implementation, append the model's main method with a few lines in which you invoke the new method and output its return. Use a calculator as oracle.

4. Add a **new method** to your model:

public String toFeetInch()

The method should return the height in feet and inches (rather than meters) rounded to the nearest foot and inch. Note that:

- The height in meter is already stored in the model's state.

- The method's return should be a `String`, not a `double`.

- The returned string must have the feet amount F followed by a single quote followed by the inch amount I followed by a double quote; i.e. F'I".

For example, if the stored height is 1.78 then the returned string should be 5'10".

You don't need to implement the conversion yourself because the `Utility` class in the i2c library (Section L0.2.c) already has a method named m2FtInch that you can use. Your implementation of toFeetInch should simply invoke m2FtInch.

To test your implementation, append the model's `main` method with a few lines in which you invoke toFeetInch and output its return. Use any online calculator as an oracle and compare your output to it.

Note:
The exercise asks you to use a library method in order to practice delegating to an API. You can also try to implement the conversion yourself, and to that end, here are a few hints:

- *Multiply the height by 3.28084 and call the product x.*
- *The integer part of x (obtainable via Math.floor) is the sought F.*
- *The fractional part of x multiplied by 12 yields I.*
- *Use String.format to round and to convert to string.*

5. Modify your app and have your activity invoke both toPound and toFeetInch of the two previous exercises and combine their returns with the return of getBMI so that the app's output when the button is tapped becomes:

   Your weight is xxx lb, your Height is F'I", and your BMI is xx.x.

For example, if the entries are as in Fig. D1.1 (90 and 1.8) then the output should be:

   Your weight is 198 lb, your Height is 5'11", and your BMI is 27.8.

Hint: To combine two strings, put the + operator between them.

6. If you have hard-coded the strings of your UI then undo this by defining these strings in `strings.xml` as was done in exercises 7 and 8 in Chapter 0. This should allow you to easily localize your app. Go ahead and make the two labels and the caption of the button **locale sensitive** by entering their translations to French as follows:

Your Weight	Votre Poids
Your Height	Votre Taille
COMPUTE BMI	CALCULER BMI

Feel free to use any other language. Deploy the app and verify that these three strings get auto-translated whenever the device default language changes.

7. Create a new project named *RandomColours* with an empty activity and use any name you like for its activity and layout. The UI consists of a button that spans the whole screen as in Fig. D1.2. Make sure the button covers the screen in both portrait and landscape orientations.

Whenever the button is tapped (or "pushed" as per its caption) its background colour (which starts off being gray) should change to some randomly chosen colour. The colour is selected from all the possible mixes of the 256 shades of red, green, and blue.

The activity method that handles the on-click of the button must follow this logic (in pseudocode):

```
- Generate a random red value in [0,255].
- Generate a random green value in [0,255].
- Generate a random blue value in [0,255].
- Combine these three values into one colour.
- Grab the button object from the view.
- Set the background colour of that object.
```

Here are some APIs from the standard Java library that helps you achieve the above.

Figure D1.2 The RandomColours app.

- The Math class has a static method named random and it returns a random number in [0,1). If we multiply it by 256 and looked at the product as an integer, it will be in [0,255). Hence, we can generate the red component using a statement like this:

$$\text{int red = (int) (256 * Math.random());}$$

- The Color class has a static method named rgb. It takes three integers representing the three components and returns a combined colour as one integer. Hence, we can combine the components using a statement like this:

$$\text{int c = Color.rgb(red, green, blue);}$$

Use the above APIs to build the app. Deploy the app and verify that you get a new background colour with every tap.

Note: We didn't need a model in this app because there is no data to be stored and the needed behaviour is readily available in the library (the activity can use the library directly without going through a model).

8. Refactor the app of Exercise 7 by adding a label below the button to show the relative values of the three colour components. In the example shown in Fig. D1.3, the red component R has a relative value 75%; i.e. its actual value is 0.75*255=191. Similarly, the actual value of the green component G is 179 and that of blue B is 206.

Add a TextView to the UI anchored it to the bottom of the screen and constrain the button between it and the top of the screen.

When your activity generate the three random colour values, divide each by 255.0 in order to compute its relative value.

Afterwards, convert these values to strings and format them with no decimals so that you can construct the sought content.

Note:
We still don't need a model in the refactored app because there is still no data to be stored and the added behaviour is readily available through arithmetic and string operations.

Figure D1.3 Adding RGB components..

9. Create a new project named *PushCount* with an
empty activity and use any name you like for its
activity and layout. The UI consists of a button that
spans the width of the screen and extends from the
top to a row at the bottom. The row displays a push
count as shown in in Fig. D1.4. Make sure the
layout of your app adheres to this requirement regardless of the device size and how it is held.

Whenever the button is tapped (or "pushed" as per
its caption) the row at the bottom is updated to
reflect the number of times the button has been
tapped so far. Initially, the count should be zero but
it is then incremented with every tap of the button.

This app has a state that it needs to keep; namely,
the tap count, so we could create a model to hold it.
Alternatively, since it is only a simple integer and we
merely increment it, we can implement this app
without a model by holding the count either in the
activity class (as an attribute) or in the UI itself. We
will use the latter approach.

Figure D1.4 The PushCount app.

Insert two side-by-side labels in the bottom row of the screen and chain them
horizontally. The left label holds the text *"Push Count ="* and aligns it to the right. The
right label holds the tap count (initially set to zero) and aligns it to the left.

Add the follow logic (shown in pseudocode) to the activity method that handles the on-
click of the button:

- Grab the text of the label that holds the tap count.
- Convert the grabbed text to an integer.
- Increment the integer.
- Set the text of the label to the incremented value.

Deploy the app on a real or virtual device and test it. Pay attention to the boundary test
case of zero; i.e. the count should 1 after the first tap.

10. Create a new project named *PushCount* with an empty activity and use any name you like for its activity and layout. The UI consists of a button that spans the width of the screen and extends from the top to a row at the bottom. The row displays the time that elapsed (in seconds) since the button was tapped last, as shown in Fig. D1.5. Make sure the layout of your app adheres to this requirement regardless of the device size and how it is held.

    When the app is first launched, the text in the bottom row should be blank.

    The functionality of this app requires that we measure the elapsed time between two events. Hence, we need to have a way of acquiring the time when the button is tapped and storing it. Later, when the button is tapped again, we re-acquire the time and subtract the two time values in order to get the inter-tap duration. This would be the algorithm to follow if we were to implement the logic ourselves. But the API of i2c provides an alternate approach that is much easier.

Figure D1.5 The PushRate app.

The Utility class in the i2c library (Section L0.2.c) has a method named mark. Whenever you invoke this method, it return to you the time that has elapsed since you invoked it last. The returned duration is measured in milliseconds and is a real number; i.e. it could include a fractional amount. Hence, all we need to do is invoke this method in our on-click handler and insert its return in the label below the button (after formatting it as in the shown UI).

Deploy the app on a real or virtual device and test it. Pay attention to the boundary test case which occurs after the very first tap.

CHAPTER 1 – LEARNING

The Landscape

L1.1 JAVA BASICS

L1.1.a About
L1.1.b Language Elements
L1.1.c Naming Convention and Style
L1.1.d Syntax, Runtime, and Logic Errors

L1.2 SEPARATION OF CONCERNS

L1.2.a The Idea
L1.2.b The Client View
L1.2.c The Implementer View
L1.2.d API Examples

L1.3 THE TESTBED PROJECT

L1.3.a Building the Project
L1.3.b Building POJO Classes

L4.4 EXERCISES

L1.1 – JAVA BASICS

L1.1.a – About

Java is an industrial-strength language that is widely used in a variety of domains. Its syntax is similar to that of C, C++, C#, and JavaScript, which makes the transition from Java to any of these languages somewhat smoother.

Java is an extremely rich language so we will follow a carefully planned route that exposes its various facades little by little in an incremental fashion and that revisits these facades at increasing depth in a layered fashion. In this section, we focus only on its program layout.

The smallest compilation unit in a Java is the **class**. Classes in Java are grouped in **packages** for obvious organization purposes (classes of similar functionalities are grouped together) and also to avoid name clashes (the package provides a namespace that allows a class in one package to have the same name as one in another). This concept is recursive so packages can themselves be grouped in a bigger package, and so on.

For example, there is a class in Java's standard library called *LocalDate* and it resides in a package named *time* which in turn resides in a package named *java*. Hence, the fully qualified name of that class is: *java.time.LocalDate*. If you need to use the services of that class in your program, you will need to either write this full name every time you use it, which is a nuisance, or **import** the class just once at the top of your program by writing:

```
import java.time.LocalDate;
```

With this statement in place, you can refer to the class in your program by writing just *LocalDate*. Note that package names are in lower case while class names are in *title* case (the first letter in every word in the name is in upper case; acronyms are all caps).

The structure of a Java class is always the same: a **package** statement to designate where the class resides, one or more import statements, and a **class block**. The class block starts with a class **header** and is followed by the class **body** surrounded by two **braces**. The class body starts with a declaration of **attributes** followed by a number of **constructor** and **method** blocks (a constructor block must have the same name as the class). Typically, the attributes are **private** and the blocks are **public** unless the API indicates otherwise.

The body of any block is made up of **statements**. Statements do things like declaring variables, assigning values, controlling flow, or commenting the code. Aside from comments (which start with // or /*), all statements are made up of a sequence of tokens delimited by **whitespace** (blanks, tabs, or newlines) and terminated with a **semicolon**. Hence a statement can optionally span several lines (but this makes the code harder to understand). Because of this, Java is **freeform**. It is also **case-sensitive** so be careful with letter case.

L1.1.b – Language Elements

One starting point for learning a programming language is to be able to classify the tokens that make up its statements. The English analogy to this would be to be able to distinguish actual English words from names of people and to recognize punctuation marks. This does not make you understand what you read but it raises your comfort level with the language.

The classification categories constitute the elements of the language and are known as its **lexical elements**. Java has the *five* such elements: Keywords, Identifiers, Literals, Operators, and Separators, and they are explained below:

Keywords
These are words that have predefined meanings in Java, and hence, you should avoid them when you name your own variables. Java has 53 keywords:

abstract	assert	boolean	break	byte	case
catch	char	class	const	continue	default
do	double	else	enum	extends	false
final	finally	float	for	goto	if
implements	import	instanceof	int	interface	long
native	new	null	package	private	protected
public	return	short	static	strictfp	super
switch	synchronized	this	throw	throws	transient
true	try	void	volatile	while	

Identifiers
These are names that the programmer chooses to use; they have no predefined meaning in Java. For example, *Rectangle* (a class name), *getBMI* (a method name), and *width* (a variable name) are all identifiers. Note that *Math*, *sqrt*, and *lang* are also identifiers (we did not choose them, but the developer of an imported class did). You can use any name you like for an identifier as long as:

- It is not a keyword,
- It begins with a letter, and
- It consists only of letters, digits, the characters $ (dollar), and _ (underscore).

Note, in particular, that no spaces are allowed. In terms of style, we must choose names that are meaningful to the context and that follow the professional software engineering guidelines that are covered in the next section.

Literals

These are constant values. They can be numeric (such as the number 2) or strings (such as "I am") or other types. Like variables, literals do have types but they don't need to be declared because their type can be inferred. For example, 2 is of the `int` type whereas 2.0 is of the `double` type

Operators

These are similar to mathematical function because they take *operands* and produce results. For example, the asterisk takes two operands and produces their product. Java's operators are made of certain combinations of the following characters:

Some operator symbols consist of just one of these characters (such as + for addition, = for assignment, and > for greater than) while others contains more than (such as ++ for incrementing by 1, == for equality testing, and <= for less than or equal).

Java's operators are either **unary** (they take a single operand), **binary** (they take two), or **ternary** (they take three). The unary operands are either **prefix** (the operator is placed before its operand as in *-x*) or **suffix** (the operator is placed after its operand as in *x++*). The binary operators are all **infix** (the operator is placed between its operands as in *x* *x+y*).

We will meet most of Java's operators as we need them. See the Appendix-A for a list.

Separators

These are used like punctuation to separate various parts of your code. Java's separators are the following 10 (the last is made up of 3 dots, an ellipsis):

We have already seen some of these separators in action, as braces in blocks and semicolons terminating statements.

L1.1.c – Naming Convention and Style

The professional developers community, together with industry, has developed a convention for naming identifiers and styling in order to make code easier to read and maintain. We will adopt these guidelines throughout.

Naming Identifiers

- Names must be meaningful (i.e. indicative) and of reasonable length. Avoid using abbreviations unless they are standard. Avoid also using generic names (such as a for area) unless the context is generic.

- For *packages*, use small case throughout even for acronyms. For example, the input-output package in Java is named: `java.io`.

- For *classes*, use *title* case; i.e. capitalize the first letter (as in `Math`), and for a multiword name, capitalize the first letter of each word as in `BigInteger`. If the name is an acronym, capitalize all its as in `URL`.

- For *variables* and *methods*, use *camel* case; i.e. lowercase characters (as in `length`). For a multiword name, capitalize the first letter of each subsequent word as in `indexOf`.

- For *finals* (a final is a variable whose value never changes throughout the program; i.e. it is a constant), use uppercase characters (as in `LIMIT`) and for a multiword name, delimit the words by an underscore character (as in `UPPER_LIMIT`).

Whitespace

- Leave exactly one space between otherwise touching keywords or identifiers.
- Leave exactly one space before and after an operator.
- Leave exactly one space after the comma separator.
- Avoid putting two statements on the same line.

Braces

We adopt the vertical alignment of braces in this textbook. Some developers prefer to have the opening braces on the same line as the header of the block, as in:

```java
public class Rectangle {
    private int width;
    ...
}
```

L1.1.d – Syntax, Runtime, and Logic Errors

Three stages are needed to execute (i.e. run) any program:

1. Create the program. The tool you use is called an **editor**. Different editors have different features, such as auto-complete, auto-styling, and auto source generation, but in the end, the editing process culminates in a file on disk containing your so-called **source** code, e.g. `Program.java`.

2. Translate your program to machine code. The tool you use is called a **compiler**. In the case of Java, the machine is called **JVM** (Java Virtual Machine) and the its code is *bytecode*. This step culminates with the translated program in a disk file, e.g. `Program.class`.

3. Launch your program. This steps involves passing your bytecode to the JVM so it can execute it statement by statement.

When you use an **IDE** (Integrated Development Environment) such as *Eclipse* or *Android Studio*, the first two stages are combined because the IDE attempts to compile your program with every change you make, which helps expose errors as you type. When such a **compile-time** error is detected, the IDE flags the statement that triggered it and even suggests a fix. Hence, these errors, albeit bothersome to the beginner, are easy to handle, which takes us to the third stage: running the program.

When the program is launched, one of two things may happen: it may *crash* (due to a so-called **runtime error**) or worse yet, may run smoothly without any problem but it produces the wrong result (i.e. wrong relative to the program's requirement specification), and this is known as a *bug* or a **logic-error**.

For example, suppose a program is supposed to take two integers from the user, add them, and output the sum. The program compiles without problems and runs. But when the user was prompted to enter the numbers, a non-numeric entry was made, and this triggered an exception which caused the program to crash (i.e. abort and return to the operating system). We say that a runtime error has occurred. If you re-run the program but this time make valid entries, such as 3 and 5, the program will not trigger a runtime error but its output may be 7 instead of 8. This is a logic error.

Both runtime and logic errors are bad, but as you can imagine, logic errors are the worst of the two because they do not manifest themselves in any way. The user, relying on the output, will make incorrect conclusions without knowing the output is wrong. And if the program is in an embedded system (e.g. part of an Internet of Things sensor) then it will actuate some action (such as increasing the beam intensity of an MRI machine or steering a car off the road) without realizing the sensed data is computed incorrectly.

Extensive research in software engineering seeks to minimize both runtime and logic errors. One theme in this research program centres on devising techniques, such as strong typing and static checking, that can transform some of these errors to compile-time errors, thereby exposing them during development. Java embraces these techniques. For example, it is strongly typed, which means every variable or method you define must have a type that you specify. Hence, unlike other languages, such as JavaScript and Python, the type cannot be misunderstood by the language, and any type mismatch will trigger an immediate compile-time error rather lurk in the code.

But besides using a well-designed language like Java, what can be done to avoid these errors? Here are some guidelines that, in the author's view, cannot be over-emphasized:

1. Most logic errors originate from misunderstanding the requirement or the API. Read the specifications carefully, parsing every word, as if you are reading a legal contract, or even a computer program.

2. Most errors originate from relying on un-validated assumptions. Hence, include code to validate every assumption you make. If you think the variable x "has got to be positive" at some point in your code, play the devil's advocate and ask "what if it is not?". The `assert` statement in Java makes assumptions explicit and verifies them at run time.

3. Runtime errors can originate from sources outside your code, such as an invalid input, a disconnected network, a missing file, or an ejected drive. Use *exception handling* whenever you deal with such sources. Java has a `try-catch` construct to implement that.

4. Runtime errors can also originate from sources within your code, such as dividing an `int` by zero, invoking a method on a `null` reference, or making an invalid cast. Use defensive strategies whenever such situations can occur.

5. Your code should be short (not terse) and easy to understand, and it should make proper use of language constructs. If you find that your code has become unwieldy, then rethink how the class is structured; avoid redundancy; and see if Java or its library already has a construct or an API that does exactly what you want.

Our last line of defense is **testing**. *Unit test* every component in your code before linking it to the rest of the system. Make sure your test cases have **coverage** (i.e. they sample the entire input range, including boundaries) and that they **execute every path** through your code. Do also *integration testing* to verify that the components work together. We end with a somber note from E.W. Dijkstra: *Testing can only show the presence of bugs, not prove their absence.*

L1.2 – SEPARATION OF CONCERNS

L1.2.a – The Idea

The complexity of computation has grown by leaps and bounds during the past few decades. If we measure complexity by the number of lines of code (for the lack of a better measure), we find that it has grown from a few hundred thousands thirty years ago to hundreds of millions today. For example, your car will soon contain over 100 million lines of code that control hundreds of processors scattered throughout its body.

In order to confront such complexity, we resort to a good-old divide-and-conquer strategy: rather than dealing with the problem as one entity, we break it into smaller pieces such that each piece is concerned with only one thing and has a protocol that allows it to interact with the other pieces. We call each piece a *concern* and refer to the overall strategy as *separation of concerns*. Once the concerns are separated, they can be solved independently, which makes the problem easier, and concurrently, which makes the process faster. And as a by-product, the solutions of the pieces can be packaged as ready-made components that can be re-used in future projects. This strategy is recursive: once the concerns are separated, each can itself be divided further into smaller concerns. This *layering* process continues until each of the final concerns is simple enough to be solved by a few lines of code.

There could be several ways to partition the problem, some better than others, but the most recurring theme is separating *what* needs to be done from *how* it is done. We thus recognize two roles: the **client** (who knows the what) and the **implementer** (who knows the how).

For example, the controller in the BMI app knows what the app should do (grab the weight and height from the view; compute their BMI; and send the result to the view) but it doesn't know how to do the computation. The model class, on the other hand, knows nothing about the app or its view but it knows how to compute the BMI. Hence, the controller here acts as a client while the model is the implementer.

Since you will be writing both the client and the implementer pieces, it is important that you are aware of the role you are playing at any given time, and not mix up the two. When you build the model, put on the implementer hat and focus only on the model; i.e. forget about the app and the Android platform. And when you build the controller, put on the client hat and use the model as an outsider.

Note that the term "client" does not refer to a person (we use *end-user* for that). Both client and implementer refer to pieces of code. When we sometimes personify the role in this book and write "you are the client", what we really mean is that you are writing the client code.

L1.2.b – The Client View

In order for the client to use the services offered by the implementer, it needs to know how to talk to it. The situation is analogous to going to a shopping mall to get something. The mall has many stores in it and each store has a sign posted on its door listing all the services it offers. By reading these signs, you locate the store that has what you want.

In programming lingo, the shopping mall is a *library* and its stores are *classes*. The sign posted on the store's door is the class *API* (Application Programming Interface). The API of a class lists the headers of all its constructors and methods and explains what each does.

If you look at the APIs of Java classes, you will notice that, in general, methods come in two categories: **static** and **instance**. The API makes it clear which is which by adding the word *static* to the header of static methods and *not* adding it if the method is of the instance type. It is important that you, as client, pay attention to whether a method is of one type or another because this affects how you invoke the method.

Here is the invocation recipe:

- If the method is static, invoke it by writing the class name followed by a dot followed by the method's name. We summarize this by saying we invoke the method *on the class*. If the class is C and the method is m then the invocation syntax is `C.m(...)`.

- If the method is not static, you *cannot* invoke it on the class. Instead, you need to first get an instance of the class and then invoke the method *on the instance*. If the instance is s and the method is m then the invocation syntax is `s.m(...)`.

But how do you get an instance of the class in the second case? There are two ways:

- If the API of the class has a constructor, use it to get the instance. If the class is C then you would instantiate it along the lines: `C s = new C(...)`.

- If the API does not show a constructor, look for a static method in the API that returns an instance. There got to be one or else we cannot get an instance, and hence, we cannot invoke any non-static method. If the class is C and the static method that returns an instance is m then you get the instance along the lines: `C s = C.m(...)`.

You can access the API of the Java library at `http://docs.oracle.com/javase` and the API of the Android library at `http://developer.android.com/reference/`. The book's website at `http://book.roumani.ca` has links to these two APIs plus that of the i2c library.

The above description of the invocation mechanics is admittedly abstract. We therefore look now at two concrete examples of static and non-static methods.

Example 1

Consider the Rectangle class whose API is shown below:

Rectangle API
Methods
`public static int getArea(int width, int height)` Return the area of the given rectangle.
`public static int getCircumference(int width, int height)` Return the circumference of the given rectangle.

How would you, as client, use the services of this class to compute the area and circumference of (say) a 3×4 rectangle?

Well, we see that the needed methods are both static, so according to the recipe, we can invoke them directly on the class. This leads us to the following client code fragment:

```
1  int x = 3;
2  int y = 4;
3  int a = Rectangle.getArea(x, y);
4  int c = Rectangle.getCircumference(x, y);
5  System.out.println(a);
6  System.out.println(c);
```

The relevant code is Statements 3 and 4. The first two statements and the last two are there merely for testing purposes. If this were a real Android app then the above fragment would be in the controller, and in that case, the first two would be replaced with code that grabs the user entries from the view and the last two would be replaced with code that pokes the two results in the view. In this scenario, the Rectangle class is the model.

Note that whenever we needed to compute something, we had to pass the needed data to the method. To compute the area of the rectangle for example, we passed 3 and 4 (the values of the two parameters x and y) to the getArea method. And in the statement immediately after, when we wanted the circumference of that same rectangle, we also had to pass 3 and 4 a second time. This shows that these methods <u>have no memory</u>; they just compute based on whatever is passed to them. Each invocation behaves as if it is done for the first time. This is reminiscent to functions in mathematics (such as sin and cos): every time you use them, you have to specify the argument—they are memory-less. That's why this approach (of a client delegating to static methods) is known as the **functional paradigm**.

Example 2

Consider a (different) `Rectangle` class whose API is shown below:

Rectangle API
Constructor
`public Rectangle(int width, int height)` Construct a rectangle having the given width and height.
Method
`public int getArea()` Return the area of this instance.
`public int getCircumference()` Return the circumference of this instance.

How would you, as client, use the services of this class to compute the area and circumference of (say) a 3×5 rectangle?

Well, we see that the needed methods are both not static, so according to the recipe, we cannot invoke them directly on the class; we can only invoke them on an instance of the class. We therefore need to create an instance first. We see that the API does have a constructor so we can use it to create the instance. This leads us to the following client code fragment:

```
1  int x = 3;
2  int y = 4;
3  Rectangle r = new Rectangle(x, y);
4  int a = r.getArea();
5  int c = r.getCircumference();
6  System.out.println(a);
7  System.out.println(c);
```

The relevant code is Statements 3, 4, and 5.

Compare and contrast the two cases. Both will correctly compute the area and circumference so the only difference is the invocation syntax.

At a deeper level, however, note that the dimensions of the rectangle was passed to the class only once (through the constructor). Afterwards, we only specify the method name without re-sending the dimensions. The instance (aka object) thus remembers our dimension. This is the essence of the **objected-oriented** paradigm.

L1.2.c – The Implementer View

It is instructive to revisit the two examples of the previous section but this time from the implementer point of view. You are not expected to be able to implement the two APIs yourself at this stage so we provide them below. You are expected to take the time to think them through by comparing and contrasting the two.

Example 1

The API in this example shows all methods as static, and hence, the class does not need a constructor (since no instances are needed). The job of the constructor is to set the state of the instance, but since no constructor is needed, then no state is needed either, and hence, no attributes. We conclude from this that the class body needs only two blocks for two public methods. The headers are already in the API so we copy them as-is to the class body and then implement the body of each.

The first method, getArea, receives the width and height of the rectangle through parameters named w and h. The area of a rectangle is the product of its width and height. Hence, we just multiple these two and return the result.

The second method, getCircumference, also receives the width and height of the rectangle through parameters named w and h. The circumference of a rectangle is the sum of its four sides, i.e. two widths and two heights. One way to do that would be to add the width and the height and multiply the sum by 2 then return the result.

The complete implementation is shown below.

```
public class Rectangle
{
    public static int getArea(int w, int h)
    {
        int result = w * h;
        return result;
    }

    public static int getCircumference(int w, int h)
    {
        int result = w + h;
        result = result * 2;
        return result;
    }
}
```

Example 2

The API in this example shows a constructor and instance (non-static) methods. Hence, we do need to hold a state, and to that end, we declare two integer attributes to store the width and the height. These must be private, not public, since they don't appear in the API.

The complete implementation is shown below.

```
public class Rectangle
{
    private int width;
    private int height;

    public Rectangle(int w, int h)
    {
        this.width = w;
        this.height = h;
    }

    public int getArea()
    {
        int result = this.width * this.height;
        return result;
    }

    public int getCircumference()
    {
        int result = this.width + this.height;
        result = result * 2;
        return result;
    }
}
```

The constructor initializes the state of the instance to be created based on the parameters it receives. Note that we always prefix attributes with ".this" when we refer to them.

The computational aspects of the other two methods is the same as they static case with one notable exception: these methods do not receive any parameters from the calling client. Instead, they use the values stored in the attributes (i.e. the state of this instance). This is why both methods end with () which signifies an empty parameter list.

Compare this implementation with that of Example 1 and you will quickly see the difference between the functional and the object-oriented paradigms: both perform the same computations but the functional one has no state.

L1.2.d – API Examples

To raise our comfort level (as clients) with APIs, let's take a look at a few from the standard Java library.

The Math class has a large number of methods that do various mathematical computations. Here is the API of two of them:

Methods (Math class)
```public static double pow(double b, double e)```   Return the power b^e (the base b raised to the exponent e).
```public static double random()```   Return a random number in [0,1).

Both methods are static, which means we can invoke it on the class itself (no instantiation) and both return a real number (a double).

As indicated, the first method returns a power computed from the two parameters we send. Hence, if we write a code fragment like this:

```
double x = 2;
double y = 3;
double z = Math.pow(x, y);
```

the value of z should be 8.

The second method also returns a double and does not take any parameters (we don't send it anything). The returned number is randomly chosen with uniform distribution over [0,1); i.e. all values in this interval are equally likely to be chosen so if we invoke this method a large number of times, the distribution of the returned values should be uniform.

Note that the interval is closed-open (bracket=closed, parenthesis=open) which means it includes 0 but exclude 1. The returned value therefore satisfies:

$$0 \quad \Leftarrow \text{ returned value} < 1$$

For example, if we write a fragment like this:

```
double x = Math.random();
double y = Math.random();
double z = Math.random();
```

then the values of x,y,z would be different every time we run the code.

We look next at this API from the String class:

Methods (String class)
`public static String format(String f, int n)` Return a string containing n formatted according to f.
`public static String format(String f, double n)` Return a string containing n formatted according to f.

The format method converts the second parameter it receives (integer or real number) to a string after formatting it using the format specified in the first parameter.

A few examples:

- `format("%d", 1234)`
  Converts the integer to a string (d indicates a decimal integer).
  Returns "1234".

- `format("%,d", 1234)`
  Converts the integer to a string and adds a thousand separator.
  Returns "1,234".

- `format("%f", 1234.567)`
  Converts the real to a string (f indicates a floating-point number).
  Returns "1234.567".

- `format("%.2f", 1234.567)`
  Converts the real to a string after rounding to 2 decimals.
  Returns "1234.57".

- `format("%,.2f", 1234.567)`
  Converts the real to a string after rounding to 2 decimals and adds a thousand separator.
  Returns "1,234.57".

- `format("%6d", 1234)`
  Converts the integer to a string of *six* characters by prepending spaces.
  Returns " 1234".

- `format("%,10.2f", 1234.567)`
  Converts the real to a string of ten characters with 2 decimals and a thousand separator.
  Returns " 1,234.57".

L1.3 – THE TESTBED PROJECT

L1.3.a – Building the Project

In order to become competent in Java development, and indeed in the computing field in general, it is critical that you work at a computer. Yes, you can study the physics of skating by reading a book, but if you ever want to actually skate, you had better go on the rink. Even when you have doubt about a simple thing, such as *"Can I write 2 or 2.0?"*, it is much faster to actually try it out than to search the Internet or ask someone. It is also better because "*it teaches you how to fish rather than just give you a fish*". It is for these reasons that we want to build a test bed that allows us to quickly write a few lines of code and run them.

Since this is about Java rather than Android, this test bed does not need a view or an activity, just a POJO. As such, follow these steps to build a new project that will be used throughout the rest of this book:

1. Launch your Android Studio. If it prompts you to update anything (whether in this screen or in any other), reject the update by closing these prompts.
2. Start a new project.
3. Name the new project *TestBed* and accept the other defaults then click Next.
4. Accept the Phone/Tablet platform and the default minimum SDK then click Next.
5. Select the *Add No Activity* choice then click Finish.

When IDE launches, if the project pane on the left is not visible, click on the Project tab on the left margin to show it.

L1.3.b – Creating Packages and Classes

We will organize our classes in packages, and we will have one package per chapter:

1. Open the *app* tree in the project pane and then the *java* subtree to see the three packages in the app, the main package and two testing ones). Right-click the main package and select *New...*, and then *Package*. When prompted the package name, enter *chapter1*. This will be a sub-package inside the main package.
2. Repeat the above step several times to create packages *chapter2*, *chapter3*, ... *chapter 5*.

The chapter exercises will ask you to create classes in these packages. To do that, right-click the appropriate package name and select *New...*, *Java Class* and then enter the class name.

L1.4 – EXERCISES

1. Consider the BMIModel class whose implementation is shown in Section D1.3.b.

    a. List five keywords that appear in it.

    b. List all the identifiers that appear in it.

    c. List one literal that appears in it.

    d. List three operators that appear in it.

    e. List three separators that appear in it.

2. For each of the following statements, determine if it is true or false and present a brief yet complete logical argument that justifies your answer:

    a. Runtime errors are worse than compile-time errors.

    b. It is a compile-time error to divide a number by zero.

    c. It is a runtime error to take the square root of a negative number.

    d. Testing can reveal the presence of compile-time errors.

3. Based on your understanding of the client and implementer roles, describe a scenario in which the implementer can act as a client.

4. Create the class **Rectangle1** in the *chapter1* package of the *TestBed* project. It is the same as the class implemented in Example 1 of Section 1.2.c except we added 1 to the name. You can copy the implementation as-is from that section except for the name change.

    To test your work, create a second class, in the same package, named *UseRectangle*. In it, put only a main method (use the *psvm* shortcut). Insert code in the body of the main method so it acts as a client for your Rectangle1 class.

    Hint: Insert code that is similar to the client code fragment shown in Section 1.2.b, Example 1.

5. Create the class **Rectangle2** in the *chapter1* package of the *TestBed* project. It is the same as the class implemented in Example 2 of Section 1.2.c except we added 2 to the name. You can copy the implementation as-is from that section except for the name change.

    To test the new class, add a few lines to the main method of the *UseRectangle* class along the lines of the client code fragment shown in Section 1.2.b, Example 2.

6. Read the API of the method **parseDouble** in class **Double** in the standard Java library. To demonstrate your understanding of its functionality, create a class named *UseDouble* in the *chapter1* package of the *TestBed* project, and in it, write only a main method (psvm) that uses parseDouble.

   You could, for example, pass the string "1022.03" to the method; capture its return in a double variable, and then output the value of that variable.

   Note that the model of your BMI app uses this method.

7. Based on your understanding of the functionality of the **pow** method of the **Math** class in the standard Java library, create a class named *UseMath* in the *chapter1* package of *TestBed*. In its main method, use pow to compute:

   a. The cubic root of 27 using 0.3 as exponent.

   b. The cubic root of 27 using 0.3333 as exponent.

   c. The cubic root of 27 using 1/3 as exponent.

   d. The cubic root of 27 using 1.0/3.0 as exponent.

8. Based on your understanding of the functionality of the **format** method of the **String** class in the standard Java library, create a class named *UseFormat* in the *chapter1* package of *TestBed*. In its main method, write code that explores the following:

   a. What happens if we try to format a 5-digit integer such as 10350 using the format specifier "%7d"?

   b. What happens if we try to format a 5-digit integer such as 10350 using the format specifier "%-7d"?

   c. What happens if we try to format a 5-digit integer such as 10350 using the format specifier "%3d"?

   d. What happens if we try to format a 5-digit integer such as 10350 using the format specifier "%7f"?

9. Read the API of the method **repeat** in class **Utility** in the i2c library. Then, create a class named *UseUtility* in the *chapter1* package of *TestBed*, and in its main method write a code fragment that demonstrates your understanding of the repeat functionality.

   Note that in order to pass a char such as an asterisk to the method, you must enclose it in single quotes, not double, e.g. '*' rather than "*".

10. Read the API of the **Equation** class in the i2c library. After wards, add code to the main method of your *UseUtility* class that uses **Equation** in order to solve the equation:

$$x^2 - 5x + 6 = 0$$

Your code must culminate with displaying the two roots of the equation; i.e. the values of x that make the left-hand side equal to zero.

Hint:
Follow the pattern shown in the client code fragment of Section 1.2.b, Example 2. Since the root finding functionality of this class is not static, you will need to create an instance of the class first, using its constructor, and then invoke the method that fetches the roots. Note that the three coefficients to be passed to the constructors for the above equation are 1, –5, and 6. Once an instance

CHAPTER 2 – DOING

Declare, Set, Go!

D2.1 REQUIREMENT

D2.1.a The MCalc App
D2.1.b UI and Behaviour

D2.2 DESIGN

D2.2.a The Model
D2.2.b The View
D2.2.c The Controller

D2.3 IMPLEMENTATION

D2.3.a Model Testing via PSVM
D2.3.b Model Testing via JUnit

D2.4 DEPLOYMENT

D2.5 EXERCISES

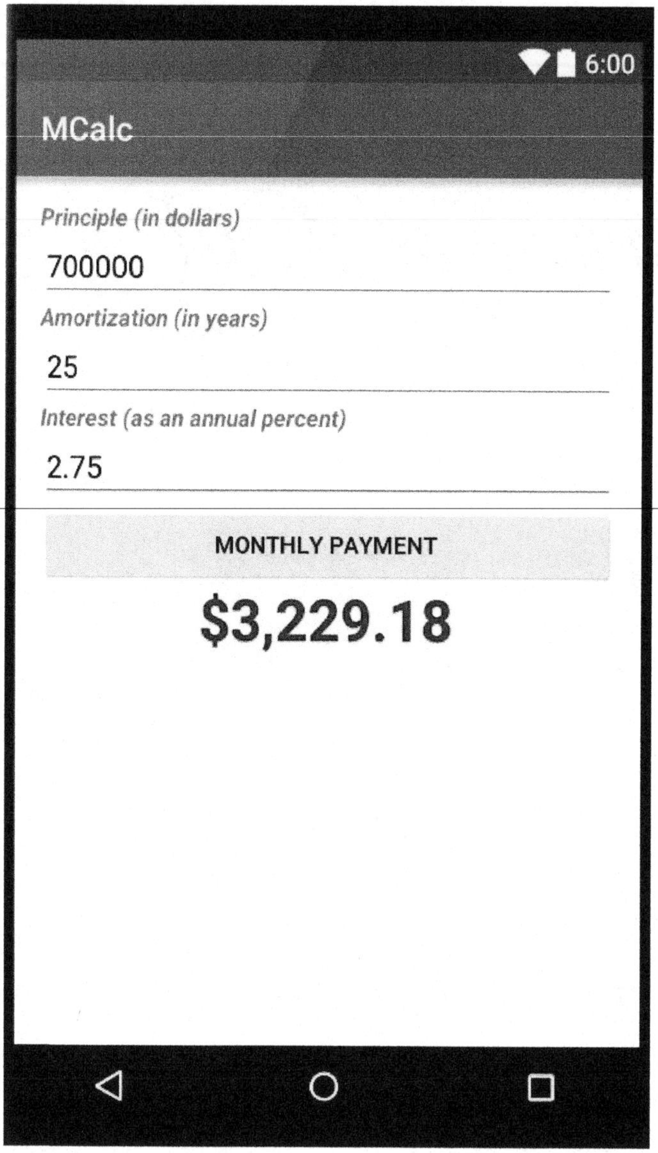

Figure D2.1 App launched, three entries made, the button tapped.

D2.1 – REQUIREMENT

D2.1.a – The Mortgage App

The objective of this project is to build an Android app to help users determine their ability to afford buying a house. If the house price is $700,000 for example, then this amount is known as the *principle*. If you don't have this amount, you would need to approach a bank to get a mortgage. If approved, the bank will purchase the house for you and you would need to pay the bank back through a sequence of monthly payments whose value is determined based on three things: the principle, the *annual interest rate* (e.g. 4.5%), and the *amortization* period (the number of years you have to keep making monthly payments). The amortization in Canada is typically between 20 and 30 years.

D2.1.b – UI and Behaviour

The UI of the sought app consists of *eight* vertically aligned widgets (see Fig. D2.1):

1. A label that says "*Principle (in dollars)*".
2. A textbox for entering the principle.
3. A label that says "*Amortization (in years)*".
4. A textbox for entering the amortization.
5. A label that says "*Interest(as an annual percent)*".
6. A textbox for entering the interest.
7. A button with caption "*MONTHLY PAYMENT*".
8. A label for displaying the answer.

The eight widgets extend across the entire width of the device (phone or tablet) regardless of device dimensions and whether held in portrait or landscape orientation. Text must be left-aligned except for the button caption and the computed payment which must be centred.

In terms of behaviour, the app must display the computed payment whenever the button is tapped. The payment (which is a real number) should be rounded to the nearest cent, should have a thousands separator, and must appear in large red text.

This release assumes, as a precondition, that all three inputs are valid.

D2.2 – DESIGN

D2.2.a – The Model

The model class is responsible for holding the data of the app (principle, interest, and amortization) and for performing the payment computation. Hence, we design its API like this:

Constructor
public MortgageModel(String p, String a, String i) Construct an instance of the class having a principle p, an amortization period a, and an annual interest rate i.
Method
public String computePayment() Return the monthly mortgage payment rounded to the nearest cent.

You can tell from the constructor that the class name is MortgageModel.java.

Note that the model communicates with the outside world through strings because this is the language of the UI. Internally, however, it should maintain its data (the attributes) and perform the computation (in the method) using the appropriate types; namely, double for the principle and interest and int for the amortization.

The computation of the monthly payment is done using this formula:

$$\frac{rP}{1 - (1 + r)^{-n}}$$

where:

- P is the principle.

- r is the *monthly* interest *percentage*, not percent.
  For example, if the user entered 4.5 then r would be 0.045/12 = 0.00375.
- n is the number of months in the amortization.
  For example, if the user entered 20 then n would be 20*12=240.

D2.2.b – The View

Name your layout file *mortgage_layout.xml*. Its content, the UI, is pretty much completely specified in the requirement. Use appropriate widgets and set their attributes according to the given specifications.

D2.2.c – The Controller

Name your activity class *EntryForm.java*. The controller should handle the tap of the button and communicate with the model. It should also poke the computed payment in the view.

D2.3 – IMPLEMENTATION

It is your job now to implement the design. Create a new project named **MCalc** and make sure its activity and layout are named as per the design document. Start by implementing the model, and to that end, use `Math.pow` for the power and `String.format` with `"$%,.2f"` for the formatting. The next two sections elaborate on testing your model.

D2.3.a – Model Testing via PSVM

As we have been doing so far in this book, we test our model by adding a `main` method to it. The method should instantiate the class and then run several test cases. Here is an outline

```
public static void main(String[] args)
{
   MortgageModel myModel = new MortgageModel("700000", "25", "2.75");
   System.out.println(myModel.computePayment());

   myModel = new MortgageModel("300000", "20", "4.50");
   System.out.println(myModel.computePayment());

   ...

}
```

When you run the main method, several output lines would appear and you would need to use your calculator as oracle to verify the correctness of each.

D2.3.b – Model Testing via JUnit

Using a main method to test your class works pretty well but it doesn't scale as the model becomes more complex in terms of the number of methods it has and the number of test cases needed. Because of this, a framework that automates the testing process has been developed and it is widely adopted in the industry. It is called JUnit and we will use it to test our model.

1. In the project pane on the left, open the app tree and open the java tree within it.
2. The java tree has three packages within it:
   a. The main package which holds our activity and model.
   b. The *androidTest* Package.
   c. The *test* Package.
3. Right-click the test package and select New... then Java class.
4. Name the class ModelTest.
5. Write only one method in the class body, as shown below:

```
@Test
public void testPayment()
{
    MortgageModel myModel;

    myModel = new MortgageModel("700000", "25", "2.75");
    Assert.assertEquals("C1", "$3,229.18", myModel.computePayment());

    myModel = new MortgageModel("300000", "20", "4.5");
    Assert.assertEquals("C2", "$3,000.00", myModel.computePayment());
}
```

As usual, the IDE will complain when you refer to any feature that has not been imported, so identifiers such as Assert or @Test will be highlighted in red. And as usual, you fix this by clicking on the highlighted word and pressing Alt-Enter.

Once, done, right-click the testPayment method header and select to run it (yes, you can run just one method in the JUnit framework). Studio will open a testing pane in the bottom and show you any case that failed. In this case, the second should fail because we intentionally used an incorrect oracle payment so you can see what happens. Replace the $3,000.00 with the correct amount and re-run. You should not get an all-green result.

A few notes about the JUnit class we just wrote:

- We named the class *ModelTest* but you could use any other name. The key requirement is to place it under the (test) package so that it can access the JUnit framework.

- We named the method *testPayment* but you could use any other name. The key require-ment is for it to be `public void` and with no parameters, and to be preceded by the `@Test` annotation. Annotation are meta-descriptions that tie the method being annotated with the JUnit framework.

- Within the method's body, we instantiate the model (as we did in the PSVM approach) and then invoke the `computePayment` method on the instance. We do this several times, once per test case. The only difference between this approach and PSVM is that rather than printing the computed payment, we assert that it is equal to the oracle's answer.

- As you can tell, `assertEquals` is a static method in the `Assert` class (part of the JUnit framework) and it takes three String parameters: a message that identifies the test case, the expected answer (coming from the oracle), and the model's answer.

JUnit seems pretty much the same as PSVM so why do we need it? Well, two reasons:

A. Separation of Concerns
Testing a class and implementing it are two different concerns. Sticking a `main` method inside the class body is a clear violation of the concern separation principle.

B. Regression Testing
It is typical for apps to have more than one model class. If your app has n model classes and you use PSVM, you will need to run n `main` methods every time a change is made in any of the classes. This is cumbersome and may lead developers to test only the modified class and forget to re-test the rest of the classes. But with JUnit, your tests appear as n `@Test` methods all residing in one class, so with one click, you can re-run all tests. The term *Regression Testing* refers to re-testing all components of an application after a change is done in any component within it.

D2.4 – DEPLOYMENT

The last step in the development process involves deploying the app on a device and doing integration testing.

D2.5 – Exercises

In order to practice your skills, augment your app by implementing these new requirements:

1. Modify the keyboard that pops when the principle, amortization, and interest boxes are focused so that only valid entries can be made. Recall that a valid amortization entry must an integer whereas the other two entries must be real. And to ensure no decimal point and no negative numbers are entered, set also the allowed characters.
    Hint: Look for two textbox attributes that control the input type and the digits.

2. Modify the app's badge to an image of a house or a building so it better reflects what the app is about. Follow the same procedure you did in Chapter 1.

3. Modify the view so that the computed payment appears in italics. Deploy the modified app and test it.
    Hint: Look for a label attribute that controls the text style.

4. Modify the view so that the computed payment appears without a thousands separator and without decimals; i.e. in dollars only. Deploy the modified app and test it.

5. Modify your model by adding this method to it:

    ### public String outstandingAfter(int x)

    Implement the new method so it returns the remaining balance to be paid to the bank if the mortgage is terminated (prematurely) after x months from its inception. This amount is computed using the formula:

    $$P - (\frac{monthlyPayment}{r} - P)((1 + r)^x - 1)$$

    where *monthlyPayment* is the payment the app computes. The return must be rounded to the nearest dollar and must have a thousands separator.

    Test your implementation using a calculator as oracle. For example, if a 25-year mortgage with a $700,000 principle at 2.75% is terminated after 5 years (during which monthly payments of $3,229.18 were made), then the outstanding balance should be $595,606.

6. Modify the UI of your app by adding a button and a label below the monthly payment label.

The new widgets enable the user to determine how much would still be owing to the bank if the mortgage were terminated after *five* years.

The UI is shown in Fig. D2.2.

Normally, a mortgage is carried to the end of its amortization period, and by making the regular monthly payments throughout this period, the balance still owing will reduce to zero after the very last payment. But if the mortgage is terminated before its amortization period then a non-zero outstanding balance remains and can be computed as shown in the previous exercise.

The modified app captures the outstanding balance after 5 years; i.e. x=5*12=60.

Figure D2.2 The modified UI.

❖ ❖ ❖ ❖

7. Create a new project named *Temperature* with an empty activity and use any name you like for its activity and layout. The UI consists of a textbox at the top and three buttons below it as shown in Fig. D2.3. Make sure the text is centered in the textbox.

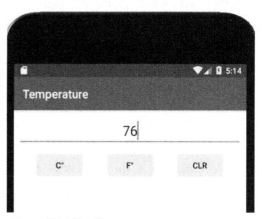

The user enters a temperature (e.g. 76) and then taps one of the three buttons. If **C°** is tapped then the entry is converted from Fahrenheit to Celsius and the result (rounded to 1 decimal) is written back in the textbox thus overwriting the entry (e.g. 24.4).

Figure D2.3 The Temperature app.

The conversion is done the other way around if **F°** is tapped. And if **CLR** is tapped then the textbox is cleared. Note that all numbers are real (double) and that the conversion formula is C=5(F-32)/9 which implies F=32+9C/5.

8. Create a new project named *Satellite* with an empty activity and use any name you like for its activity and layout. The UI (shown in Fig. D2.4) consists of a label prompt at the top, an entry textbox under it, a button, and finally a label to hold the result.

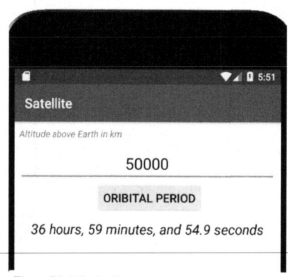

Figure D2.4 The Satellite app.

The app computes the orbital period P of a satellite (i. e. how long it takes it to go around the Earth once) given its height A above the Earth surface. The user enters A (in kilometers) and then taps the button. The result is shown in terms of the hours (integer), the minutes (integer), and the seconds (real, rounded to 1 decimal).

The design phase revealed that the following formula is to be used:

$$P = K \, (A + R)^{3/2}$$

Here, P is the orbital period in seconds, A is the altitude in kilometers, and K and R are constants: K=0.00995, R=6378.

Note that the formula gives P in seconds, so in the example shown (A=50,000), P works out to be ~133194.895. You will need to express this in hours, minutes, and seconds.

As a second test case, if the altitude is 1,000 km then the app's output should be:

1 hours, 45 minutes, and 5.7 seconds

CHAPTER 2 – LEARNING

Declare, Set, Go!

L2.1 – DECLARE

L2.1.a – The int Type

The term **type** refers to a set of values <u>and</u> a set of operations on these values. To distinguish one type from another, we give each a unique name. The set of values must be **closed** under all the operations; i.e. if we operate on the values in the set using any of the operations, we should end up with a result that is also a member of the set.

For example, consider the set of integer values in $[-2G, +2G-1]$ (where $G = 2^{30} \approx$ one billion) together with the five operations:

- **+** for addition,
- **–** for subtraction,
- ***** for multiplication,
- **/** for division, and
- **%** for remainder (aka modulus), e.g. 7%3=1 and 2%4=2

Note that division here refers to integer division, so 7/2=3 (*not* 3.5) and 2/4=0 (*not* 0.5). But is the set closed under these operations? No! Adding two integers in the set, for example, could yield a sum outside the set, and the same happens with subtraction and multiplication. To ensure closure, Java *wraps* the set (i.e. treats it as circular) so the number that comes after +2G-1 is -2G. This takes care of all problems except for one: division by zero. Java's solution is to make such a division illegal by crashing any program that attempts it.

With these fixes in place, this becomes a "*respectable*" type and it is called int.

Every variable in your program must be **declared** before it is used. The declaration specifies the name of the variable and the type of values that it is intended to hold. The declaration statement has the general form:

> *type variableName;*

where *type* is the name of the type and *variableName* is the name of the variable.

For example, to declare that you intend to have a variable named count in your program and that you will store in it values that belong to the int type, you would write:

```
int count;
```

The declaration is valid (and hence the variable can be used) starting from the statement that follows its declaration and ending at the end of the smallest block that encloses the declaration. This area is known as the **scope** of the variable.

You cannot refer to a variable outside its scope; doing so would lead to a compile-time error. Hence, if a method in your class declared a variable with name count and a second method declared a variable with the same name then this is OK because these two variables reside in different scopes and are completely unrelated (and can conceivably have different types). Because of this, any variable declared within a method is known as a **local variable**. In contrast, attributes are declared outside all methods, so their scope is the entire class, and that is why they are sometimes known as *global variables*. Nevertheless, you should always prefix any attribute with "this." when you refer to it in constructors and methods within the class.

L2.1.b – The double Type

Also known as *double precision*, this type is intended for storing real numbers, such as amounts of money and scientific measurements. Its operations are the same five as the int type but division here refers to real division, so 7.0/2.0=3.5 and 7.5%3.0=1.5. The value-set consists of all real numbers whose values belong to the interval [-2F, +2F], where $F = 10^{308}$, and whose *significant digit count* does not exceed 15. The significant digit count of a number is its digit count aside from leading or trailing zeros. Hence, 100.0 has 1 whereas 100.01 has 5 significant digit.

Unlike the int case, the value-set here could not be specified by just a range because there are infinitely many real numbers in any range. That is why we see an additional restriction related to accuracy. Whenever you use double to store a value in the range, it is rounded to the nearest 15-significant-digit value. This may seem like a minor issue, and it is for a single number, but if the program involves repeated computations, these *round-off errors* may add up. Handling these errors is beyond the scope of this book but lack of precision should always be kept in mind when it gets to double.

How about closure? Since the operations always round, their results will always be in the set except for two cases: going outside the range and dividing by zero. Java has a creative fix for each: it adds three elements to the value-set: +Infinity, -Infinity, and NaN. If an operation leads to a result outside the range, it is replaced by ±∞, so the result would be in the set! The same applies for dividing by zero. And if we computed (3.0/0.0)*0.0 (i.e. infinite times zero) then the result is set to NaN (Not a Number) which is also in the set.

With these fixes in place, **double** becomes a "*respectable*" type. To declare a **double** variable named price, we write:

```
double price;
```

The fact that **double** and **int** share the same symbols for their operators and their literals creates an ambiguity. For example, when we write the literal 2 in a program, do we mean for it to be **double** or **int** ? And does / imply real or integer division?

When a symbol such as 2 or / has more than one meaning, we say it is *overloaded* and we look for rules to resolve the ambiguity. Here are the rules for the int/double overloading:

1. A numeric literal is **int** unless it contains a decimal point or it is suffixed with D or it is suffixed with E and an exponent. For example, 200 is int whereas 200. and 200.0 and 200D and 2E2 are all double (and all equal). The E/D suffix is case insensitive.

2. An operator in {+,-,*,/,%} resolves its type by looking at its two operands. If either is **double** then it is the **double** operator. In other words, it is an **int** operator only if both operands are **int**.

Based on the above, **1/2 = 0** whereas **1./2 = 1d/2 = 0.5**.

L2.1.c – The boolean Type

Perhaps the simplest of all types, it has the value-set {true, false} (recall that these two are keywords and must always be written in lowercase) and the operations:

- ! for *negate* (a unary operation)
- && for *and*
- || for *or*
- ∧ for *exclusive or*

Hence, ! toggles between true and false, && leads to true only if both operands are true, || leads to false only if both operands are false, ∧ leads to true if its operands are different.

The set is manifestly closed under these operations, so **boolean** is a "*respectable*" type.

Since this type may be not be as familiar as the numeric ones, the fragment below highlights how it can be used in a computation:

```
1  boolean x, y, z;
2  x = true;
3  y = false;
4  z = x && y;
5  boolean t = !z;
6  System.out.println(z);
7  System.out.println(t);
```

The firs statement declares three boolean variables. Statements 2 and 3 sets the values of two of them. Statement 4 sets the value of z as the *and* of x and y, and since y is false then z would be false. Statement 5 sets the value of t as the negation of z so t would be true. This reasoning leads us to predict that the two outputs of the fragment are false and true.

L2.1.d – Other Primitive Types

In addition to the three types we covered (int, double, boolean), Java has five more types:

- **byte** is similar to int but has a narrower range.
- **short** is similar to int but has a narrower range.
- **char** is similar to short but accepts non-negative values only.
- **long** is similar to int but has a wider range.
- **float** is similar to double but has a narrower range and lower accuracy.

The table below lists all eight types and provides additional details about each.

Primitive Type	Size (bytes)	Approximate Range min	max	Sig. Digits	Operators
byte	1	-128	+127	N/A	+ – * / %
short	2	-32,768	+32,767	N/A	+ – * / %
char	2	0	65,535	N/A	+ – * / %
▶ int	4	-2×10^9	$+2 \times 10^9$	N/A	+ – * / %
long	8	-9×10^{18}	$+9 \times 10^{18}$	N/A	+ – * / %
float	4	-3×10^{38}	$+3 \times 10^{38}$	7	+ – * / %
▶ double	8	-2×10^{308}	$+2 \times 10^{308}$	15	+ – * / %
▶ boolean	1	true / false		N/A	! && || ^

As you can see, the five additional types are all numeric and they use the same five operators as int and double. As such, they are only used in situations that have memory size restrictions or specific range requirement. In fact, our three basic types (the ones with ▶ next to their rows in the table) are sufficient to implement all the apps developed in this book.

These eight data types are known as Java's *primitive types*. They are called "primitive" because they are supported by the language itself rather than by its library. Specifically:

- Their type names (int, double, boolean, etc.) are keywords, *not* identifiers.
- Their value-sets are predefined and fixed (as in the table above).
- Their operations are carried out via operators, *not* methods.

L2.1.e – Non-Primitive Types

The eight primitive types enable us to store and process numeric and boolean values but the world around us is full of other types of entities. For example:

- A fraction (such as ½ or ¾) is neither an integer nor a real number and is certainly not a boolean. Its "value" involves two integers (numerator and denominator) and its operations (e.g. add two fractions) is more complex than a simple integer addition.

- A picture is also something that primitive types cannot capture because its "value" involves lots of attributes (e.g. pixels, date taken, location, etc.) and its operations (e.g. crop, brighten, overlay) are more complex than addition and multiplication.

- A phrase (such as "Toronto, Canada") is also something that primitive types cannot capture because its "value" involves several characters and its operations (e.g. split, capitalize, concatenate) are quite different from arithmetic and boolean operations.

In order to accommodate such entities, Java supports three *non-primitive* types:

1. The Class Type

Probably the most versatile of all types, the class type allows us to define any value-set we like and any operation. For example, we can define a new class type named `Fraction` and use it to declare variables using a statement like this:

```
Fraction x;
```

Unlike primitive types, the name of a class type is a user-defined identifier (*not* a keyword) and its operations are carried out via methods (*not* operators). The Java and Android libraries come with thousands of ready-made class types that you can use. The `i2c.jar` library associated with this book also has several class types that you can leverage in your programs. And when we don't find the needed functionality in a library class type, we define our own. For example, `MortgageModel` is a class type that we created to capture a mortgage: an entity whose value-set consists of three strings (principle, amortization, and interest) and whose operation allows us to determine the monthly payment.

2. The Array Type

This type captures a homogeneous collection of entities. By "homogeneous" we mean that all these entities must have the same type (which can be primitive or non-primitive). The name of the array type is derived from the entities' type by appending it with `[]` (open and closed brackets). For example, an array of `int` entities is declared using a statement like this:

```
int[] bag;
```

Once an array is populated, you can refer to its individual elements using the element's index; e.g. `bag[0]` gives you the first int element and `bag[1]` gives the second, and so on.

The array type comes with one operation only: it is named length and it returns the number of entities in the array. For example, if the bag array declared above contains 20 elements then bag.length would be 20.

3. The Interface Type

This type captures design specifications of class types. For example, any text messaging app must, at a minimum, provide two functionalities: one to start a new conversation and one to send a message. The app designer can capture this by creating the interface Messageable which describes these two functionalities without indicating how they are implemented; i.e. the interface contains the method headers but not their bodies. When the app is built, its class header would look as shown below (the **implements** clause declares that this class has the complete bodies of all the methods specified in the interface):

```
public class TextingApp implements Messageable
```

Since the interface type does *not* specify a value-set, only operation headers, you can think of it as an API that Java understands and enforces.

A Note About Strings

All types in Java are either primitive or non-primitive but there is one particular type that is rather confusing: the String type. It is a class type, and hence non-primitive, but unlike other non-primitive types, it is supported by the language itself (not just its library), which makes it resemble primitive types!

Because strings are quite common in applications, Java has added syntactical sugar to make string programming "sweeter". Specifically,

1. A sequence of characters enclosed in double quotes is recognized by the language as a *String literal*, e.g. "Hello". Because of this, String variables can be declared and set as if they were primitive, e.g.

    ```
    String s = "Hello";
    ```

    All other non-primitive types have no literals associated with them, and hence, the process of declaring and setting their variables is not as simple as the above.

2. The *string concatenation* operation, which joins strings, is carried out by an operator, not a method. For example, the statements:

    ```
    String s = "Hello";
    String t = s + " from Canada";
    ```

    result in t being the string "Hello from Canada".

Keep this special treatment in mind when you deal with strings.

L2.2 – SET

L2.2.a – The Assignment Statement

The assignment statement has the following general form:

variableName = value;

The left-hand side (LHS) is the name of a variable that has already been declared. The right-hand side (RHS) is the value to be assigned to the variable. For example, to declare count as an int variable and assign the value 3 to it, you write:

```
int count;
count = 3;
```

You can optionally combine declaration with assignment by writing:

```
int count = 3;
```

Once a value is assigned to a variable, we say that the variable has been *set* or *initialized*.

To execute the assignment statement, the following algorithm is followed:

1. If the LHS is not a declared variable, issue a compile-time error.
2. Evaluate the RHS until you culminate in a value.
3. If the type of RHS is not compatible with that of LHS, issue a compile-time error.
4. Set the LHS to the RHS value.

In light of this, let us analyze this code fragment:

```
1  int x, y;
2  double z;
3  x = 7;
4  t = 5;
5  y = 2.5;
6  z = true;
7  boolean w = 1;
```

The fragment contains five assignment statements of which only one (Statement 3) is valid. Can you see why?

The one on Line 4 refers to an undeclared variable while the one on Line 5 is trying to assign a double value to an int. The next two statements also involves incompatible types.

The value on the right-hand side can be one of three things:

- A **literal**.
- A **variable** that has already been declared and set.
- An **expression** involving a combination of the above two.

This is demonstrated in the following fragment:

```
1  int x, y, z;
2  x = 5;
3  y = x;
4  z = 1 + x;
5  x = 3;
```

- The first statement declares three int variables.
- The second has a literal in its RHS. At this point, x is 5 while y and z are not set.
- The third has a variable in its RHS. At this point, x is 5, y is 5, and z is not set.
- The fourth has an expression that evaluates to 6 in its RHS. Now, x is 5, y is 5, and z is 6.
- The fifth statement has a literal in its RHS. At this point, x is 3, y is 5, and z is 6.

The = operator in between LHS and RHS is the *assignment* operator, and it is important that you think of it as performing the algorithm described above rather than an equality between two things. The point is best seen in light of the above code fragment. If you think of = as an equality then you might be led to believe that the value of y at the end of the fragment should be 3, not 5, because if the third line declares an equality between y and x, then since x became 3 then so should y. This common mistake (mistaking assignment with mathematical equality) can be avoided by always treating = as an algorithmic task that does some work and then ends. Its work does not persist beyond its statement. Incidentally, the notion of equality does appear in Java in the context of testing if two things are equal, and in that context, its operator is == but this is has nothing to do with assignment so *don't* mix = up with ==.

L2.2.b – Memory Allocation

In this section we take a look "under the hood" in order to understand what really happens inside the computer when we declare or set a variable. These mechanisms operate at a layer below the abstraction level at which we have been operating in this book, but we feel it will be helpful to take a peek at them in order to form a correct mental model.

Computer memory can be viewed as a one-dimensional arrangement of cells each of which is called a *byte* and is denoted by B. The total number of bytes in memory is known as RAM *(Random Access Memory)* and is measured in multiples of bytes, e.g. GB (~ 1 billion bytes).

The bytes are numbered sequentially as shown, starting with 0, and this number is known as the memory *address* of the byte. The partitioning wall between one byte and the next can be thought of as removable, so if we need to store something that doesn't fit in one byte, we can make room by removing some walls.

When you make a declaration such as:

```
int count;
```

the system needs to reserve a spot in memory to hold the future value of count. It knows that `int` needs 4 bytes so it looks for 4 consecutive bytes that are free, removes the walls between them, and then associate their starting address (which is 16 in the figure) with `count`. From that point on, `count` is 16 in the eyes of the system, so if you later wrote:

```
count = -5;
```

the system interprets the assignment as saying: "*Take the RHS value (which is -5) and store it in the location reserved for the LHS (which is 16)*". In this sense, the word "variable" is a misnomer at this abstraction level because its "value" never changes! This observation gives us a glimpse of the fact that different abstraction levels, albeit each correct on its own, can seem contradictory. At the higher level, we don't see addresses, and since we can change the value assigned to the identifier, we call it a variable. But at the deeper level, the identifier is just an address of a memory spot (so it never changes) whereas the value is the content of that spot.

As an analogy, think of memory as the seating plan of a theatre, and imagine purchasing a ticket to see a show. The ticket says *"Admit One to Seat #16"* so it doesn't matter who uses it; you can use it yourself or give it to a friend. Declaring a variable is like purchasing a ticket, so the variable is the ticket. Assigning a value to the variable is like using the ticket, so whoever goes to see the show (and sit in the seat) is the value.

Finally, we shed some light on the strange-looking ranges of the value-sets of integer types. Each memory byte is itself divided into 8 smaller cells each of which is called a *bit*. One bit can store only one of two things, e.g. 0 or 1. Hence, a byte can store one of $2^8=256$ different things. If we want to store an integer in one byte (which is appropriate for the `byte` type), there can only be 256 elements in the value-set, so if we start at -128, we end up at +127. Similarly, if we want to store an integer in 4 bytes (appropriate for `int`), there can only be $2^{32}=4G$ elements, so if we start at -2G, we end up at +2G-1.

Similar arguments apply for other types such as `double`. The ranges in all these types derive from the fact that the number of elements in the value-set must be equal to 2^{8N}, where N is the number of bytes reserved for each element.

L2.2.c – Setting Class-Type Variables

The assignment statement can also be used to set variables of class types. Consider for example the following fragment:

```
Fraction x;
x = new Fraction(1, 2);
```

The first statement declares the variable (as was done in Section L2.1.e) and the second sets it to the fraction ½. The algorithm of the assignment statement is the same as in Section L2.2.a, namely, the RHS is evaluated and the result is assigned to the LHS. In this case, RHS involves the new operator and a class constructor and its evaluation leads to creating an instance of the Fraction class. The assignment thus makes x *point at* that instance. We will examine this construct in depth in Section L3.1.b. Here we focus only on the assignment and its syntax. As in primitive types, declaration and assignment can optionally be combined:

```
Fraction x = new Fraction(1, 2);
```

Recall from Section L2.1.e that class types (other than strings) have no literals associated with them, so when a class-type variable is to be set, the RHS of the assignment statement cannot be a literal. Recall also that these types have no operators associated with them so the RHS cannot be an expression either. Hence, the RHS of an assignment of a class-type variable can only be one of three things:

- The new operator together with a constructor.
- A variable that has already been declared and set.
- The special keyword null.

This is demonstrated in the following fragment:

```
1  Fraction x, y, z;
2  x = new Fraction(1,2);
3  y = x;
4  z = null;
```

- The first statement declares three Fraction variables.
- The second has new and a constructor in its RHS.
  At this point, x is the fraction ½ while y and z are not set.
- The third has a variable in its RHS.
  At this point, x is ½, y is ½, and z is not set.
- The fourth has keyword null in its RHS.
  At this point, x is ½, y is ½, and z is null.

L2.3 – Go

L2.3.a – Expression Evaluation

We saw earlier that the value on the right-hand side of an assignment statement can be either a literal or a variable or a combination thereof. In the third case, we have an expression that contains some variables (which have already been declared and set), some literals, and some operators acting on them. An example is shown in the last statement of this fragment:

```
int a = 4;
int b = 3;
int v = 5 + (a - b) / 5 - 2 * b % a;
```

To evaluate an expression with more than one operator, we need to know which one should act first because the rules we learned in Math do not apply here. If parentheses are present, then they guide the process, but what do we do in the absence of parentheses?

Java resolves this by specifying a precedence and an associativity for each operator. Precedence is a number and operators with higher (less negative) precedence act first. If you have two operators of the same precedence, you break the tie based on associativity, which is an arrow (a direction) that determines whether they act left-to-right or right-to-left. The shown table lists some operators and indicate for each whether it is binary-infix, unary-prefix, or unary-postfix. The last column shows the precedence level and the associativity direction. For this subset of operators, the association rule is always left to right and unary postfix should act before any other. See the book's Appendix-A for a similar table for other operators.

+	in	-5
–	in	→
*	in	
/	in	-4
%	in	→
+	pre	-2
–	pre	→
++	post	-1
--	post	→

Based on this, here is a step by step evaluation of the above expression (check your understanding by verifying that the operation to be done first is the underlined one):

v = 5 + (4 – 3) / 5 – 2 * 3 % 4

v = 5 + 1 / 5 – 2 * 3 % 4

v = 5 + 0 – 2 * 3 % 4

v = 5 + 0 – 6 % 4

v = 5 + 0 – 2

v = 5 – 2

v = 3

Beyond the basic five arithmetic operators that can appear in expressions, Java adds a couple of shortcuts relating to incrementing / decrementing a variable and to variable self-update. They are widely used in the developer community and you may want to use them yourself:

Increment / Decrement

We often need to increment a variable in our programs in order to count something. You could of course just add 1 to the variable or you can do this:

```
int x = 4;
int y = x++;  // same as: int y = x + 1
```

This unary postfix operator is known as *auto-increment* and it simply adds 1. Note that its precedence is quite high so it should act early if present with other operators in an expression. A similar *auto-decrement* operator is available with symbol --.

Variable Self-Update

As a generalization to auto-increment, Java adds an assignment shortcut that applies when you update the value of a variable to one computed from its old value. Here is an example:

```
int x = 4;
x += 3;      // same as x = x + 3
x /= 2;      // same as x = x / 2
```

This assignment shortcut works with any operator **op**. Here is the general case:

$$v = v \text{ op } \textit{expression;} \quad \text{can be replaced with} \quad v \text{ op= } \textit{expression;}$$

L2.3.b – Relational Operators

Many computations require that we compare numbers (e.g. to determine if they are equal or if one is less than the other) so we need a few operators in addition to the arithmetic five and their shortcuts. They are called *relational* operators because they establish relationships among their operands. Before describing these operators, we should note from the outset that, unlike all other operators, they

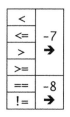

<	
<=	-7
>	→
>=	
==	-8
!=	→

don't have closure because they operate across types: they take operands of any numeric type (such as int or double) and produce results that are always of type boolean. The table to the right shows these operators along with the precedence and associativity of each. The first four are for less-than, less-than-or-equal, greater-than, and greater-than-or-equal. The last two are for equal and not-equal. Here is an example:

```
boolean x = (2 < 4);
```

The < operator compares 2 to 4 and culminates in a boolean result being true, which will be assigned to x. Here is a second example:

```
int m = 2;
int n = 5;
double x = 3.5;
double y = -4.0;
boolean b = (m == n);
boolean c = (x > y);
boolean d = (b || (n <= m)) && c;
```

Go through the statements in this fragment and try to predict the final value of d. Verify by placing the code in the main method of a class and running it. The correct result is false.

Relational operators allow us to do selective computations; i.e. do one thing if a condition is met and do something else otherwise. We will see later how these operators are used in if statements to do that. For now, we will use them to do selective assignments in conjunction with Java's ternary operator, and we will do that through an example:

Suppose we are to implement the following method which receives a purchase amount and computes and returns the sales tax of that purchase:

```
public static double getSalesTax(double amount)
```

We are told by the system designer that the sales tax rate is 13% unless the purchase is more than $500 in which case the tax rate is 11%.

In order to implement the condition, we will use the ternary operator whose general syntax looks like this:

```
x = (boolean condition) ? a : b;
```

This operator uses the ? and : symbols and performs a selective assignment as follows: if the boolean condition is true, it sets x to a, otherwise it sets x to b. As usual in any assignment, the variable on the left-hand-side must be declared and a and b must be values (i.e. literals or variables or expressions) whose types are compatible with x.

Here is the answer:

```
public static double getSalesTax(double amount)
{
   double rate = (amount <= 500.0) ? 0.13 : 0.11;
   double result = amount * rate;
   return result;
}
```

L2.3.c – Mixing Primitive Types

All the examples we have encountered in this chapter involved assignments in which both sides were of the same type. Even when we used relational operators, which operate on one type and produce another, the two sides of any assignment statement were of the same type. And when we want to declare a variable x as double and set it to 2, we write:

```
double x = 2.0;
```

rather than:

```
double x = 2;
```

to maintain the type equality of the two sides. We have also maintained this attribute when we had complex expressions that involve several values. But what if this "clean" behaviour is *not* maintained? Here is a code fragment in which every statement violates this behaviour:

```
1  int m = 3.5;
2  double x = (2.5 > 2.0);
3  boolean b = 3 / 7;
4  double y = 2;
5  double z = 3 - 2 / 7 * 7.0;
```

- The first statement is attempting to store a double in an int. Java does not tolerate this and the compiler will generate a compile-time error. This is because any kind of double-to-int conversion will lead to some loss of accuracy, and Java does not want to take the responsibility for that. If you are willing to be responsible for the repercussions then you can force the conversion by adding a cast like this:

```
int m = (int) 3.5;
```

The cast *demotes* the double to int. Always avoid, or at least be careful with, such casts

- The second statement is attempting to store a boolean in a double. Java does not tolerate any conversion to or from boolean, so this will generate a compile-time error. There is no escaping this (you cannot cast yourself out of it).

- The third statement is attempting to store an int (the number 0) in a boolean. which is a no-no as indicated above, cast or no cast.

- The fourth statement is attempting to store an int in a double. Java *tolerates* this by converting the int to the closest double. Java calls this *automatic promotion*.

- The fifth statement involves a mixed-type expression. Again, the only tolerance is promoting int to double, and it is done automatically <u>upon</u> encounter. Here is a step-by-step evaluation:

z = 3 - <u>2 / 7</u> * 7.0

z = 3 - <u>0 * 7.0</u>

z = 3 - <u>0.0 * 7.0</u>

z = <u>3 - 0.0</u>

z = <u>3.0 - 0.0</u>

z = 3.0

Note that promotion occurs only when needed, which happens when one of the operands is int and the other is double, and not before. In the above example, the fact that the left-hand side is a double, and the fact that the very last literal (i.e. 7.0) is also a double, did not stop the (overloaded) division operator from being integer division.

Casting is actually an operator in Java and has a relatively high precedence (-3) so it acts before most other operators. To appreciate this, let us do a quick computation: suppose we were asked to implement a method that computes the hit rate of some website:

```
public static double getHitRate(int hits, int seconds)
```

The method parameters are the hit count and the number of seconds during which the hits occurred, e.g. the site received 30 hits in 60 seconds. The sought hit rate is the average number of hits per second and is computed by simply dividing the hit count by the duration. In the above example, the method should return 0.5 hit/sec. Here is the method's template:

```
public static double getHitRate(int hits, int seconds)
{
    double result = ...   // fill in the blanks!
    return result;
}
```

Here are *four* different ways to fill in the blanks:

1. `double result = hits / seconds;`

2. `double result = (double) (hits / seconds);`

3. `double result = (double) hits / seconds;`

4. `double result = hits / (double) seconds;`

Based on your understanding of this section, argue that only 2 of these implementations are correct. Use your TestBed project to verify your conclusion by creating a scratch class with a main method. Note the role that precedence plays in the 3rd implementation. In the absence of parentheses, only precedence can tell whether the cast applies to hits or to the quotient.

L2.3.d – Mixing Non-Primitive Types

Casting and automatic promotion are not limited to primitive types as they also apply to non-primitive types. But how do you decide if a conversion is automatic, allowed, or forbidden? In the case of primitive types, it is rather intuitive that `int` to `double` is automatic; that `double` to `int` is allowed (with a cast); and that `int` to `boolean` is forbidden. But when it gets to class types, how do we know if `String` can be converted to `Rectangle` automatically, or via a cast, or not at all? The answer comes from the API. At the top of the API of some class X, you will find a header like this:

    public class X extends B

This means that X is considered a *child* (aka *subclass* or *descendent*) of B. In this case, converting from X to B is automatic (promotion) and from B to X is allowed (demotion via a cast).

As an example, the three Android widgets: `Button`, `EditText`, and `TextView` are all children of the `View` class, so they can all be automatically promoted to `View`, and a `View` can be demoted to any of them via a cast.

The above observation gives us a glimpse of the hierarchies that exists among Java classes. This hierarchical structure is known as *inheritance*, and while we use it every time we build apps in this book, its foundational concepts lie beyond the scope of this book.

Let us then summarize the rules regarding type mixing:

- **For Primitive Types**
  If a double is expected then an int is accepted.

- **For Class Types**
  If a class is expected then any of its descendants is accepted.

- **For Interface Types**
  If an interface is expected then any class that implements it is accepted.

- **For Array Types**
  No type mixing is allowed.

These rules apply whenever variables and values that appear in the same context, e.g. two sides of an assignment, two operands of a binary operator, an argument and its corresponding parameter in a method) are expected to be of the same type.

A subtle point but worth noting: the word "accepted" in the above has different meanings in primitive versus non-primitive types. In the former, it amounts to coercion (the `int` is converted to `double`) whereas in the latter, it amounts to tolerance (the descendent maintains its type even after it substituted for an ancestor –a *polymorphic* behaviour).

L2.4 – EXERCISES

1. Present a brief yet complete logical argument to prove that these statements are false:

    a. You can use an `int` to store the number of milliseconds that have elapsed from the *Epoch* (midnight Jan 1, 1970) until midnight tomorrow.

    b. You cannot use a `double` to store the world GDP ($107.5 trillion) because this figure is made up of 16 digits.

    c. If you set a `boolean` to zero, its value becomes `false`.

    d. The output of the following fragment is zero because x has not been initialized:

        ```
        double x;
        System.out.println(x);
        ```

    e. The expression `a*b*c/d` will be evaluated as `((a*b)*(c/d))`.

2. Given a declared and set `int` variable `x`, which of the following statements increments it?

    ```
    x = x + 1;
    x++;
    x = x + 1/2 + 1/2;
    x += 1;
    x = x + 0.5 + 0.5;
    ```

3. The following fragment is intended to compute the arithmetic mean of three numbers:

    ```
    int x = 4;
    int y = 1;
    int z = -3;
    double mean = x + y + z) / 3;
    ```

    Identify the compile-time error and correct it. Will the fragment accomplish its goal after the error is corrected?

4. Under what condition will b be `true` below (x is a declared and set `int` variable):

    ```
    boolean b = 2 / x * x;
    ```

5. In Math, we learned that `(x*y)/z` is the same as `x*(y/z)`. Show that this is *not* always the case for `int` variables. Recall that to prove that something is not true, you only need one counterexample.

6. In Math, we learned that (x*y)/z is the same as x*(y/z). Show that this is *not* always the case for double variables. Recall that to prove that something is not true, you only need one counterexample.

7. The pow method of the Math class is intended to compute powers, and since taking the square root is the same as raising to an exponent of a half, we can use pow to compute square roots. For example, the following fragment *should* compute the square root of 2:

    ```
    double base = 2;
    double expo = 1 / 2;
    double root = Math.pow(base, expo);
    ```

    Does it? Try it out and examine the result. Explain why the logic fails and provide a fix. Provide a critique of this approach to computing square roots compared to using sqrt (also in the Math class).

8. Read the API of the two methods floor and ceil in the Math class to understand what they do and write a main method that demonstrates their functionalities. After wards, refactor your main method so that it also demonstrates the difference between these two methods and rint which has a similar signature and is also in the Math class.

9. Create the class **Rectangle2** in the *chapter2* package of the *TestBed* project. Its body is the same as its namesake in the *chapter1* package so you can simply copy and paste (but note that the top line in the class should have *chapter2* as the package). Add a second constructor to the class; i.e. do not delete the old constructor–it is OK for a class to have more than one constructor as long as they are different in the parameters they receive. The new constructor should have this header:

    ```
    public Rectangle2()
    {
        ...  ← add your code here
    }
    ```

    Unlike the first constructor which creates an instance having a given width and height, this one assigns the width and height **randomly** in the range [1, 5]. In order to create a random integer in this range, use a statement like this:

    ```
    int x = (int) (1 + 5 * Math.random());
    ```

    Test the class by adding code to the main method in which you create several instances using the new constructor and output for each the return of the toString method.

10. Create a class named *UseFraction* in the *chapter2* package of the *TestBed* project as follows:

```
public class UseFraction
{
    public static void main(String[] args)
    {
        Fraction x = new Fraction(83, 100);
        Fraction y = new Fraction(5, 9);
        Fraction z = new Fraction(667, 1000);
        Fraction t = new Fraction(-2, 3);

        x.add(y);
        t.add(z);
        x.divide(t);

        System.out.println(x.toString());
        System.out.println(x.toProperString());
    }
}
```

The `main` method uses the `Fraction` class from the book's i2c library (Section L0.2.c). It creates four instances of that class and then performs a computation and generates two outputs. Complete the tasks below in the order shown:

- Read the API of `Fraction`, particularly the methods used above.

- Predict the two outputs of the method. Use may a calculator.

- Run the `main` method.

- Compare the run to your prediction and reflect.

CHAPTER 3 – DOING

A Symphony of APIs

D3.1 REQUIREMENT

D3.1.a The MCalcPro App
D3.1.b UI and Behaviour

D3.2 DESIGN

D3.2.a The MPro API
D3.2.b The Toast API
D3.2.c The IME API
D3.2.d The TTS API
D3.2.e The Accelerometer API

D3.3 IMPLEMENTATION

D3.3.a Building the View
D3.3.b Mortgage Data
D3.3.c Exception Handling
D3.3.d Voice Output
D3.3.e Clear on Shake

D3.4 EXERCISES

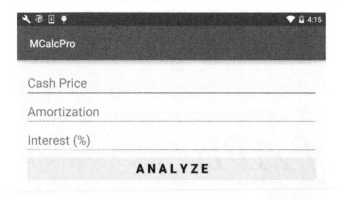

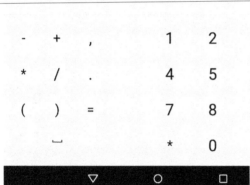

Figure D3.1 Upon launching the app.

MCalcPro

400000

20

5

ANALYZE

Monthly Payment = 2,639.82

By making this payments monthly for 20 years, the mortgage will be paid in full. But if you terminate the mortgage on its nth anniversary, the balance still owing depends on n as shown below:

n	Balance
0	400,000
1	388,051
2	375,490

Figure D3.2 Upon tapping the ANALYZE button.

D3.1 – REQUIREMENT

D3.1.a – The MCalcPro App

This Mortgage-Calculator-Pro app is similar to the one built in the previous chapter except for two key differences:

- A professional look-and-feel on the outside, and
- Full API delegation on the inside.

The former means the app is feature-rich and crash-proof, and the latter means we don't implement anything ourselves! The result is a symphony in which we are the maestro.

D3.1.b – UI and Behaviour

The visible UI consists of *five* vertically aligned widgets: three textboxes (for the cash price, amortization, and interest), a button captioned "$A \, N \, A \, L \, Y \, Z \, E$", and label for displaying the output (see Figures D3.1 and D3.2). The widgets extend across the entire width of the device (regardless of size) in portrait and landscape modes.

As to behaviour, the app must:

1. Equip each textbox with a **hint** (in lieu of a label) to prompt the user. The hint gets overwritten by the input and it reappears whenever the input is cleared.

2. Display a soft keyboard that is **appropriate** for the input. The keyboard's **next** button must move the focus to the next input field, if any.

3. **Validate** the input when the button is tapped: the cash price (aka the principle) must be a positive real number; the amortization must be an `int` in `[20,30]`; and the interest rate percent must be a non-negative real number `<= 50`.

4. Issue an **error message** in a brief, floating bubble if any exception is thrown.

5. Display the **analysis** for valid input below the button with vertical **scrolling** as needed.

6. The analysis consists of the **monthly** payment (**rounded** to the nearest cent) and a **table** that shows the balance owing (rounded to the nearest dollar) if the mortgage is stopped after `0,1,2,3,4,5,10,15,20` years. All amounts must have thousands separators.

7. The monthly payment must be **spoken** (voice output) in addition to being displayed.

8. All entries and any output must be **cleared** if the device is **shaken** strongly; specifically, whenever the device acceleration exceeds 20 m/s^2.

Based on this requirement, the soft keyboard that pops when the cash price receives focus must allow the user to only enter a real number (i.e. digits with an optional decimal point), while the amortization keyboard must allow only integers. Such soft keyboards cut down on invalid inputs (such as entering letters) but does not completely eliminate them. Specifically, the user can still manage to make invalid inputs in two ways:

- **Make Non-Numeric Entries**
  For example, the user can simply leave one of the input fields blank. In this case the entry cannot be parsed into a real number and must be handled or else the app will crash.

- **Make Out-Of-Range Entries**
  For example, the user can enter 12 for the amortization or 75 for the interest. These will not create parsing problems but must still be handled as per the requirement.

Requirement specifies that invalid input must be handled (i.e. it must not be allowed to reach the computation part of the app) and the handling must culminate in an error message. This message must indicate why the input is invalid, must appear for a short time (and then disappear), and must float "above" the UI. Fig. D3.3 is shows an example of the error message that must appear briefly when the entered interest is not within the specified range.

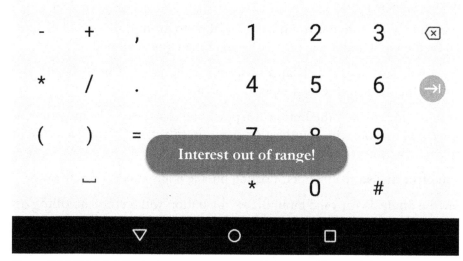

Figure D3.3 This brief, floating error message appears if the entered interest is invalid.

Note that your app must examine the entries in the order of their appearance in the UI and reports the first invalid one. For example, if the user left all entries blank and tapped the analyze button, then the error message would be "Cash Price not numeric!".

If the input is valid, the app displays the analysis as shown in Fig. D3.4. The screenshot on the left appeared when the button was tapped. But since the device could not accommodate the full height of the analysis, the user had to scroll down, which led to the right screenshot.

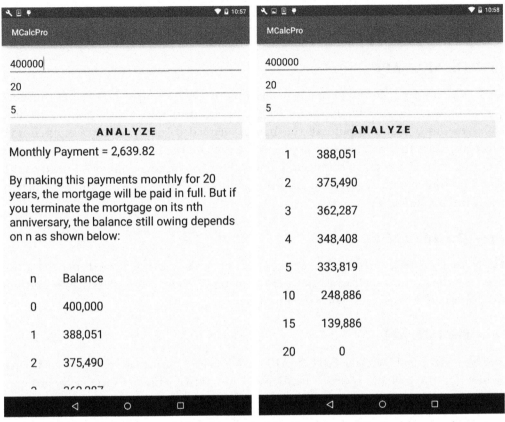

Figure D3.4 The analysis appears as in the left screenshot. Scrolling down leads to the right screenshot.

The analysis starts with a line that shows the monthly mortgage payment properly formatted (this is the line that must be read aloud). Below this line is a fixed explanatory paragraph and then a table of two columns and ten rows (including a header row). The formatting of these elements should be as close as possible to the above screenshots. In particular, the figures in the second column should be rounded to the nearest dollar with a thousand separator.

The table shows how much is still owing to the bank if the mortgage is terminated before its amortization. For example, if this mortgage is terminated on its 5th anniversary, you would need to pay the bank \$333,819. The table shows the outstanding balance (still owing) on the 1st, 2nd, 3rd, 4th, 5th, 10th, 15th, and 20th anniversaries. The 0th anniversary (termination on start) is there as a self-check and its outstanding balance must be the full cash price.

D3.2 – DESIGN

As advertised earlier, this project is about orchestrating the required functionality by piecing together a bunch of APIs. As such, there is no model for us to build—our activity will rely on ready-made components whose APIs are described in the following sections.

D3.2.a – The MPro API

The textbook's library (i2c.jar) contains a class named MPro whose API fulfills our needs. It allows us to create an instance having a user-supplied principle, amortization, and interest, and it has methods that compute all the figures needed to compose the required analysis. Moreover, the class has mechanisms in place that validate the user input and return messages that we can display if any entry is invalid. Hence, this class has everything we need to validate the input and to generate the output. Add the textbook's library to your project's dependencies as shown in Chapter 0.

D3.2.b – The Toast API

A ready-made class named Toast has an API that provides methods for displaying a floating message (a *toast*) to the user for a brief period of time. Hence, this class has everything we need to display error messages when the input is invalid.

D3.2.c – The IME API

This ready-made Input-Method-Editor API allows us to customise the soft keyboard that pops when a textbox widget receives focus. We can control what keys the keyboard contains and what happens when the keyboard's *action key* is tapped (e.g. move to the next entry).

D3.2.d – The TTS API

This ready-made Text-To-Speech API allows us to synthesize voice from any string in many languages. We simply create a default instance and then mutate it for our locale. After wards, we simply invoke the speak method and pass to it the text to be spoken.

D3.2.e – The Accelerometer API

This ready-made API allows us to monitor the acceleration sensor on the device. Whenever the device is accelerated, an event is fired and a method in our activity is invoked with the three components of the acceleration vector passed to it. We simply clear the fields if the length of that vector exceeds the threshold specified in the requirement.

D3.3 – IMPLEMENTATION

Create a project MCalcPro with activity MCalcPro_Activity and layout mcalcpro_layout.

D3.3.a – Building the View

Add three textboxes *pBox*, *aBox*, and *iBox* and set the *hint* attribute of each to the prompts as shown. Set the *Input Type* attribute of the *p* and *i* boxes to *numberDecimal* and that of the *a* box to *number*. This attribute is part of the IME (input-method-editor) API and it dictates the type of soft keyboard that pops and the allowed characters. Next, add a button with a caption and connect its *onClick* attribute to a method in the activity (see Fig. D3.5).

Figure D3.5 The UI elements.

Below the button, add a *ScrollView* and anchor it under the button and make it extend to both sides and to the bottom edge of the screen. Use the techniques you learned in Chapter 0 This way, it would extend sideways and down to the edge of the device in both portrait and landscape modes.

Scroll view is a container widget that can hold other widgets inside it. Its role is to enable scrolling: if the contents in the widgets inside it do not fit in the visible device window, it enables the end user to swipe up and down and thus be able to see the content that is hidden "below" the edge of the device. It is a good idea (though not specified in the requirement) to set the *scrollingIndicators* attribute to *right* so that the user can see where about the scrolling window lies.

Finally, add a label named *output* to the scroll view; i.e. it should be *inside* the scroll view with match_parent for the layout width. The component tree should thus look as shown in Fig. D3.6. Set the *fontFamily* attribute of output to *monospace* because this allows us to easily align the tabular part of the analysis.

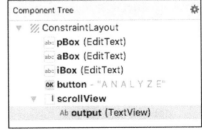

Figure D3.6 The UI component tree.

The requirement does not specify any particular size or colour for the output so set these as you see fit.

D3.3.b – Mortgage Data

This ready-made class performs the needed analysis. Its API shows this constructor:

MPro Constructor
`public MPro()` Construct an instance having zero principle, AMORT_MIN amortization, and zero interest.

The first observation we make here is that the description refers to "AMORT_MIN". These are known as *fields* in API lingo and represent public constants. Indeed, we see a field section in the API (in addition to constructors and methods) and it looks like this:

MPro Fields
`public static final int AMORT_MIN` The minimum amortization period allowed (value=20).
`public static final int AMORT_MAX` The maximum amortization period allowed (value=30).
`public static final double INTEREST_MAX` The maximum interest rate percent allowed (value=50).
`public static final double EPSILON` A small number that sets the resolution in this class. Any real number less than it in absolute value is deemed to be zero (value=0.001).

As you can see, all these fields are `final` (hence they are constants) and are all `static` (so you refer to them in code using the class, rather than the instance, name before the dot). For example, a client of MPro can include this line in its code:

```
double x = MPro.INTEREST_MAX;
```

This effectively transfers a value across classes (from MPro to the client class). Syntax-wise, you can easily tell a field from a method by the absence of parentheses after the name.

Note that the API not only describes the contents of fields but also specifies their values. Nevertheless, client code should refrain from referring to these values. For example, this statement:

```
double x = 50;
```

is 100% equivalent to the one above (since INTEREST_MAX is 50) yet it should not be used. Can you think of a reason why not?

In general, you should strive to avoid including numbers (other than 0 and ±1) in your code because doing so makes your programs difficult to understand (by others and even by you after a few weeks) and difficult to maintain (e.g. modify). Such so-called *magic numbers* can be avoided by prefixing any declaration with the word `final`. For example, if the variable z holds a period measured in years and you want to convert it to months, you may be tempted to write:

```
z = z * 12;    // don't use magic numbers!
```

But based on the above guideline and best practices, you should instead write:

```
final int MONTHS_PER_YEAR = 12;
z = z * MONTHS_PER_YEAR;
```

It may take a few more seconds to write two lines instead of one but experience has shown that this can save *months* of work down the road. It makes it easier for someone reading the code to understand why z was multiplied by 12 (e.g. was it to convert feet to inches?).

In the case of MPro, the developer followed the above guidelines to handle the constants that determine the interest and amortization range, so we, as clients, should continue the practice. For example, to ensure that the interest is within range, we should ensure that:

```
interest < MPro.INTEREST_MAX
```

rather than:

```
interest < 50
```

because this makes our code clearer and keeps it correct even if a new version of MPro came out and it changed the maximum allowed interest from 50 to 60.

The second observation we have about the constructor is that it does not allow us to set the state of the created instance. We thought the constructor should take three parameters so we can pass to it the principle, amortization, and interest as entered by the user. Instead, this constructor sets the state based on some default values (zero principle, 20 year amortization, and zero interest rate) all chosen by the developer! Hence, when we write:

```
MPro mp = new MPro();
```

the created instance (with reference mp) is not of direct use to us. What we need is the ability to *mutate* this instance (i.e. change its state without creating a new instance). As we shall see, the API fortunately includes methods (known as *mutators*) that allow us to do just that.

This approach to object construction (create a default instance and then mutate it) is quite common and is often motivated by performance consideration in iterative situations as it is much faster to mutate an instance then to create a new one.

The API lists three methods that modify the state:

MPro Methods
`public void setPrinciple(String p)` The principle mutator. Throws an Exception if p is not numeric or not positive.
`public void setAmortization(String a)` The amortization mutator. Throws an Exception if a is not numeric or not in [AMORT_MIN,AMORT_MAX].
`public void setInterest(String i)` The interest mutator. Throws an Exception if i is not numeric or not in [0,INTEREST_MAX].

A mutator is a method that mutates (i.e. modifies) the state, and as a matter of convention, it is named setX if it mutates the attribute x. Given these methods, we can now have any state we want by creating a default state and then mutating it. Something like this:

```
MPro mp = new MPro();
mp.setPrinciple("400000");
mp.setAmortization("20");
mp.setInterest("5");
```

This is just an example; the three parameters in the real activity class will come from the view to reflect the user entries. For example, the `"400000"` string literal would be replaced with the following value:

```
((EditText) findViewById(R.id.pBox)).getText().toString()
```

The API lists two methods that perform computations:

MPro Methods
`public String computePayment(String fmt)` Compute the monthly payment of this instance and return it formatted as specified in the fmt string.
`public String outstandingAfter(int years, String fmt)` Compute the balance that is still outstanding after the given number of years and return it formatted as specified in the fmt string.

The first method computes the monthly payment, and as a bonus, it also formats it any way we like. The second computes the outstanding balance after a given number of years (needed for the analysis table) and returns it formatted as we like. For example, here is a fragment that outputs the monthly payment (rounded to the nearest cent with a 1000-separator) and the outstanding balance on the 2nd anniversary (rounded to the nearest dollar, with a 1000-separator, and right-justified in a field of 16 characters):

```
MPro mp = new MPro();
mp.setPrinciple("400000");
mp.setAmortization("20");
mp.setInterest("5");
System.out.println(mp.computePayment("%,.2f"));
System.out.println(mp.outstandingAfter(2, "%,16.0f"));
```

This fragment should output 2,639.82 in the first line and 375,490 in the second.

As you can see, the MPro API provides all the pieces needed to compose the sought analysis. The composition would start with something like this:

```
String s =  "Monthly Payment = " + mp.computePayment("%,.2f");
s += "\n\n";
s += "By making this payments monthly for ";
. . .
```

The idea is to build the analysis string s little by little using the + operator. To insert a new-line in your string, embed "\n" in it. This is known as an *escape sequence* and it allows us to embed characters that cannot be typed in, such as the ENTER, TAB, and non-English letters.

The rows of the analysis table are then appended to s by using something like this:

```
. . .
s += String.format("%8d", 0) + mp.outstandingAfter(0, "%,16.0f");
s += "\n\n";
s += String.format("%8d", 1) + mp.outstandingAfter(1, "%,16.0f");
. . .
```

The usage of fixed field widths (8 for the first column, 16 for the second) enables us to make the output look like a table without using complex tabular UI widgets.

Once the composition of s is completed, we poke it in the view:

```
. . .
 ((TextView) findViewById(R.id.output)).setText(s);
```

D3.3.c – Exception Handling

Looking at the mutators API, you may have noticed the sentence about an exception being thrown if the provided parameter is invalid. For example, if you invoke setPrinciple and pass an invalid parameter, such as an empty string or a negative number, the method will *not* mutate the state. Instead, it will throw an exception which would crash the app.

Exception handling allows us not only to prevent the crash but also to capture the message of the thrown exception so that we can display it to the user. What we need to do is to sandwich the code in a **try-catch** block, like this:

```
try
{
    MPro mp = new MPro();
    mp.setPrinciple("400000");
    mp.setAmortization("20");
    mp.setInterest("5");
    String monthly = mp.computePayment("%,.2f");
    ...
}
catch (Exception e)
{
    // display e.getMessage()
}
```

This construct allows us to avoid crashing the app when a runtime error occurs. The system runs the code in the try block as usual, and if everything is fine, the catch block is skipped. But if any statement in the try block triggered an exception, the rest of the try block is skipped and control transfers to the catch block in which we can handle the exception. The runtime error appears in the catch block as an instance named e on which we can invoke the method getMessage to grab a textual description of the error.

The exceptions thrown by the MPro mutators have the exact error messages specified in the requirement. For example, if you invoke setInterest and pass a value greater than 50, the thrown exception would have the message "Interest out of range!". Hence, all we need to do is to display the message of any thrown exception.

Requirement specifies that the error message should appear to be floating on top of the UI (rather than being part of it) and that it should appear for a brief period of time and then disappear. In Android lingo, such a label is known as a *toast*.

A view that is not part of the original XML layout must be created programmatically. *Toast* is our first encounter with a *dynamically created* view. We will see more examples in the exercises.

To create a toast, we use the Toast class whose API is shown below:

Toast Fields
`public static final int LENGTH_LONG` A long display duration.
`public static final int LENGTH_SHORT` A short display duration.
Toast Methods
`public static Toast makeText(Context c, String s, int d)` Create an instance containing the given string s and lasting for the duration d. The duration has to be either LENGTH_LONG or LENGTH_SHORT.
`public void show()` Display this instance.

To display a toast we need to use the show method, but since this method is not static, we must first create an instance. The above API does not list a constructor but it has a static method makeText that returns an instance. The method takes three parameters:

1. **Context**
   This is the activity over which the toast should float (needed if an app has more than one activity). In our case, we can simply pass this which refers to the invoking activity.

2. **String**
   This string contains the text to be displayed inside the toast.

3. **integer**
   This specifies how long the toast should remain visible. The value you pass here should be one of the two fields specified in the API.

Based on this, the usage pattern for displaying a message msg looks like this:

```
Toast label = Toast.makeText(this, msg, Toast.LENGTH_SHORT);
label.show();
```

In particular, we can use this pattern to display error messages by placing the above fragment in a catch block and replacing msg with e.getMessage(). This way, any exception thrown in the try block will be caught and its error message will appear in a toast.

D3.3.d – Voice Output

The text-to-speech engine has a simple API, but since it runs asynchronously with our code, there is a little bit more overhead involved in using it. Specifically, in addition to us creating an instance of it and invoking methods, we should also *listen* to it; i.e. provide a method in our code that the engine can invoke in order to talk back to us.

Because of this added complexity, we will just list the needed steps:

1. Our activity class must have an **implements** clause added to its header to declare that it can act as a listener to the text-to-speech engine:

```
public class MCalcPro_Activity implements TextToSpeech.OnInitListener
```

2. Add an attribute tts to hold the TextToSpeech instance:

```
private TextToSpeech tts;
```

3. Initialize the attribute in the onCreate method:

```
this.tts = new TextToSpeech(this, this);
```

The constructor takes two parameters: the activity class and the listener class. Since our activity class is also the listener, we passed this for both parameters.

4. Add a listening method to your activity:

```
public void onInit(int initStatus)
{
    this.tts.setLanguage(Locale.US);
}
```

This is where the engine communicates with us. The constructor starts the engine, and during its initialization phase it invokes our onInit method and passes initStatus to tell us if it managed to start successfully (if its value is 0) or not (value -1). We did not check the value in the above but we can do so for debugging purposes. In addition, the onInit method enables us to query the available languages and choose the one we want. Not all languages are supported on every device. We chose the US locale.

5. Whenever you want to read aloud a string s, write:

```
tts.speak(s, TextToSpeech.QUEUE_FLUSH, null);
```

This is finally where the action happens. The speak method takes the string s to be read aloud and a constant to indicate if s is to replace (QUEUE_FLUSH) whatever is still pending in the engine's queue (not spoken yet) or to be appended to it ((QUEUE_ADD).

D3.3.e – Clear on Shake

The accelerometer sensor API is different from the norm in that we don't talk to it! Instead, it talks to us. Hence, there is no instance to create or methods to invoke. We just need to listen to the sensor by having two methods in our activity.

Here are the needed steps:

1. Our activity class must `implement` a second listener:

    ```
    implements TextToSpeech.OnInitListener, SensorEventListener
    ```

    This declares that our activity will listen to the accelerometer sensor in addition to listening to the text to speech engine.

2. Add a listening method to your activity:

    ```
    public void onAccuracyChanged(Sensor arg0, int arg1)
    {
    }
    ```

    Leave the body empty as we don't need to do anything if the accuracy changed.

3. Add a second listening method to your activity:

    ```
    public void onSensorChanged(SensorEvent event)
    ```

    This method will be invoked whenever the device is shaken. Hence, we need to put the logic that implements the required app behaviour in its body.

Whenever the device is moved, its acceleration changes, and this causes the accelerometer sensor to invoke our `onSensorChanged` method. The parameters sent to us in that invocation is a reference `event` to an object that has information about the acceleration. Specifically, it has an array attribute called `values` and it holds the three components of the acceleration vector along the x, y, and z directions (with z being vertical).

We can thus write:

```
double ax = event.values[0];
double ay = event.values[1];
double az = event.values[2];
```

Given the three components, we compute the length a of the vector from:

```
a² = ax² + ay² + az²
```

The requirement document specifies that all fields should be cleared if this length is more than `20`. Otherwise, nothing should happen.

Clearing the three input and one output field is simple; we just set their text contents to an empty string:

```
((EditText) findViewById(R.id.pBox)).setText("");
((EditText) findViewById(R.id.aBox)).setText("");
((EditText) findViewById(R.id.iBox)).setText("");
((TextView) findViewById(R.id.output)).setText("");
```

What is left is execute the above statements if the length is greater than 20 and to skip them otherwise. This can be achieved using the *if construct* as you can see in the full implementation shown below:

```
public void onSensorChanged(SensorEvent event)
{
    double ax = event.values[0];
    double ay = event.values[1];
    double az = event.values[2];
    double a = Math.sqrt(ax*ax + ay*ay + az*az);
    if (a > 20)
    {
        ((EditText) findViewById(R.id.pBox)).setText("");
        ((EditText) findViewById(R.id.aBox)).setText("");
        ((EditText) findViewById(R.id.iBox)).setText("");
        ((TextView) findViewById(R.id.output)).setText("");
    }
}
```

If the device is accelerated beyond 20 m/s^2, the boolean expression (a > 20) will evaluate to true, and this will trigger the execution of the block following the if statement, which in turn will trigger the clearing of the four fields. On the other hand if (a > 20) evaluated to false, the block following the if statement will be skipped, and the method will end with no change to the displayed screen.

D3.4 – EXERCISES

1. The IME API enabled us (through the soft keyboard) to prevent the user from entering letters into numeric fields. Answer the following two questions about IME:

    a. What if the user launched a different app on the device; typed some letters; copied them to the clipboard; and pasted them in our app? Can the user thwart the IME by bypassing the soft keyboard this way?

    b. When the soft keyboard pops, it blocks the analysis area from view. The user can of course lower the keyboard but this is a nuisance. Is there a way to automatically remove the keyboard when the ANALYZE button is tapped?

2. How long does a toast last when created using the **LENGTH_SHORT** field? Use your watch to estimate this duration after deploying the app on a device. Next, re-do the experiment for a toast created using the **LENGTH_LONG** field.

3. Modify your app so that the entire analysis (not just the monthly payment) is read aloud (spoken) via the `tts` API.

4. The activity of your app needs an `MPro` instance in order to perform the computation. It can create this instance in one of two places:

    a. In the method that handles the button's `onClick` event.

    b. In the `onCreate` method.

    If we adopt the latter approach, where should the reference of that instance be declared?

    Refactor your app so it uses the latter approach and argue that this is better, performance wise, than the former approach.

5. The code that generated the analysis string included many statements that are essentially identical—they differ only by the year value. Such code is an ideal candidate for loops because loops allow us to generate these statements automatically rather than manually.

    a. Refactor your app so it would use a loop to replace the statements that handle the 0th, 1st, ... 5th anniversaries.

    b. Refactor your app so it would use a loop to replace the statements that handle the 10th, 15th, and 20th anniversaries.

6. It is instructive to actually see the values of the three components of the acceleration:

    a. Refactor your onSensorChanged method so it displays these three numbers at the bottom of the analysis (after the table). Show the numbers comma delimited on a line by themselves and round any decimals in them.

    b. Explain why one of the components is not zero even when the device is not moving.

❖ ❖ ❖ ❖

7. Create a new app named *Tabulate* as shown in Fig. D3.7. The UI consists of 2 textboxes at the top to enter the from/to values, a button, and a scrollable area underneath to display the tabulation: a table of 3 columns. The table has a row for every integer in [from, to] range. Each row has three columns that display the integer, its square, and its square root.

In the shown example, the user entered 1 and 30 and then tapped the generate button. The app produced a table of 30 rows. The second row, for example, shows that the square of 2 is 4 and that the square root of 2 is 1.41421.

The values in the first columns are formatted with %5d, those in the second with %10d, and those in the third with %12.5f.

If the number of rows exceed the screen size then the user can swipe up and down to scroll the table. This works the same in both landscape and portrait orientation and is independent of device size.

The IME API is used to ensure that only non-negative integers can be entered. If from is less than to then nothing is displayed.

The challenge in this app is not so much in its computation but rather in the view. We need to generate the tabular view dynamically in code rather than statically in XML.

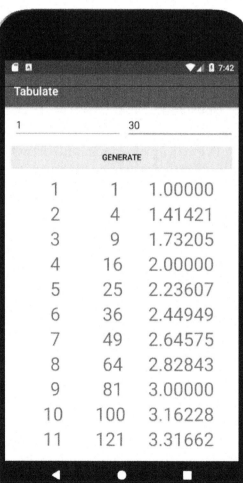

Figure D3.7 The Tabulate App.

The layout of the app is straightforward. Simply place the two textbox widgets as a chain at the top and place a button under them. Next insert a **ScrollView** container below the button and anchor it to the screen sides horizontally and from the button to the screen bottom vertically. Set the ID attribute of the scroll view container to **sv**.

No other widgets are needed. We will generate the table dynamically in Java. Specifically, the table is created using an aggregate of objects as follows:

- A **TableLayout** object residing inside the ScrollView.

- A **TableRow** object, one per row, residing inside the TableLayout.

- A **TextView** object, one per column, residing inside the TableRow.

The following code fragment demonstrates the APIs that you will need to use:

```
ScrollView sv = (ScrollView) findViewById(R.id.sv);
sv.removeAllViews();

TableLayout tl = new TableLayout(this);
sv.addView(tl);

TableRow row = new TableRow(this);
row.setGravity(Gravity.CENTER_HORIZONTAL);
tl.addView(row);

TextView tv = new TextView(this);
tv.setGravity(Gravity.CENTER_HORIZONTAL);
tv.setTextSize(TypedValue.COMPLEX_UNIT_DIP, 32);
tv.setText("Hello!");
```

Notes:

- The removeAllViews method ensures that every tap starts with an empty table.

- Invoking setGravity method on a row ensures that the row is centered.

- Invoking setGravity method on a TextView ensures that its text is centered.

To avoid having too many repeated code in your onClick method, you may want to create a private method that takes a string and returns a TextView that holds that string and that has the desired gravity and text size.

Aside from the above, your onClick needs a loop that spans the desired range and invokes the above private method three times.

8. Create a new app named *TaxCalc* as shown in Fig. D3.8. The UI has a textbox at the top to enter the annual income, a button to compute the *i2c tax* on that income, and a large, screen-wide scrollable area extending from the button down to the bottom of the screen in which the output is displayed.

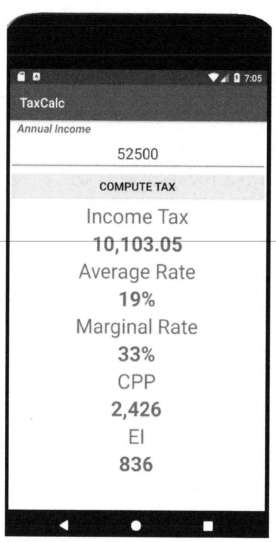

Figure D3.8 The TaxCalc App.

When the user taps the button, the app computes and displays *five* quantities as shown in the figure. Note that the designed UI does not have individual textviews for the five quantities and their titles; it only has one large ScrollView. The ten needed textviews will be created dynamically in code.

Albeit a bit abstract, creating views in code is as easy as creating them at design time. Start by fetching the scroll-view area (with ID sv) and remove all views from it:

```
ScrollView sv = (ScrollView) findViewById(R.id.sv);
output.removeAllViews();
```

Next, put a linear layout inside the scroll view. We need a vertical linear layout so that when we add the textviews to it, they will be aligned vertically:

```
LinearLayout output = new LinearLayout(this);
output.setOrientation(LinearLayout.VERTICAL);
sv.addView(output);
```

Now that everything is in place, we create 10 textviews and add each to the linear layout that we called output. The following code fragment demonstrates creating a text view, setting its attributes, and inserting it in the linear layout.

```
TextView tv = new TextView(this);                       // create a new text view
tv.setGravity(Gravity.CENTER_HORIZONTAL);               // centre its text
tv.setTextSize(TypedValue.COMPLEX_UNIT_DIP, 32);        // make its text 32 dp
tv.setTypeface(null, Typeface.BOLD);                    // make it bold
tv.setText("Hello!");                                   // set its text to some string
output.addView(tv);                                     // add it to the linear layout
```

You may want to create a private method in your activity to create and return a textview that has certain attributes set so as to reduce redundancy in your code.

The only remaining challenge is the tax computation. We will adopt a taxation model for our (fictitious) *i2c* country that resembles that of Canada but is much simpler. Given the annual income, the income tax rate is computed as follows:

- For the part of the income that is less than or equal to **$11,475**, the tax rate is **0%**.

- For the next **$33,808** part of the income, the amount is **22.79%** of that part.

- For the next **$40,895** part of the income, the amount is **33.23%** of that part.

- For the next **$63,823** part of the income, the amount is **45.93%** of that part.

- For the remaining part of the income, the amount is **52.75%** of that part.

As an exercise, show that an income of $52,500 will trigger a tax of $10,103.05. The calculation is shown below.

For an income of **$52,500**:

- The first **$11,475** is exempt so the tax on it is 0.
- The remaining income is **$41,025**.
- The next bracket leads to a tax of 33,808 * 22.79% = 7,704.84.
- The remaining income is **$7,217**.
- The next bracket leads to a tax of 7,217 * 33.23% = 2,398.21.
- The remaining income is **$0**.
- Hence, the total tax is: 0 + 7704.84 + 2398.21 = $10,103.05.

The **Average Tax Rate** is defined as the tax amount divided by the income. It is expressed as a percent without decimals, e.g. if the division leads to 0.277, we express it as 28%.

For the above example, the average tax rate is equal to: 10103.05 / 52500 = **19%**.

The **Marginal Tax Rate** is defined as the highest tax rate used in the tax calculation; i.e. it is the tax rate on the last dollar earned. It too is expressed as a percent without decimals.

For the above example, the marginal tax rate is equal to: **33.23%**.

The **CPP** (Canada Pension Plan) figure is obtained as follows:

- For the part of the income that is less than or equal to $3500, the amount is zero.
- For the remaining part of the income, the amount is 4.95% of that part.

CPP is capped at $2,564.10.

For the above example, CPP on first 3500 is zero, leaving 52500-3500 = 49000. CPP is thus 49000 * 4.95% = **$2,425.50** (cap does *not* apply).

The **EI** (Employment Insurance) figure is obtained as follows:

- EI is 1.63% of the income.

EI is capped at $836.19.

For the above example, EI is 52500 * 1.63% = 855.75 so it gets capped at **$836.19**.

Hint:
Create a model class that takes the annual income in its constructor. Declare and set the tax brackets and their tax rates as final attributes. Add methods for computing the tax, the EI, and the CPP. The average and marginal tax rates can be computed in the same method that computes the tax.

9. Create a new app named *TaxTable* as shown in Fig. D3.9. The UI has there textboxes to allow the user to enter an income range (from/to) along with an increment. It also has a button and a large, screen-wide scrollable area under the button. As you see in the figure, the app computes the five tax-related figures (as in Exercise 8) for every income in the specified range, and displays the result in a table.

Hint:
- Use the *model class of Exercise 8 as is (copy-and-paste).*
- *Create the table dynamically in code: insert a table layout inside the scroll view, and insert in it a table row to hold the six text views as columns (as shown in Exercise 7).*

Annual Income

From 10000   250000   5000|
          To   Inc

TABULATE

INCOME	TAX	Avg	Mgn	CPP	EI
10,000	0.00	0%	0%	321.75	163.00
15,000	803.35	5%	23%	569.25	244.50
20,000	1,942.85	10%	23%	816.75	326.00
25,000	3,082.35	12%	23%	1,064.25	407.50
30,000	4,221.85	14%	23%	1,311.75	489.00
35,000	5,361.35	15%	23%	1,559.25	570.50
40,000	6,500.85	16%	23%	1,806.75	652.00
45,000	7,640.35	17%	23%	2,054.25	733.50
50,000	9,272.30	19%	33%	2,301.75	815.00
55,000	10,933.80	20%	33%	2,549.25	836.19
60,000	12,595.30	21%	33%	2,564.10	836.19
65,000	14,256.80	22%	33%	2,564.10	836.19
70,000	15,918.30	23%	33%	2,564.10	836.19
75,000	17,579.80	23%	33%	2,564.10	836.19
80,000	19,241.30	24%	33%	2,564.10	836.19
85,000	20,902.80	25%	33%	2,564.10	836.19
90,000	23,049.70	26%	46%	2,564.10	836.19
95,000	25,346.20	27%	46%	2,564.10	836.19
100,000	27,642.70	28%	46%	2,564.10	836.19
105,000	29,939.20	29%	46%	2,564.10	836.19
110,000	32,235.70	29%	46%	2,564.10	836.19
115,000	34,532.20	30%	46%	2,564.10	836.19

Figure D3.9 The TaxTable App.

10. Tax brackets and tax rates (such as those used in the previous exercises) are examples of constants whose values cannot be modified while the program is running. We have been using the **final** keyword to declare and set such constants. For example:

```
private final double EI_RATE = 0.0163;
private final double EI_CAP = 836.19;
```

While this serves the purpose of making them unmodifiable, it violates the separation of concerns principle because we are mixing data (which may change from one year to the next or from one locale to another) with the logic that manipulates that data in one file. For example, the combined Federal-Provincial tax brackets in Canada are not the same in all provinces. Similarly, the above declarations involve Employment Insurance figures that change from one year to the next. To change the values, you will need to re-edit the program and re-compile it, which can potentially trigger unintentional code change and possibly introduce bugs.

For such constants, the professional, best-practice approach would be to *externalize* them; i.e. store them in a file external to the program. The program can then read them into `final` variables. For example, you can store the above EI values in the `strings.xml` file:

```
<resources>
    <string name="app_name">TaxCalc</string>
    <string name="EI_RATE">0.0163</string>
    <string name="EI_CAP">836.19</string>
</resources>
```

These string resources can now be accessed by name in your activity and then passed to the model:

```
String ei_rate = this.getResources().getString(R.string.EI_RATE);
String ei_cap  = this.getResources().getString(R.string.EI_CAP);

double rate = Double.parseDouble(ei_rate);
double cap  = Double.parseDouble(ei_cap);
TaxModel model = new TaxModel(rate, cap);
```

But how does the model treat them as constants? The solution comes from a feature in Java known as *blank finals*. These are declared as final attributes but are not assigned a value. Instead, their values are set in the class constructor, as shown below.

```
public class TaxModel
{
    private final double EI_RATE;
    private final double EI_CAP;
    ...

    public TaxModel(double rate, double cap)
    {
        EI_RATE = r;
        EI_CAP = r;
        ...
    }

    ...
```

Edit any one of your projects that contain final values by turning them into blank finals. Add name-value entries for them in XML and modify your activity and model classes accordingly.

CHAPTER 3 – LEARNING

A Symphony of APIs

L3.1 – A DAY IN THE LIFE

L3.1.a – Anatomy of an API

There are *three* key sections in any API: *fields*, *constructors*, and *methods*.

Fields

Fields are attributes that the developer has made public. This is *not* typical because the value of a public attribute can be changed by the client and developers don't like that (they prefer to maintain control over the state). The only exception is when the attribute is `final` because then, its value is constant and cannot be changed. Such fields are typically made `static` to allow a client to access them without creating an instance. Here are a few examples:

Fields (Math class)
`public static final double PI` The ratio of the circumference of a circle to its diameter.

Fields (Integer class)
`public static final int MAX_VALUE` The maximum value an `int` can have ($2^{31} - 1$).

To use a field in client code we employ the same technique as for methods: precede by the class name if the field is static and by the instance name if not. For example, this fragment uses the `PI` field of the `Math` class to compute the area of a circle:

```
double radius = 2.5;
double area = Math.PI * radius * radius;
```

Constructors

Constructors are intended to initialize the state of the instance being created. They have the following attributes:

• Must have the same name as the class.

• A class can have more than one constructor, and since they must all have the same name (an overloaded name), they must have different parameters.

Let us take a look at the constructor section of the `MPro` class:

Constructors (MPro class)
`public MPro()` Construct an instance having zero **principle, AMORT_MIN amortization**, and zero interest.
`public MPro(String p, String i)` **Construct an instance having the given principle and interest and amortization AMORT_MAX.**
`public MPro(String p, String a, String i)` Construct an instance having the given principle, amortization, and interest.

Since the state of any instance of MPro must have a principle, an amortization, and an interest rate, the third constructor in the above list is perhaps the most natural. The client passes the principle in p, the amortization in a, and the interest in i, and the constructor sets the state accordingly.

A client that uses the second constructor is leaving it to the class to apply a default amortization. For example, a bank may choose to default to 30-year amortization unless the customer indicates otherwise.

The first constructor is known as the *default constructor* because it creates an instance whose state is *not* specified by the client; e.g. zero principle and interest and 20-year amortization. This constructor can be used by a client that does not know yet what the user wants (e.g. before the user makes any entry). In such cases the client creates the default instance and then uses mutators to mutate the state once the desired one is known.

Methods

The behaviour of objects is controlled by methods. They provide state management through accessors and mutators, identity services through toString and equals, and computations. Methods have these attributes:

- A method can return *at most one value*; i.e. either one value or no return at all.
- Data transfer into and out of the method is done by value.
- The method header contains four key parts (in the order shown):
    1. **public** or **private** (cannot be private if it appears in the API)
    2. **static** or nothing (nothing means not static)
    3. **return type** (or void if no return)
    4. **signature** = name + parameter types

The *signature* must be unique within the class so if two methods have the same name (overloaded methods) then they must have different parameters.

Here is an example:

```
public static int getArea(int x, int y)
```

This method is public; is static; returns an int value; and its signature is:

```
getArea(int, int)
```

Note that the signature cares only about the order and type of parameters, not their names.

Here is a second example:

```
public String computePayment(String format)
```

This method is public; not static; returns a String, and takes a String.

If the class in question extends another then all the methods in the parent class are inherited and appear in the child's API. And if the class implements some interface then the methods specified in that interface must also appear in the class's API.

L3.1.b – The Birth of an Object

Given a class C, a client can create an instance of it using a statement like this:

```
C x = new C();
```

Let us shed some light on the elements of this statement. The C that appears on the left-hand side is a type declaration for the variable x. Indeed, we could have split the above statement in two; one to declare x and one to set it:

```
C x;
x = new C();
```

The variable x is known as the *object reference* (aka *pointer* in other programming languages). It is *not* the object itself, just a reference to it (just like a key to a car is not the car but merely a mean to access it). The right-hand side contains the keyword new. It is this keyword that does the actual creation of the object. Specifically, it allocates a block in memory big enough to hold the state (i.e. the values of all the attributes) of the object. The last element on the right hand side is C() which is the constructor. Its role is to determine the state to be stored in the allocated block. And once this process completes, the address of the allocated block is stored in x. For example, the statement:

```
MPro mp = new MPro("400000", "20", "5");
```

Allocates a block in memory to hold the state at address100 (say). It uses the three-parameter constructor to set the values in that block. It also declares the variable mp to be of type MPro and sets its value to 100.

You can think of the object reference as a name given to the object upon its birth but keep in mind that an object may have more than one name. Consider the fragment:

```
MPro x = new MPro("400000", "20", "5");
MPro y = x;
MPro z = new MPro("400000", "20", "5");
```

Here, we have two objects in memory (because we used new twice). Lets assume the first object resides at address 100 and the second at 200. In this case, both x and y will be 100 and z will be 200. Hence, the object at 100 has two names, just like you can make a duplicate key for your car and both keys would open it. Two object references that point at the same object are known as *aliases* and they are equal; i.e. if you evaluate:

```
boolean b = (x == y);
```

you will find it equal to true.

L3.1.c – Objects at Work

Objects do work through the methods we invoke on them. Methods that manage the state of the object are known as *accessors* and *mutators* (aka *getters* and *setters*). Accessors allow clients to read the state whereas mutators allow them to mutate (change) the state.

For example, this fragment demonstrate accessors and mutators of MPro. Its output should be the string "300000":

```
MPro mine = new MPro("400000", "20", "5");
mine.setPrinciple("300000");
System.out.println(mine.getPrinciple());
```

Not every class has state accessors and mutators. Some have none, some have accessors only (thus providing immutable, read-only state), and some have mutators only. The String class, for example, has no mutators, so Java strings are immutable after creation. (This is done to optimize their storage and manipulation.)

All classes have obligatory methods that they inherit and two of them are often used: equals and toString. The former tests the equality of the *states* of two objects (not their references) and the latter returns a useful, textual representation of the object. Note that the equality of objects is contextual. In a particular application, for example, two rectangles may be considered equal if they have the same area (even if they have different widths and heights).

Note also that two objects may be equal even though their references are not. The fragment above (with x, y, and z) has x.equals(z) being true even though x==z is false.

L3.1.d – The Death of an Object

Like any variable, the object reference dies when it goes out of scope. The object dies when no reference is pointing at it—it becomes an **orphan**. To see this, examine the fragment below and ask: *How many objects and how many references are there after each statement is executed?*

```
1  MPro a = new MPro("400000", "20", "5.0");
2  MPro b = new MPro("500000", "25", "3.5");
3  MPro c = new MPro("400000", "20", "5.0");
4  MPro d = b;
5  b = a;
6  d = null;
```

After executing statement #4, we have *three* objects and *four* references in memory. To better visualize them, a *memory diagram* like Fig. L3.1 is instructive: draw all created objects as ovals (with the state of each inside it) and write down the names of all declared references. When a reference is set, draw an arrow that connects its name to the object it points at.

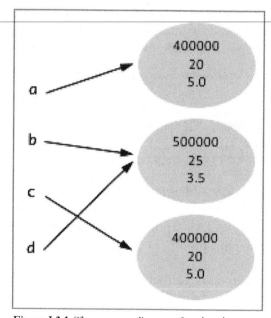

Figure L3.1 The memory diagram after d = b.

We can now easily see from the diagram that **a == c** is false (because these two references point at different objects) whereas **a.equals(c)** is true (because the two referenced objects, albeit distinct, have identical states).

After executing statement #5, reference b will point at the first object as depicted in Fig. L3.2. We still have 3 objects and 4 references and: **a.equals(c)** is true (as before), **d == b** is no longer true, and **b == a** is now true.

At this point the first object has two *aliases* (a and b) and the second object is still alive (even though b no longer points at it) because d is still pointing at it. As to the third object, no changes has occurred to it or to the reference c that points at it.

After executing statement #6, reference d becomes null. When a reference is set to null, it would no longer point at any object, and as such, you cannot invoke any method on it (doing so would lead to the infamous *null-pointer exception*). This does not mean the reference is dead; it simply means it is not connected to an object as depicted in Fig. L3.3.

At this point, we still have 4 references but only 2 objects, the first and the third. This is so because the second object died when it became an orphan (no reference pointing at it). You can keep it in the diagram (as we did) or remove its oval completely.

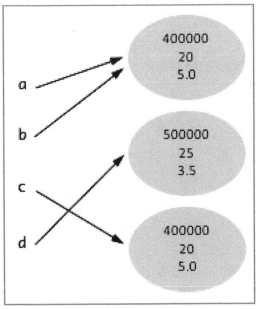

Figure L3.2 The memory diagram after b = a.

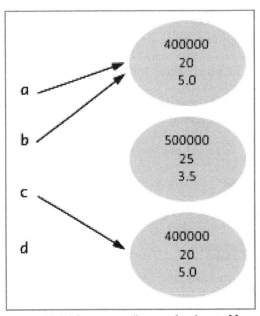

Figure L3.3 The memory diagram after d = null.

We mention for completeness that removing dead objects from memory does not happen synchronously in Java. Instead, a garbage collector (aka *gc*) runs asynchronously (in a separate thread) and it removes dead objects as needed without blocking our programs.

L3.2 – CONTROL STRUCTURES

L3.2.a – The if Statement

Whether implementing a tax computation or a cooking recipe, most computations present a choice (a fork in the road) and require that we do one thing or another depending on some condition. The *if statement* is a Java construct that allows us to implement such selection. In its simplest form, it has this syntax:

```
statement-1
if (boolean)
{
    ... // one or more statements
}
statement-2
```

If the boolean evaluates to true then we execute statement-1, then the statements inside the if block, and then statement-2. Otherwise, we execute statement-1 then statement-2, thus skipping the entire if block.

The more general form of this statement incorporates an else block:

```
statement-1
if (boolean)
{
    ... // one or more statements
}
else
{
    ... // one or more statements
}
statement-2
```

If the boolean evaluates to true then we execute statement-1, then the statements inside the if block, and then statement-2. Otherwise, we execute statement-1, then the statements inside the else block, and then statement-2.

For example, implement the following method which takes the mark that a student received in a test and returns "PASS" if the mark is not less than 50 and returns "FAIL" otherwise.

public String assess(int mark)

The algorithm here calls for a choice so selection control is natural. Here is the complete implementation:

```
public String assess(int mark)
{
   String result;
   if (mark >= 50)
   {
      result = "PASS";
   }
   else
   {
      result = "FAIL";
   }
   return result;
}
```

Note that as a matter of best practice, methods should not have multiple returns within them and that is why we declared a `result` variable at the top and returned it at the bottom. If you prefer to default the value of that variable, then that is acceptable too:

```
String result = "FAIL";
if (mark >= 50)
{
   result = "PASS";
}
return result;
```

The `if` statement can be nested. For example, suppose you are to implement the following method which takes an integer and validates it as a positive even integer; i.e. if it is positive and even then the return must be `true`, otherwise, it must be `false`.

Here is the implementation:

```
public static boolean isValid(int x)
{
   boolean result = false;
   if (x > 0)
   {
      if (x % 2 == 0)
      {
         result = true;
      }
   }
   return result;
}
```

A second option would be to combine the two conditions using the boolean *and* operator and thus use only one `if` statement, as shown below.

```
public static boolean isValid(int x)
{
   boolean result = false;
   if (x > 0 && x % 2 == 0)
   {
      result = true;
   }
   return result;
}
```

The above implementation uses one `if` statement instead of two, but as a matter of fact, you don't need any `if` statement to implement this method, as shown below:

```
public static boolean isValid(int x)
{
   boolean result = (x > 0 && x % 2 == 0);
   return result;
}
```

As a matter of best practice, try to avoid using an `if` statement in order to set a `boolean` variable. By the same token, avoid testing a `boolean` variable using `==` so instead of writing "`if (b == true)`" write "`if (b)`". Here is a full example to illustrate the second point. You are to implement the following method:

`public static double withTax(boolean isTaxed, double price)`

It takes a `boolean` that indicates if an item is taxable or not, and the price of that item. If the item is not taxed, return the price as is; otherwise, return it inflated by 13% (i.e. multiplied by 1.13). Avoid using `==` to test `isTaxed`.

Here is the complete implementation:

```
public static double withTax(boolean isTaxed, double price)
{
   double result = price;
   if (isTaxed)
   {
      result *= 1.13;
   }
   return result;
}
```

L3.2.b – The for Statement

One of the obvious differences between computer and calculator usage is *iteration*: the ability to repeat certain operations several times. Java implements this control structure through the *for* statement which has the following syntax:

```
for (statement-x; boolean; statement-y)
{
    ... // one or more statements
}
statement-after
```

The execution algorithm follows these steps:

1. Execute **statement-x**, if present.
2. Evaluate the **boolean** and if false then skip to statement-after.
3. Otherwise, execute all statements in the loop's **body**.
4. Execute **statement-y**, if present.
5. **Go** to step #2.

As a first example, argue that this fragment will print all integers in [0 , 9].

```
for (int i = 0; i < 10; i++)
{
    System.out.println(i);
}
```

Note that statement-x is executed only once; the boolean is checked at the start of every loop iteration; and statement-y is executed at the end of every loop iteration. Note also that if a variable is declared in statement-x then it is considered to be part of the for block, and hence, would be out-of-scope after the loop.

As a second example, argue that invoking log2(32) will return 5 where log2 is this method:

```
public int log2(int n)
{
    int result = 0;
    for (int r = n / 2; r > 0; r = r / 2)
    {
        result++;
    }
    return result;
}
```

In summary, we learned that a for loop always starts with statement-x. After wards, it goes through the cycle of executing the boolean-check, the body, and statement-y. The boolean specifies the condition for staying in the loop and it is the only way to get out of the loop. For historical reasons, however, Java includes two keywords (break and continue) that disrupt the regularity of this cycle and allow for a sudden transfer of control. **Do not** use them! Research has shown that such abrupt transfers make programs hard to read and difficult to maintain. We always avoid using them in this textbook and so should you (especially in tests and job interviews). The example below may prompt some to use these dreaded constructs.

As a third example, implement the method:

> public static int largestFactor(int n)

It receives a positive integer and returns its largest factor. For example, largestFactor(24) is 12 and largestFactor(7) is 1. To find the largest factor of n, we try all integers from 1 to n-1 and find the largest one that divides it. If n is prime, the answer would be 1. Note that the method's contract assumes that n is positive *as a precondition.*

Take some time to sketch how you would implement the method yourself before reading on.

A possible implementation starts by defaulting result to 1 and then setting up a loop that goes through the integers from 2 to n-1. For each, we check to see if it divides n, and if so, we update result (thereby overwriting its previous value). The last such update occurs when we reach the largest factor. If n is prime, no integer in the loop's range would divide it, so no update would take place, and result remains 1. Here is the full implementation:

```java
// Precondition: n > 0
public static int largestFactor(int n)
{
    int result = 1;
    for (int i = 2; i < n; i++)
    {
        if (n % i == 0)
        {
            result = i;
        }
    }
    return result;
}
```

Create a class in the TestBed project to hold this method and run it for n=24624561 and then for n=67867979. The oracle answers for these two test cases are 8208187 and 1, respectively.

Just like the `if` statement, `for` can be nested; i.e. you can place one loop inside another. Any variable declared in the outer loop can be accessed in the inner. Consider the fragment:

```
int count = 0;
for (int i = 0; i < 5; i++)    1, 2, 3, 4, 5
{
    for (int j = 0; j < 3; j++)   1, 2, 3
    {
        count++;   1, 2, 3 → repeats 5 times
    }              Total = 15
}
```

The outer loop sets i to 0 and then the inner loop starts. It starts with j being 0 and it makes `count=1`. It then sets j to 1 and makes `count=2`. Next it sets j to 2 and makes `count=3`. Afterward, it sets j to 3 but this makes the boolean `false` so the loop exits. Hence, the first iteration of the outer loop ends with `count=3`. After wards, i becomes 1 and the inner loop will again increment `count` three more times thus making it 6. Continuing along these lines, we can see that the final value of `count` will be 15.

When a code fragment contains non-trivial logic, a *trace table* can be used for reasoning about it. A trace table captures the values of relevant variables in the fragment at a certain location in it and records them in a row (one variable per column). If loops are involved then you will end up with one row per iteration. For example, consider this fragment:

```
int count = 0;
for (int i = 0; i < 5; i++)
{
    for (int j = i+1; j < 3; j++)
    {
        count++;
    }
}
```

The fragment is similar to the one above except that j does not start at 0 but rather at a value that depends on the outer loop's iteration.

To determine the final value of `count`, we construct the trace table shown to the right and record in it the values of the variables i, j, and count immediately after `count` is incremented in the inner loop. Whenever control reaches this point, we start a new row. As you can see, once i becomes more than 1, the inner loop is not entered. We therefore conclude that the final value of `count` is 3.

i	j	count
0	1	1
0	2	2
1	2	3

L3.2.c – The try-catch Blocks and throw

When a running program asks the processor to perform an illegal operation (such as dividing an int by zero or invoking a method of a null reference), the processor responds by throwing an exception and crashing the program. Exceptions in Java are object oriented; i.e. every possible illegal operation has an exception class associated with it. So to throw an exception, the processor locates the class that corresponds to the illegal operation; creates an instance e of it; and presents the program with a choice:

❖ *Handle e or I will crash you!* ❖

To handle an exception, the offending statement must be present in a **try** block or else the program will crash. When the exception occurs, the rest of the a **try** block is skipped and control is transferred to the **catch** block. Here is an example:

```
int x = 5;
int y = 0;
try
{
    int z = x / y;
    System.out.println("The result of the division = " + z);
}
catch (Exception e)
{
    System.out.println("Division not possible!");
    System.out.println("The error message is: " + e.getMessage());
}
```

The fragment attempts to divide by zero and show the result, but if an exception occurred, and it will, the fragment indicates that and shows the error message by invoking getMessage on the thrown exception instance. This fragment will *not* crash.

We mentioned earlier that Java has, not just one, but numerous exception classes, e.g.

- RuntimeException
- IOException
- NullPointerException
- IndexOutOfBoundsException
- PatternSyntaxException

Does this mean we have to anticipate all the exceptions that our code may trigger and have a catch block per each? Fortunately no, because all these classes belong to one family whose great grandparent is the Exception class; i.e. all exception classes **extend** this class. Hence, by catching this class, we catch all of them.

As a second example, implement the following method which takes a string s that contains an integer and returns a string containing three times that integer:

public static String triple(String s)

For example, if s="4" then the return should be the string "12". If the parameter s does not contain an integer then the method should return the string "0".

Here is the implementation:

```
public static String triple(String s)
{
    String result;
    try
    {
        int x = Integer.parseInt(s);
        x = 3 * x;
        result = String.format("%d", x);
    }
    catch (Exception e)
    {
        result = "0";
    }
    return result;
}
```

The error messages that come with the exception classes are intended for the developer, and hence, are rather cryptic in the eyes of the end user. Furthermore, most requirement documents specify custom error messages. In these situations, it is common to have the model class perform the validation by catching the standard exceptions and then re-throwing them (in the catch block) as new exceptions but with custom messages. The re-thrown exceptions are thus not handled in the model so they propagate to the controller and get caught there.

For example, consider the method:

public static String root(String s)

It is supposed to take a string s containing a non-negative real number and return a string containing the square root of that number. For example, if s="2.5" then the return should be the string "1.581139". On the other hand, if the parameter s does not contain a real number (e.g. s="Canada"), or if it contains a negative (e.g. s="-25"), then the method should throw an exception, specifically a RuntimeException with the custom message:

"String must contain a non-negative real!"

Here is the implementation:

```
public static String root(String s)
{
    String result;
    try
    {
        double x = Double.parseDouble(s);
        if (x < 0)
        {
            throw new Exception();
        }
        x = Math.sqrt(x);
        result = String.format("%f", x);
    }
    catch (Exception e)
    {
        throw new RuntimeException("String must contain a non-negative real!");
    }
    return result;
}
```

Let us use this method to review how custom exception messages are created. This method's contract dictates that we throw an exception *with a specific message* if:

- The given string s does not contain a number.

- The given string s contains a negative number.

The first case causes the parse method to throw an exception (NumberFormatException) but its message would be cryptic to the end user. Hence, we catch it using the grandparent of all exception classes and then re-throw it using our own custom message.

The second case does *not* cause any exception because Math.sqrt accept negative numbers (and returns NaN as their square root). Hence, we need to detect this case ourselves (via an if statement) and manually throw an exception. That exception is caught in the catch block, as in the first case, and gets re-thrown with our custom message.

The client of this method must thus be prepared when invoking it. The invocation will either return the sought square root if all is well, or trigger an exception. In a typical app, the client is a controller which captures either the method's return or the exception message and pokes them in the view.

L3.3 – OTHER FLOW CONSTRUCTS

The `if` and `for` control structures enable us to meet the flow requirements of any algorithm. Nevertheless, most modern programming languages come with additional control structures: `switch`, `while`, and `do-while`. Albeit less powerful than `if` and `for`, it is instructive to take a look at these three because:

- They help us better understand `if` and `for` via compare-and-contrast.
- You may encounter them in code you come across.
- You may prefer to use them for certain coding patterns.

The following sections define them and give an example of each.

L3.3.a – The switch Statement

This statement (inherited from C) can replace the `if` statement in certain (very narrow) situations to implement selection. It can only be used if the selection condition tests the equality of an `int` variable and a literal, or a `String` variable and a literal. In particular, it cannot be used if the variable is a double or if the condition uses > or ≤.

For example, a parking lot has three zones and it charges $10 if you park in zone #1, $7.5 in zone #2, and $2.5 otherwise. Implement this method to compute the charge given the zone:

```
public double charge(int zone)
```

Here is the implementation with `if` (on the left) and with `switch` (on the right):

```
public double charge(int zone)
{
   double result;
   if (zone ==1)
   {
      result = 10.0;
   }
   else if (zone == 2)
   {
      result = 7.5;
   }
   else
   {
      result = 2.5;
   }
   return result;
}
```

```
public double charge(int zone)
{
   double result;
   switch (zone)
   {
      case 1:  result = 10.0;
               break;
      case 2:  result = 7.5;
               break;
      default: result = 2.5;
               break;
   }
   return result;
}
```

The syntax involves putting the variable to be tested between parentheses after the switch keyword. Afterwards, list all the values you want to handle by putting their literals after the case keyword (or after the default keyword to handle all the remaining values). The break keyword is important[†] after every case in order to skip the cases below it. If you forget it, control will *fall through* the remaining cases! For example, if you omit break in the above, the method will always return the last handled case, which is 2.5 in the above example. Comparing the two implementations, some may argue that the switch syntax is more natural than the if. It is really a matter of personal preference.

As a second example, suppose you want to implement this method:

```
public int daysInMonth(int month)
```

It takes a month number (should be in [1,12]) and return the number of days in that month ignoring leap years; i.e. February is always 28 days. If the received parameter is not in [1,12] then the method should return -1.

Here is the implementation using with switch:

```
public int daysInMonth(int month)
{
    int result;
    switch (month)
    {
        case 1: case 3: case 5: case 7: case 8: case 10: case 12:
            result = 31;
            break;
        case 2:
            result = 28;
            break;
        case 4: case 6: case 9: case 11:
            result = 30;
            break;
        default:
            result = -1;
            break;
    }
    return result;
}
```

Notice how we benefited from the fall through in this example. When you write a case without a terminating break (or without any body at all) then all statements in subsequent case clauses are executed until a break is encountered.

[†]We warned against using break in loops, but for switch, it is acceptable; in fact, often necessary.

L3.3.b – The while Statement

This statement (inherited from C) can replace the for statement to implement iteration. It is less versatile than for (in the sense that it can always be replaced with a for) but its syntax is admittedly more intuitive. The table below shows the general while syntax on the left and the equivalent for syntax on the right:

| ```while (condition)
{
    loop body
}``` | ```for (; condition;)
{
    loop body
}``` |
|---|---|

As you can see both loops iterates as long as the boolean condition is true, which corresponds to the English meaning of while, i.e. *"keep looping while a condition holds"*. Unlike for, the while loop has no initial statement (often used to declare and set the for loop counter) and no post-body statement (often used to increment the counter). But like for, the while loop will skip its entire block if the condition happened to be false at the start.

As an example, let us re-implement the log2 method of Section L3.2.b using a while instead of a for. The table below shows the original implementation on the left and the one based on while on the right.

| ```public int log2(int n)
{
    int result = 0;
    for (int r = n / 2; r > 0; r = r / 2)
    {
        result++;
    }
    return result;
}``` | ```public int log2(int n)
{
    int result = 0;
    int r = n / 2;
    while (r > 0)
    {
        result++;
        r = r / 2;
    }
    return result;
}``` |
|---|---|

Notice how the local variable r had to be declared and set before the while (in a separate statement) whereas its declaration and initialization were bundled in statement-x (within the for statement). Similarly, the updating of r after each loop iteration was done seamlessly via statement-y of the for whereas the update was placed within the while's body.

Keep in mind that the differences pointed out above are merely syntactical; i.e. the method's return is the same whether implemented one way or the other.

L3.3.c – The do-while Statement

This statement (inherited from C) can also replace the for statement to implement iteration. It is also less versatile than for but it has one feature that neither for nor while possess: *it always iterates at least once.*

Recall that both for and while rely on a condition, and that this condition is checked before the loop starts and after each iteration. The do-while statement also relies on a condition but it is checked only at the end of the body, *not* before the loop starts. Hence, the statements of its body are never skipped even when the condition is false from the start.

The syntax of the new loop reflects the lack of initial checking:

```
do
{
    loop body
} while (condition);
```

As an example, let us re-visit the log2 method. In Section L3.3.b, we showed its implementation once using a for and once using a while. Let us try to implement using the do-while loop. Here is a first attempt:

```
public static int log2(int n)
{
    int result = 0;
    int r = n / 2;
    do
    {
        result++;
        r = r / 2;
    } while (r > 0);
    return result;
}
```

The logic *looks* equivalent to the for and while one but careful inspection of the flow should reveal a difference. If not, the acid test is to try out a few test cases and compare with an oracle we trust.

The oracle says:

$$\log2(1) = 0, \ \log2(2) = 1, \ \log2(10) = 3, \ \log2(15) = 3, \ \log2(32) = 5$$

Does the above code produce these results?

L3.4 – EXERCISES

1. Consider the fragment:

```
int x = 1;
boolean b1 = (x > 0);
boolean b2 = false;
boolean b3 = b1 && !b2;
if (b3 || x == 1)
{
    x++;
}
```

Create a table (known as a *trace table*) with four columns, one per variable, and one row. Fill the row with the values of the variables at the end of the fragment.

2. Consider the fragment:

```
final int A = 3;
final int B = 10;
int count = 0;
int sum = 0;
for (int i = A; i < B; i = i + 2)
{
    count++;
    sum = sum + i;
}
```

Create a trace table with three columns for the variables (count, sum, and i) and several rows, one per loop iteration. Each row in the table must be filled with the values of the three variables *at the end* of each iteration; specifically, after executing the loop body but before executing statement-y, which for this loop is i = i + 2.

3. Implement the following method which takes two int parameters a and b and returns the sum of the squares of all integers in [a,b]. For example, sumSquares(3,5) should return 50 (because $3^2+4^2+5^2 = 50$). The method should return 0 if a is not less than b.

```
public int sumSquares(int a, int b)
```

Create a class in this chapter's package (in the Testbed project) to hold the method and test your work using PSVM or J-Unit.

4. Implement the method shown below which computes the price of a movie ticket based on this algorithm: On Wednesdays (day code W), the price of the ticket is $8. On all other days, the price depends on the age of the customer. For a child who is less than 10, the price is $8, and for a teen who is between 10 and 17, the price is $10, and for a senior who is 60 or over, the price is also $10. For other ages, the price is $12:

    `public static double moviePrice(int age, String dayCode)`

    Create a class in this chapter's package (in the `Testbed` project) to hold the method and test your work using PSVM or J-Unit.
    Hint: do not use == to test the equality of two string objects!

5. Implement the method shown below which computes the factorial of n if n belongs to the interval [0,12], and throws a `RuntimeException` with message *"Number must not be negative"* if n is negative, and throws a `RuntimeException` with message *"Number must not be greater than 12"* if n is greater than 12. For example, `factorial(4)` should return 24.

    `public static int factorial(int n)`

    Create a class in this chapter's package (in the `Testbed` project) to hold the method and test your work using PSVM or J-Unit.

6. Implement the following method which takes two int parameters a and b and returns the number of perfect squares in [a,b]. A perfect square is an integer whose square root is also an integer. For example, `calc(4,15)` should return 2 because there are two integers in the [4,15] interval that are perfect squares (4 and 9). The method should throw a `RuntimeException` with an appropriate message if a > b and with a different appropriate message if both a and b are negative.

    `public int calc(int a, int b)`

    Create a class in this chapter's package (in the `Testbed` project) to hold the method and test your work using PSVM or J-Unit.

7. Given a positive integer n, return the number of *p-additions* needed to make it a palindrome (reads the same left-to-right as right-to-left). A p-addition is the addition of the number to its inverse. For example, if n=159, the first p-addition yields 159+951=1110, and the second p-addition yields 1110+111=1221, which is a palindrome. Hence, the return for 159 is 2. If n is a palindrome to begin with then return zero, and if the number does not become a palindrome after 10 p-additions then return -1.

    `public static int palindroCount(int n)`

    Implement this method and test it in the `main` method of a class.

8. Given two integers, if n <= m then return the sum of the reciprocals of all integers from n to m (inclusive) rounded to 2 decimals. Otherwise, return n/m (this is real division) also rounded to 2 decimals.

    public static double reciprocalSum(int n, int m)

    Implement this method and test it in the main method of a class. Here are two test cases you can use: reciprocalSum(-5,-3) is -0.78 and reciprocalSum(5,3) is 1.67.

9. This method computes the sum of the infinite series:

    x / (1*1) - x / (3*3) + x / (5*5) - x / (7*7) + ...

    The terms alternate in sign and each is a fraction whose numerator is x and whose denominator is the square of the next odd integer starting with 1. The method keeps adding these terms until it reaches a term whose absolute value is less than the received e parameter. At that point it returns the computed sum.

    public static double sum(double x, double e)

    Implement this method and test it in the main method of a class. For example,

    sum(10.0, 0.1) *is* 9.21 *(approximately)*

10. This method receives an integer n and returns the smallest integer that is greater than n and in which the sum of the digits is divisible by 11:

    public static int nextCRC(int n)

    For example,

    nextCRC(100) = 119

    This is because 119 is the first integer greater than 100 and the sum of its digits 1+1+9=11 is divisible by 11.

    Here are two more examples:

    nextCRC(-100) = -92
    nextCRC(20) = 29

CHAPTER 4 – DOING

String Land

D4.1 REQUIREMENT

D4.1.a   The KryptoNote App
D4.1.b   UI and Behaviour

D4.2 DESIGN

D4.2.a   The Vigenère Cipher
D4.2.b   File Storage

D4.3 IMPLEMENTATION

D4.3.a   Building the View
D4.3.b   The Cipher Model
D4.3.c   The Activity-View Connection
D4.3.d   File I/O

D4.4 EXERCISES

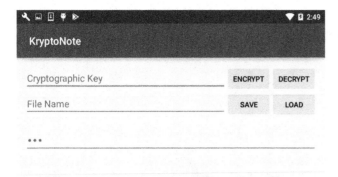

Figure D4.1 Upon launching the app.

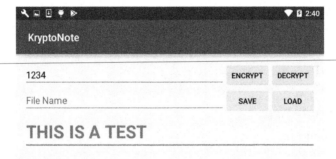

Figure D4.2 After entering the cryptographic key and some text.

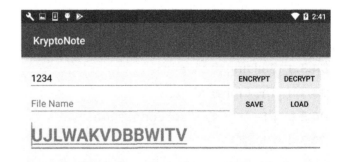

Figure D4.3 Upon tapping the ENCRYPT button.

D4.1 – REQUIREMENT

D4.1.a – The KryptoNote App

This app allows the user to create encrypted notes and save them on the device or optionally send them as text messages or emails.

D4.1.b – UI and Behaviour

The visible UI consists of *seven* visible widgets (see Fig. D4.1):

- A textbox (with a hint) for entering the encryption key and two buttons captioned *Encrypt* and *Decrypt* to the right of it.

- A textbox (with a hint) for entering the file name and two buttons captioned *Save* and *Load* to the right of it.

- Below these two lines is a textbox (with hint …) occupying the rest of the screen for entering the note to be encrypted or decrypted or saved.

For example, in the use-case shown in Fig. D4.2, the user entered "1234" as the encryption key and "THIS IS TEST" as the note. After wards, the user tapped the "ENCRYPT" button. In this use-case, the user wants to encrypt this note using the entered key. As a result, the app reacted as shown in Fig. D4.3. It encrypted the entered note using the entered key so it be–came "UJLWAKVDBBWITV". This is known as the *ciphertext*. As you can see, the app displayed the ciphertext in the same note textbox, thus overwriting the entered "THIS IS A TEST", which is known as the *plaintext*.

At this stage, the user has a number of options:

- Select the ciphertext, copy it, and paste it in another app, e.g. to email it.

- Enter a filename and tap Save in order to store the ciphertext in the indicated file on the device for later retrieval.

- Tap Decrypt so the app would decrypt the ciphertext (using the same key), which should lead back to the original plaintext as entered.

More formally, the requirement for the app behaviour is as follows:

1. The app must allow only digits for the key, only letters and digits for the filename, and only uppercase letters and spaces in the note textbox.

2. If the Encrypt button is tapped then the app must encrypt the entered note using the Vigenère cipher together with the entered key and display the result back in the note textbox (thus overwriting its contents).

3. If the Decrypt button is tapped then the app must decrypt the entered note using the Vigenère cipher together with the entered key and display the result back in the note textbox (thus overwriting its contents).

4. If the Save button is tapped then the app must save the content of the note textbox in the indicated file and then display the toast "Note Saved" to confirm.

5. If the Load button is tapped then the app must load the content of the indicated file into the note textbox (thus overwriting its contents).

6. If an exception occurred for any reason (e.g. invalid entries or file not found), the app must display a toast with an appropriate error message.

Here are a few typical use cases:

•   Launch the app; enter a note; enter a key; tap ENCRYPT; enter a filename; tap SAVE.

•   Launch the app; enter a filename; tap LOAD; enter a key; tap DECRYPT.

•   Launch the app; enter a note; enter a filename; tap SAVE (no encryption involved).

•   Launch the app; enter a note; enter a key; tap ENCRYPT; long press; select all and save to the clipboard; switch to an SMS or email app; paste.

The algorithm of the Vigenère cipher is explained in the Design section.

This app will expose us to string processing techniques and give us a glimpse of cryptography. And like all apps developed in this textbook, it will be designed with separation of concerns in mind so different ciphers can easily be plugged in (in place of Vigenère) without affecting the implementation of the view or the behaviour.

D4.2 – DESIGN

We will leverage the platform's APIs to implement file storage and handle flow / exceptions. As to encryption, and since the Vigenère cipher is not implemented in any of the platform libraries (nor in i2c), we will have to implement it ourselves in our model.

D4.2.a – The Vigenère Cipher

In order to better understand the algorithm, we will assume that the alphabet of the plaintext to be encrypted consists of the uppercase English letters and the space character (i.e. only 27 characters). Furthermore, we will assume that the alphabet of the encryption key consists of digits; i.e. the key is just a pin. It is straightforward to relax both conditions once the gist of the algorithm is understood.

```
ALPHABET = " ABCDEFGHIJKLMNOPQRSTUVWXYZ"
```

Given a plaintext such as "THIS IS A TEST" and a key such as "1234", the encryption process starts by creating a string known as the *pad* which has the same length as the plaintext and which is constructed by replicating the pin (**p**ersonal **i**dentification **n**umber). Imagine placing the pin repetitively under the plaintext, as shown here:

```
THIS IS A TEST
12341234123412
```

In this case, the pad contains 4 replicas of the key, the last of which has two characters only to keep the pad length the same as the text. Note that this process is always possible as long as the key has at least one character (i.e. it is not an empty string).

We now encrypt the plaintext characters one by one by shifting each of them forward in the alphabet a number of times equal to the pad digit under it. For example, the first character in the text is "T" and the pad digit under it is "1" so we shift it once. This makes it "U". Similarly, the second character "H" must be shifted "2" times so it becomes "J". This leads to:

```
THIS IS A TEST   <-- plaintext
12341234123412   <-- pad
--------------
UJLWAKVDBBWITV   <-- ciphertext
```

And in order to handle the case in which shifting forward takes us beyond the end of the alphabet, we treat the shift circularly (just like addition in int). For example, shifting "Z" one time makes it a space, and shifting it twice makes it "A", and so on.

Decryption works the same but by shifting backward (also circularly) in the alphabet.

Based on this, we seek a model class (call it `Cipher`) with the following API:

Cipher Fields
`public static final String ALPHABET` The characters of the plaintext (and the ciphertext) belong to this set of characters (`value=" ABCDEFGHIJKLMNOPQRSTUVWXYZ"`).
Cipher Constructor
`public Cipher(String k)` Construct an instance having the given key.
Cipher Methods
`public String Encrypt(String note)` Encrypt the given string and return the ciphertext.
`public String Decrypt(String note)` Decrypt the given string and return the plaintext.

D4.2.b – File Storage

File storage in the Android platform is similar to that of most other operating systems. The smallest unit of storage is the *file*, and in order to organize files and provide a namespace, the storage area is divided into *directories* (aka folders). The storage medium is non-volatile (does not lose content if power is lost) and is typically divided into *internal* and *external* areas. The internal area is built-into the device and files stored in it by an app are only accessible by that app (and will be removed when that app is uninstalled). The external area is removable (e.g. an SD card) and files in it can be shared by different apps.

Your activity class has methods (inherited from the parent activity class) that allows your code to access both the internal and the external areas.

Once you gain access to the root directory of either area, the `File` API allows you to manage that area as you wish. You can, for example, divide it into directories; remove directories; list all files and directories to determine their names and dates created; and view or change the permissions of each entry. It also allows you to create a new file and write to it or read the contents of an existing file.

Since this rich API is already available in the platform, we don't need to implement any model for it. Any needed functionality can be accessed directly from the activity.

D4.3 – IMPLEMENTATION

Create a new project with these names:

Project: KryptoNote
Activity:KryptoNoteActivity
Layout: kryptonote_layout

D4.3.a – Building the View

Start by adding the top row: a textbox (with id *key* and hint as per the requirement) and two buttons (with id's *encrypt* and *decrypt* and captions as per the requirement). These should be chained together as explained in Chapter 0 (see Fig. D4.4).

Repeat the above process for the second row of widgets using *file* for the id of the textbox and *save* and *load* for the id's of the two buttons. This chain is constrained under the one above.

Place a Scroll View below the second chain and make sure its width extends across the screen. Place a textbox with id *data* and hint "..." inside it to hold the note. The textbox must have a match_parent layout width so that it too extends across the entire screen.

Figure D4.4 The UI elements.

The requirement does not specify any particular size or colour for the note textbox so set these as you see fit.

Once all eight widgets are set, the component tree should thus look as shown in Fig. D4.5.

To verify that the components are correctly constrained, switch to landscape mode (see Chapter 0 if you don't know how) and make sure the layout in that mode looks OK. In particular, the data textbox must spread across the screen.

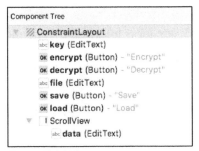

Figure D4.5 The UI component tree.

Finally, Make sure you set the *input type* attributes of all three textboxes to meet the validation requirement.

D4.3.b – The Cipher Model

The designer's API requires a field and a constructor that takes a key. This immediately tells us that we must have two attributes in the class:

```
private String key;
public static final String ALPHABET = " ABCDEFGHIJKLMNOPQRSTUVWXYZ";
```

The constructor should simply set the key attribute. We will not do validation in this release but will return to this point in the exercises.

Both the encrypt and decrypt methods need to create a pad based on the key attribute and the size of the plaintext. It therefore makes sense (to avoid code redundancy) to perform this work in a private method:

```
private String makePad(String note)
{
    String pad = this.key;
    for (; pad.length() < note.length(); )
    {
        pad += this.key;
    }
    return pad;
}
```

Take some time to examine this code. Note that this for statement has no statement-x and no statement-y, only a boolean. It keeps iterating as long as, or *while*, the boolean is true, so you can refer to it as a *while loop*. This is by no means the only way to implement this method or to write the loop. You could, for example, rewrite the same thing like this:

```
String pad;
for (pad = this.key; pad.length() < note.length(); pad += this.key);
return pad;
```

A for loop followed by a semicolon works as usual except it has no statements in its body.

The encrypt method needs to go through the given text, character by character, from left to right. At each position, it needs to extract the character at that position:

```
for (int i = 0; i < note.length(); i++)
{
    String c = note.substring(i, i + 1);
```

The substring method extract a substring starting from position i and ending *before* position i+1, which means it extracts the character at i.

Given the character c, we need to determine its position in the alphabet so that we can shift it forward. To do that, we use the indexOf method:

```
int position = ALPHABET.indexOf(c);
```

Next, we need to determine the shift amount based on the corresponding digit in the pad:

```
int shift = Integer.parseInt(pad.substring(i, i + 1));
```

The last step would be to determine the new position. It is simply position+shift except we need to handle the circularity of the shift. You can do this with an if statement:

```
int newPosition = position + shift;
if (newPosition > ALPHABET.length())
{
    newPosition = newPosition - ALPHABET.length());
}
```

Or you can benefit from the fact that the % operator works circularly:

```
int newPosition = (position + shift) % ALPHABET.length();
```

Here is the complete implementation:

```
public String encrypt(String note)
{
    String pad = makePad(note);
    String result = "";
    for (int i = 0; i < note.length(); i++)
    {
        String c = note.substring(i, i + 1);
        int position = ALPHABET.indexOf(c);
        int shift = Integer.parseInt(pad.substring(i, i + 1));
        int newPosition = (position + shift) % ALPHABET.length();
        result = result + ALPHABET.substring(newPosition, newPosition + 1);
    }
    return result;
}
```

The implementation of the decrypt method is almost identical to this except you need to shift backward rather than forward. This means the new position is obtained by *subtracting* rather than adding. Here, the circular nature of the shift means we must guard against the lower end of positions; i.e. avoid negative positions.

Implement decrypt and then test your model class.

D4.3.c – The Activity-View Connection

We have 4 buttons in our UI so we can glue them to 4 methods in out activity class:

- `public void onEncrypt(View v)`
- `public void onDecrypt(View v)`
- `public void onSave(View v)`
- `public void onLoad(View v)`

The needed code in the first two methods involves creating a `Cipher` instance (passing the entered key to it), invoking either `encrypt` and `decrypt`, and then poking the return in the `data` textbox. Enclose the body with `try-catch` construct.

The needed code in the last two methods involves leveraging the file API that was highlighted in the design section. The details are discussed in the next section.

D4.3.d – File I/O

Writing to a file involves the following sequence of steps:

1. Determine the directory to create the file in.
2. ~~Create a new file with the given name.~~
3. Create a file writer.
4. Write the data to the file.
5. Close the file writer.

The first step is easy thanks to a method that is already available in our activity class:

Activity Methods
`public File getFilesDir()` Returns a reference to a `File` instance that points at the directory (in the internal storage area) that is set aside for our app.

Hence, our `onSave` method would start like this:

```
String name = ((EditText) findViewById(R.id.file)).getText().toString();
File dir = this.getFilesDir();
```

The first statement captures the entered filename and the second captures the directory (in the internal storage area) in which our app can create its own files.

For Step 2, we examine the `File` API shown below and then append the above code with:

```
File file = new File(dir, name);
```

File Constructor
`public File(File directory, String name)` Construct an instance in the given directory having the given name.

File Methods
`public long lastModified()` Returns the time at which the file of this instance was last modified (the number of milliseconds since the epoch, Jan 1, 1970).
`public long length()` Returns the size (in bytes) of the file of this instance.
`public String[] list()` Returns an array of the names of all files and directories in this instance.

To implement the remaining steps, we examine the `FileWriter` API:

FileWriter Constructor
`public FileWriter(File name)` Construct an instance that can write to the given file. *Throws an exception if the instance cannot be created.*
`public FileWriter(File name)` Construct an instance that can write to the given file. *Throws an exception if the instance cannot be created.*

FileWriter Methods
`public void write(String data)` Writes the given string to the file. *Throws an exception if the operation cannot be completed.*
`public void close()` Flush any buffered data and disconnects the code from the file. *Throws an exception if the operation cannot be completed.*

Since all features in this API throw exceptions, we sandwich the entire body of our onSave method in a try-catch block and show a toast in the catch to display the error message.

Here is the complete implementation:

```
public void onSave(View v)
{
   try
   {
      String name = ((EditText) findViewById(R.id.file)).getText().toString();
      File dir = this.getFilesDir();
      File file = new File(dir, name);
      FileWriter fw = new FileWriter(file);
      fw.write(((EditText) findViewById(R.id.data)).getText().toString());
      fw.close();
      Toast.makeText(this, "Note Saved.", Toast.LENGTH_LONG);
   }
   catch (Exception e)
   {
      Toast.makeText(this, e.getMessage(), Toast.LENGTH_LONG);
   }
}
```

For the onLoad method, we need to examine the FileReader API:

FileReader Constructor
`public FileReader(File name)` Construct an instance that can read from the given file. *Throws an exception if the instance cannot be created.*

FileReader Methods
`public int read()` Reads one character from the file and return its code or -1 if there are no more characters in the file. the given string to the file. *Throws an exception if the operation cannot be completed.*
`public void close()` Disconnects the code from the file. *Throws an exception if the operation cannot be completed.*

The method's body is similar to onSave except we need to read the file one character at a time and concatenate these characters into a string. This requires a loop that keeps reading until -1 is returned as shown below.

```
// given a FileReader instance named fr:

String show = "";
for (int c = fr.read(); c != -1; c = fr.read())
{
    show += (char) c;
}
fr.close();
((EditText) findViewById(R.id.data)).setText(show);
```

Spend some time to understand how the loop constructs the string from the individual characters read from the file. The only question that may arise is:

Why is the char cast needed?

This has to do with how characters are stored in memory. Rather than storing the character itself (i.e. its glyph), computers store an integer that denotes the character. For example, instead of storing the letter "A" as an image, computers store the integer 65. This is surely far more economical (memory wise and performance wise) than storing an image. When we manipulate strings in our programs, we are actually manipulating their codes. The code gets transformed back into a glyph whenever we output the character. The table that maps characters to integers is known as the *Unicode Table* and it accommodates the characters of all known languages. (In the past, the mapping was based on the ASCII table which only supports English.) See Appendix-C for more details about character codes.

The read method of FileReader has an int return. Hence, if the file contains the character "A", the return will be 65. Had we not casted the return to a char, the displayed string would be "65" instead of "A", which is not what we want.

Complete the implementation of onLoad along the same lines followed in onSave.

D4.4 – EXERCISES

1. Change the default app badge to one that is more indicative of the app's functionality. For example:

    - An image of a note with a lock or a key is a good idea.
    - Another would be an image of superman *weakened by kryptonite!*

2. Add a new feature to the app so it helps the user locate a document if its name is forgotten. Specifically, if the user entered a question mark (?) as a filename and tapped Load, the app would generate a listing of all available files in the data textbox.

    Modify your onLoad method to provide this functionality.

    Hint: Look in the File API for a method that does that.

3. As built, the app displays *generic* error messages when the entered cryptographic key is empty or not numeric. This is unprofessional for the developer and not helpful for the end user.

    Modify your app so it would instead display the following meaningful error messages:

    - *The key should not be empty.*
    - *The key should consist only of digits.*

    The Cipher constructor should do the validation and throw a runtime exception that will bubble up to the activity where it is caught.

    Hint: Use either a loop or a regular expression to detect numeric-only strings.

4. The Encrypt and Decrypt methods have almost the same logic. To eliminate *code redundancy*, replace them with one method named onCipher. The onClick attribute of both the Encrypt and Decrypt buttons should point to it. The new method receives a View object reference and should use it to tell which button was tapped based on its id accessor.

5. Enhance your app by supporting an **expanded** alphabet. Rather than only capitals and a space, allow the note to include lowercase letters and a few punctuation signs. Note how the structured design of the app and the separation of concerns principle enable you to make this high-impact change elegantly and with minimal effort.

6. Enhance your app by supporting an arbitrary cryptographic key rather than a digit-only pin. This means the shift is based on the Unicode of the key characters rather than their values. For example, if the key is "ABCD" then the first letter of the plaintext is shifted forward by 65 positions (circularly) and the second by 66 positions and so on.

   Hint: Rather than using parseIn to determine the shift, use charAt.

   ❖ ❖ ❖ ❖

7. Create a new app named *Calc* as shown in Fig. D4.6. The UI consists of a label at the top and 12 buttons under it. The buttons are arranged in 4 rows, 3 per row.

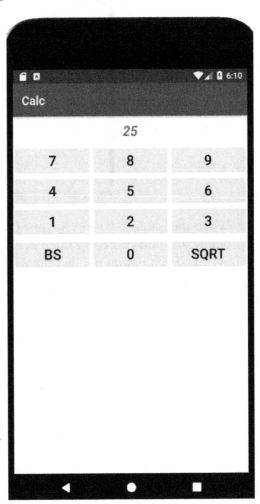

– When a digit [0-9] button is tapped, then its corresponding digit (which is its caption) is appended to the top label. For example, if the user tapped the 2 button and then the 5 button then the label would display 25.

– When the SQR button is tapped, the square root of whatever appears in the top label is computed and displayed in that label rounded to 5 decimals; i.e. it overwrites whatever was displayed.

– When the BS (back-space) button is tapped, the app removes the rightmost digit from the label.

– If the BS button is tapped twice within half a second; i.e. at most 500 ms between two taps, then the entire label is cleared. This is useful when the label has many digits to be cleared; so instead of tapping BS many times (once per digit), you just tap it twice rapidly.

Hints:
Use only one method to handle the on-click of all 10 digit buttons and identify the digit based on the text of the passed view object. For timing, use the mark method in Utility in i2c or the getNano method in System in the Standard Java library.

Figure D4.6 The Calc App.

8. Create a new app named *REX* as shown in Fig. D4.7. The UI consists of three check boxes at the top to control the regex generation process, a button to trigger the generation, a label to display the generated regex, a textbox to enter a string, a button to test the string against the regex, and a scrollable log area in the rest of the screen.

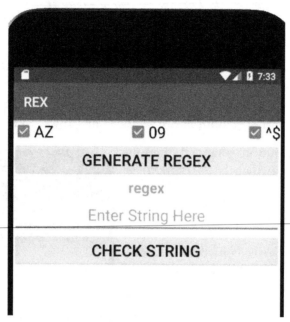

Figure D4.7 The REX App.

When the generate button is tapped, the app generates a regex and displays it in the label below that button. Seeing the regex, the user needs to enter a string that matches it then tap the check button. At that point, the app tests the string to see if it matches the regex or not and updates the log area accordingly.

For example, if the generated regex were:

$$\wedge[936]\{1\}[sct]\{3\}[0-9]\{1\}[zyq]*\$$$

and if the entered string were:

936sct9zyq

then the app would insert the following entry in the log:

```
regex = ^[936]{1}[sct]{3}[0-9]{1}[zyq]*$, string = 936sct9zyq ----> false
```

The entry shows the regex and the string and indicates that there is no match. Note that the entry is *prepended* to the log, not appended, so as to keep the latest entry at the top.

To implement the app's algorithm, create a model class named RexModel:

```
public class RexModel
{
    private String regex;
    private boolean digit, letter, anchor;
```

The attributes hold the generated regex and three boolean flags that indicate if the user likes the generated regex to include a digit pattern, a letter pattern, and anchors. The checkboxes at the top of the app's screen control these three attributes.

In addition to a constructor, the model needs to have *six* methods. Here is the sought API:

RexModel API
Constructor
`public RexModel()` Construct an instance having an empty regex attribute and true for the three boolean attributes.
Methods
`public boolean doesMatch(String s)` Determine if a given string matches the current regex.
`public void generate()` Generate the regex of this instance (and set the regex attribute).
`public String getRegex()` The regex accessor.
`public void setAnchor(boolean anchor)` The anchor mutator.
`public void setDigit(boolean digit)` The digit mutator.
`public void setLetter(boolean letter)` The letter mutator.

It is straightforward to implement all but the generate method. The constructor sets the default state and there is an accessor and three mutators. The doesMatch method simply delegates to the matches method of the String class.

Implementing the generate Method

The generated regex must have the following structure:

- The regex is anchored via ^ and $ (if any).
- The regex is made up of two pieces (always).
- A piece is a digit pattern (if any) followed by a letter pattern (if any).
- A pattern is a selector followed by a quantifier (always).
- A selector is a range (50% of the times) or a set (50% of the times).
- A quantifier is either a repetition count or + or * or ? (25% of the times each).

To understand this terminology let us look at an example of such a regex:

[936]{1}[sct]{3}[0-9]{1}[zyq]*

As you can see the first piece is **[936]{1}[sct]{3}** and its digit pattern has the set selector **[936]** with **{1}** as the repetition count quantifier.

The second piece is **[0-9]{1}[zyq]***. Its digit pattern has the range selector **[0-9]** with **{1}** as the repetition count quantifier. Its letter pattern has the set **[zyq]** with * as the quantifier.

The generate method starts with a call to Math.random which yields a real value in [0,1). If this value is less than 0.5 then it picks a range, otherwise it picks a set. Similarly, it generates a second random number and sets the quantifier to one of the above 4 possibilities based on whether the number is in [0,0.25) or [0.25,0.5) or [0.5,0.75) or [0.75,1.0).

The beginning and ending values of the range are chosen randomly by calling Math.random() for each and multiplying the return by 10.

The set is always composed of three elements and they too are generated randomly by calling Math.random() for each element and multiplying the return by 10.

Implementing the Activity

- Add a RexModel attribute and initialize it in onCreate.
- When the generate button is tapped, mutate the model's state based on state of the checkboxes and then invoke the model's generate and display its return.
- When the check button is tapped, invoke the model's doesMatch and update the log.

Updating the Log

The log area consists of a label placed inside a ScrollView. To insert a new entry at the top, start by reading the label's text. Next, create a string by concatenating the new log entry, a newline "\n" , and the label's text. Finally, set the label's text to this string.

9. Create a new app named *Investor* as shown in Fig. D4.8. The UI consists of three widgets: a textbox (with a hint) to enter the investment; a button captioned ANALYZE next to it; and a scroll view (not visible in the figure) extending across the screen and all the way to the bottom) to hold the analysis.

    The investment entry is a string that consists of four comma-delimited fields: an equity

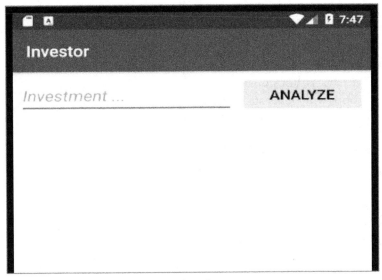

Figure D4.8 The Investor App upon launch.

symbol, the number of units, the book value (the price per unit when the equity was purchased), and the purchase date.

When an entry is made and the button is tapped, the app displays the analysis as shown in Fig. D4.9. Here, the user indicated that on Sept. 9, 2015, 24 shares of the stock whose symbol is .ad were purchased at $138.45 each. The analysis 8x2 table echoes back the four entry fields and adds fours:

- The name of the company whose symbol was entered.
- The current market value of the entered stock.
- The number of days between the purchase date and now (April 17, 2018).
- The annual yield (gain or loss) percentage of this investment.

The yield is defined like this:

$$\text{yield} = (\text{marketValue} - \text{bookValue}) / \text{bookValue}$$

The *annualized* yield is the average yield per year and is computed like this:

$$\text{annualizedYield} = \text{yield} * 365 / \text{daysHeld}$$

The entries in the first column of the table are bold and left-justified whereas those in the second column are right-justified.

Note that the delimiter in the investment entry may include one space after the comma.

The analysis shown in the figure reflects the status as of 5:00 pm on April 17, 2018. Since the market value of stocks vary continuously and the number of days is not constant, the results that your app will generate will be different from the ones in the figure.

The analysis table must be created dynamically in code as shown in Exercise #7 of Section D3.4. You will need to insert a table layout in the scroll view and then insert a table row (8 times) inside the table layout. Each table row would have two text views inside it, one per column.

Aside from the UI, the remaining challenge involves: parsing the entry and capturing its fields, determining the company name and the current price of the stock, computing the number of days between two dates, and computing the yield. We will create a model class named Equity to handle all this.

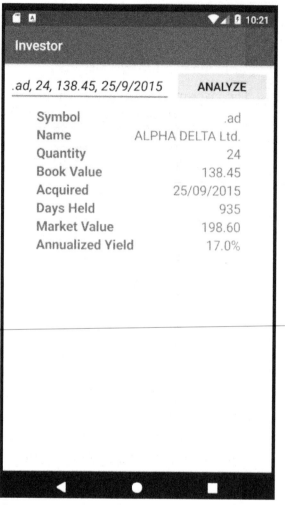

Figure D4.9 The Investor App analysis.

But first, a few business terminology from thee requirement analysis document:

EQUITY INVESTMENTS

An equity investment involves purchasing a number of shares of a company in the hope that it will prosper and its share price will increase. (There is also the hope that the company will distribute dividend to its shareholders but we will not be concerned with that in this app.) The purchase of shares is done in a market known as the *exchange* and it is there that stocks of companies are traded. For the purposes of this app, a unique stock exchange was created. It is known as the *Abstract Stock Exchange* and you can visit its website at the following URL:

http://project.roumani.ca/ase/

Each stock has an associated **symbol** (aka *ticker*) and you are invited to visit the above URL and enter a stock symbol such as .QC (a dot followed by two letters) and see the name of the company and its current price. The price may of course change if you get a quote later. As an example, suppose you purchased a few shares of the .QC stock for $7.50 each. This purchase price per share is known as the **book value** of the stock. The book value is thus constant and does not change with time. On the other hand, the **market value**, which is the current price per share on the exchange, is variable and does change with time.

INVESTMENT YIELD

The yield of an investment at any given time is defined as the profit or loss made if the investment is sold at market value at that time, divided by the book value of the investment, and then annualized. As a second example, let us assume that we purchased a number of .QC shares at $7.50 each back on *Jan. 20, 2003*. To compute the yield of this investment on *Feb 20, 2016*, we start by finding out the market value of that share. Assuming it is *$12.34*, we compute the yield like this:

$$[(12.34 - 7.50) / 7.50] * [365 / \#of\ days]$$

The initial bracket yields 64.5% but this gain needs to be annualized based on the number of days between the purchase and (assumed) sale transactions, which is 4779 days in this case. The second bracket is therefore 0.076, so the investment yield is 4.9%.

THE ABSTRACT STOCK EXCHANGE API

In order to obtain the name and the current market price of an equity investment, we need to connect to the URL of a stock exchange. Since our app deals with the special dot-letter-letter equities on the Abstract Exchange, we will employ the API of a class named Stock in the i2c library.

Hints:

- *Create a class named Equity with eight attributes corresponding to the eight rows in the analysis table.*

- *The class constructor takes one string, the investment entry, and parses it to set the eight attributes. It also uses the Stock class to determine the name and market value of the given stock symbol.*

- *To determine the number of days between two Date objects (to target devices that don't have Java 8), use the getTime method and simply subtract the purchase time from the current time. The difference can then be converted from milliseconds to days by dividing.*

- *To determine the number of days between two LocalDate objects (for devices with Java 8), use the invocation ChronoUnit.DAYS.between(now, purchase).*

10. Refactor the *Investor* app of the previous exercise to enable the user to *optionally* enter the *investment name* rather than its four-field details as shown in Fig. D4.10.

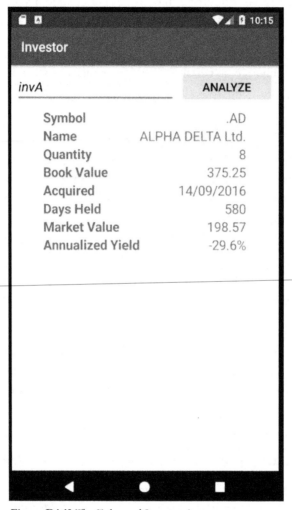

Figure D4.10 The Enhanced Investor Apps.

Here, the user entered *invA* as the investment name and then tapped the button. The app detected that this is a name entry because it does not contain any commas. As such, it looked up the entered name in the strings.xml file (in the app value resources) and used its value for the computation.

Note that in this example, the stock was purchased for $375.25 and its current value (when the button was tapped) is $198.54. This loss, 580 days after the purchase leads to an average annual loss of 29.6%.

To store the investment names, define them in the `strings.xml` file like this:

```
<string name="invA">.AD,8,375.25,14/9/2016</string>
```

You can define as many such names as you want.

To access these definitions in code, use this pattern:

```
int id = getResources().getIdentifier(entry, "string", getPackageName());
entry = getString(id);
```

Here, `entry` refers to the string that the user entered (and we have verified that it does not have commas in it). The first statement translates it into an id. The second statement uses the id to fetch the actual value of that string as defined in XML. The fetched value is used to re-define the `entry` string. This way, the rest of your activity would work as if the user had entered the investment details.

Hints:

- *Detect the presence of at least one comma in the user's entry. If not found, use the entered string as shown above to access the investment details in XML.*

- *Sandwich all your code that looks up the string in XML (as well as the code that parses its fields) in a try-catch block. This guards against a non-existent string name as well as an invalid investment details.*

- *If the entry if invalid (the catch block), use a toast to display an appropriate error message.*

CHAPTER 4 – LEARNING

String Land

L4.1 – THE STRING API

L4.1.a – The Basics

Here is the basic API of the String class:

Constructor (String class)
`public String(String s)` Construct an instance holding the passed string.
Methods (String class)
`public int length()` Return the number of characters in this instance.
`public substring(int from, int to)` Extract from this instance the substring residing in [from, to). This interval is a closed-open [includes, excludes). Throws an exception if from>to or if from is negative or if to exceeds the length of the string.
`public int indexOf(String other)` Determine if other is present as a substring in this instance. Return –1 if not and return the position where it starts if present.

The constructor is never used explicitly thanks to the *syntactical sugar* that Java provides to strings in order to make them easy to use. When you write:

```
String s = "Toronto";
```

You are actually using the constructor because the compiler replaces this, primitive-like declaration and assignment to a constructor invocation. This implicit replacement along with the + operator that concatenates strings are unique to the String class—no other class has direct syntax that supports it within the language itself.

The basic three methods in the above API are best understood through examples, which we present next, but a few remarks are in order:

- Positions in a string are numbered left to right starting with zero.
- The last position in a string is 1 less than its length.
- An *empty* string has 0 length. A null string is just a null reference (no object).
- Strings are immutable. The only way to change a string is to create a new one.

As a first example, suppose we want to count the number of times the letter "e" appears in a given string s. One approach would be to set up a loop that goes through every position in the string

```
for (int position = 0; position < s.length(); position++)
```

In each iteration of the loop, we extract the character residing at the current position:

```
String c = s.substring(position, position + 1);
```

We now check to see if this character is an "e":

```
if (c.equals("e"))
```

Note that we want to check if the *state* of our string is the same as the state of "e" string (i.e. we are comparing objects, not references) hence we use equals rather than ==.

The full fragment looks like this:

```
// count the number of "e"'s in s
int count = 0;
for (int position = 0; position < s.length(); position++)
{
    String c = s.substring(position, position + 1);
    if (c.equals("e"))
    {
        count++;
    }
}
```

As a second example, let us re-do the count using indexOf. This method can tell us in one shot if "e" is present and where, but this only covers the first occurrence. To move on to the next occurrence, we cut off the first part of the string and re-use indexOf on the remaining part. The process continues until no more occurrences are found:

```
int count = 0;
for (int p = s.indexOf("e"); p!= -1; p = s.indexOf("e"))
{
    count++;
    s = s.substring(p+1, s.length());
}
```

Note that the full String API has many other methods (in addition to, and overloaded with, the ones shown above) so other approaches are also possible.

L4.1.b – Transformers

The following String methods change the contents of a string, but since strings are immutable, they do so by creating and returning a new string:

Methods (String class)
`public String toUpperCase()` Return a new instance having the same state as this instance but with all letters converted to capitals.
`public String toLowerCase()` Return a new instance having the same state as this instance but with all letters converted to lower case.
`public String trim()` Return a new instance having the same state as this instance but with any leading or trailing spaces removed.

The functionality of these methods is self evident from the API.

L4.1.c – Comparators

The following String methods change the contents of a string, but since strings are immutable, they do so by creating and returning a new string:

Methods (String class)
`public boolean equals(String other)` Return true iff this and the passed instance have the same state.
`public boolean equalsIgnoreCase(String other)` Return true iff this and the passed instance have the same state case-insensitive.
`public int compareTo(String other)` Return a measure of the distance between this string and the passed one. The metric is based on a lexicographic comparison of the Unicode values.

The functionality of the equals methods is clear but a few words are in order regarding the algorithm that compareTo follows.

Given two strings s and t, compareTo compares the first character in s with the first one in t (left to right). The comparison is done but subtracting the Unicode values of the two characters. If the answer is negative or positive then the process ends and the computed difference is returned. But if the difference is zero (the two characters are the same) then the process moves on to compare the second character in s with the second one in t. Again, if the difference is non-zero then it is returned; otherwise, the process continues at the third character, and so on.

If one of the strings ended before the other then the method returns the length difference (rather than the Unicode difference).

Evidently, the algorithm is designed to support the sorting (i.e. ordering) of strings, an as such, we interpret the return of the invocation:

```
s.compareTo(t)
```

as follows:

- If negative then s is less than t (lexicographically).
- If positive then s is greater than t (lexicographically).
- If zero then s is equal to t (i.e. s.equals(t) is true).

L4.1.d – String-to-Number

Given a numeric string (one whose contents can be interpreted as a number) then we can convert its state to a numeric type using one of these methods:

- `Integer.parseInt`
- `Double.parseDouble`

For example, if the string s is supposed to contain a real number then we can extract it as a double type like this:

```
double x = Double.parseDouble(s);
```

You should be careful, however, when you use the parse methods because they may throw exceptions if the string does not hold the expected state (an integer or a real number). For example, an exception is thrown if the number has a thousands separator or if it has leading or trailing spaces (in which case you should pass s.trim() instead of s).

As a rule, use the try-catch construct (and log or display the error message) whenever you use the parse methods.

Conversely, if we have a numeric type and we want to convert its value to a string, we either use the + operator with the empty string or the static `format` method. Example:

```
int n = 125;
String s = "" + n;
String t = String.format("%d", n);
```

The first technique (which produced `String s`) relies on the fact that when one of the operands of the + operator is a `String`, the other operand is coerced to a `String`.

The second technique is more powerful as it allows us not only to convert but also format the string, e.g. by rounding or adding a thousands separator.

L4.1.e – String-to-Character

Given a string `s`, we saw that we can extract a character at position p in it like this:

```
String c = s.substring(p, p+1);
```

There is a second way to do this but it is not quite the same:

```
int n = s.charAt(p);
```

This method returns the Unicode value of the character rather than the character itself. For example, if `c` were "A" then `n` would be 65.

The first technique (using `substring`) is more versatile because it can extract a substring, not just one character. If you prefer to use both techniques, keep in mind that the first returns an object whereas the second returns a primitive type. This means you should use `equals` with the first and `==` with the second.

Conversely, if we have the Unicode value x of a character and we want to convert it to the corresponding character as a string, we would use the `(char)` cast and then the + operator:

```
String t = "" + (char) x;
```

This often occurs in input streams which reads characters from a file or a network socket. These streams return the Unicode value of each read character (with -1 to indicate the end of the stream) rather than the character themselves.

L4.2 – REGULAR EXPRESSIONS

L4.2.a – Pattern Description Language

The String API enables us to perform string queries that have a definite criterion. For example, we can determine if a particular character, or a substring, occurs in a string and find the position where it occurs. But what if the search criterion is not exact? For example, how do we determine if a given string has a phone number or a postal code embedded within it? In such cases, the criterion is not something for which we seek an exact match but rather a *pattern*. A Canadian postal code pattern, for example, involves three uppercase letters, three digits, and possibly a space, arranged in a particular way. How do you search for that?

To solve such problems, we need a language that can describe a pattern, and this language is known as the *regular expression* (aka *regex*) language. This language originated in Unix but is now adopted in all platforms and supported by all languages.

A regex is a string that describes a pattern in a formal, unambiguous fashion. Let us start with a simplified Canadian postal code pattern—think of a postal code like "M3J 1P3". Since it must start with a capital letter, our regex starts like this:

```
String regex = "[A-Z]";
```

The brackets indicate a *single* character selected from whatever is inside the brackets. In this case, it is a letter between A and Z (inclusive). Next we need a digit, which leads to:

```
String regex = "[A-Z][0-9]";
```

Next we need an uppercase letter, which leads to:

```
String regex = "[A-Z][0-9][A-Z]";
```

Next we need a space, which is simply [ ] (two brackets delimited by a space). This space, however, is optional so we need to quantify it as repeating once or not at all. This is done via the ? quantifier:

```
String regex = "[A-Z][0-9][A-Z][ ]?";
```

Continuing along the same lines, we reach the regex:

```
String regex = "[A-Z][0-9][A-Z][ ]?[0-9][A-Z][0-9]";
```

Now, how do you use this regex to find postal codes in the string below?

```
C3F8)F& ZU6S*R7B O1L+8MG1Q(H2K*7'C#JJ3L7'BM5IM2X *9V7B30&9H6L 7G0U0OK4EM9J%
W83KP1H%2-SN1MN9H.D6H$E3L/Z9E)3+C5/O8%D4- R0+YL3K'K0M0V3Y05G'9V7-LI302I860S
P3H'9)FF7SA2B .8W3J9V)M8DC5A/9C85&KE5Z#F5J#R1N3/Y4+G8'D8& KC6EQ2U3&U2&KE3E(
1V2U6M0+JN2K(K2UD3HZ2GY7P-7L5Z1RG8E/5U5S5RF9C)P0C0R7J%0/ I4$T9#HY1G*U0M+A0S
```

The power of regex is that there is an API that allows you to mine all matches of any pattern as long as you provide its regex. We will see the code in the next section, but for now, let us imagine using the API on the above string using the regex we developed. If we did that, the API would report *five* matches:

H6L 7G0, K0M0V3, I302I8, V2U6M0, P0C0R7

Indeed, we can see where these matches appear in our string:

```
C3F8)F& ZU6S*R7B 01L+8MG1Q(H2K*7'C#JJ3L7'BM5IM2X *9V7B30&9H6L 7G0U00K4EM9J%
W83KP1H%2-SN1MN9H.D6H$E3L/Z9E)3+C5/08%D4- R0+YL3K'K0M0V3Y05G'9V7-LI302I860S
P3H'9)FF7SA2B .8W3J9V)M8DC5A/9C85&KE5Z#F5J#R1N3/Y4+G8'D&& KC6EQ2U3&U2&KE3E(
1V2U6M0+JN2K(K2UD3HZ2GY7P-7L5Z1RG8E/5U5S5RF9C)P0C0R7J%0/ I4$T9#HY1G*U0M+A0S
```

We can appreciate the power of regex, even in this simple example, because approaching this problem with only the basic string methods would have been quite cumbersome and messy. This power scales well to complex problems such as finding a particular pattern in a DNA strand—a string containing millions of *A, C, G, T* nucleotide bases.

Let us make our example more realistic by incorporating two additional facts about postal codes in Canada:

- The letters {D,F,I,O,Q,U} are never used anywhere in the code.
- The letters {W,Z} are never used as the first letter of the code.

To incorporate these conditions, we need to restrict the criterion of the character class [A-Z] by adding that it *shouldn't* be in the set [D,F,I,O,Q,U]. The negation in regex is done by prefixing the set elements with ^. This leads us to the regex (written on 7 lines for clarity):

```
[A-Z&&[^DFIOQUWZ]]
[0-9]
[A-Z&&[^DFIOQU]]
[ ]?
[0-9]
[A-Z&&[^DFIOQU]]
[0-9]
```

Running the regex engine with the new regex on the above string yields:

H6L 7G0, K0M0V3, P0C0R7

Finally, if we are only after Ontario codes (first letter must be in {K,L,M,N,P}), we change the first character class in the regex to [K-N,P]. Running the matcher with the final regex yields only one Ontario code in the above string:

K0M0V3

The ? quantifier is not the only one that regex supports:

?	once or not at all
*	zero or more times
+	one or more times
{m,n}	between m and n times
{m,}	m or more times

As a second example, let us write a regex that describes a real number pattern. Such a number could be positive or negative but the sign is sometimes omitted if the number is positive. Hence, the pattern starts with:

`[+-]?`

After the sign comes the integer part of the number, which must have at least one digit:

`[+-]?[0-9]+`

Next comes a decimal, point but since the point has a special meaning in regex (it match any character), we must escape that default meaning by prefixing with \:

`[+-]?[0-9]+[\.]`

Finally, the decimals, if present, consist of 0 or more digits:

`[+-]?[0-9]+[\.][0-9]*`

Note that for a real number to fit this pattern it must have at least one digit before the point and it must have a point. Hence, 123 and .5 will *not* be matched. If we want to match these as well, we expand our regex using the *or* of two patterns:

`[+-]?[0-9]+([\.][0-9]*)?|[\.][0-9]+`

This says: an optional sign followed by at least one digit and then one of two things:

- An optional decimal point followed by optional digits, or
- A decimal point followed by one or more digits.

You can find more details about the regex language in Appendix-B. In particular, if you surround a regex by the anchors ^ and $ then the string must consist only of the pattern (rather than having it embedded in it). For example, the regex ^[+-]?[0-9]+$ will only be matched by a string that contains an integer (and nothing else). Anchors are ideally suited for applications requiring validation whereas a regex without anchors is ideally suited for mining applications which require finding all embedded matches.

L4.2.b − Pattern Recognition

The regex API in Java involves two classes, Pattern and Matcher, and provides a mechanism by which we can easily iterate through all matches. Given a regex regex and a string s, use the following fragment as a template for your regex-related code:

```
Pattern pattern = Pattern.compile(regex);
Matcher matcher = pattern.matcher(s);
for (; matcher.find(); )
{
    // match found from position matcher.start() to position matcher.end()
}
```

The first statement compiles the regex to optimize the matching engine. The second returns a Matcher instance. This instance has three methods of interest:

- find(): returns true if there are still matches.
- start(): returns the position at which a match begins.
- end(): returns the position just after a match ends.

You can tailor this template to serve the logic on hand depending on whether you are after all matches or just a yes/no. For example, to determine if a string s can be parsed to an integer, you could validate like this:

```
Pattern pattern = Pattern.compile("^[+-]?[0-9]+$");
Matcher matcher = pattern.matcher(s);
if (matcher.find())
{
    System.out.println("The string " + s + " is valid.");
}
else
{
    System.out.println("The string " + s + " is invalid.");
}
```

On the other hand, if you want to output all integers embedded in s, you would write:

```
Pattern pattern = Pattern.compile("[+-]?[0-9]+");
Matcher matcher = pattern.matcher(s);
for (; matcher.find(); )
{
    System.out.println(s.substring(matcher.start(), matcher.end()));
}
```

The regex language comes with a few predefined character classes that offer a convenient shorthand. For example, \d means a digit (i.e. the same as [0-9]) and \s means a whitespace digit (e.g. a space, a tab, a newline, etc.). For example, the regular expression:

```
\d+[ABC]*\s?\p
```

describes a pattern that has:

- One or more digits,
- Followed by zero or more characters each of which is either A or B or C,
- Followed optionally by one whitespace character,
- Followed by one punctuation symbol.

For example, the strings "7A !", "1B?", "3!", and "4BBA ;" all match this regex.

Before presenting a concrete coding example, we need to point out a syntactical issue related to backslashes in Java strings. The backslash character "\" has a special meaning in the regex language as it is used to designate predefined classes and as an escape character. But the Java language also uses the backslash as an escape in its strings. This means when you write a regex that contains a backslash as a Java string then you need to escape it twice; i.e. repeat it. For example, th above regex example would appear in a Java program like this:

```
String regex = "\\d+[ABC]*\\s?\\p";
```

As a final example, implement the method shown below which takes an arbitrary string and return the number of timestamps embedded in it.

```
public static int countTimestamps(String s)
```

A timestamp has the form:

> hh:mm *followed optionally by some whitespace and then either* am *or* pm *(case insensitive)*

where hh is the hour (two digits) and mm is the minute (also two digits). Examples of matches are "09:30 am", "12:00 pm", "05:47PM" and "11:10aM".

We build the regex as follows: the first hour digit can be either 0 (in which case the second hour digit would be 1-9) or 1 (in which case the second hour digit would be 0-2. The first minute digit is 0-5 while the second is 0-9. This leads us to:

```
(0[1-9]|1[0-2]):[0-5][0-9]
```

Next, we need zero or more whitespace (which is \s*) and a case-insensitive am/pm:

```
(0[1-9]|1[0-2]):[0-5][0-9]\s*[aApP][mM]
```

Here is the complete implementation:

```
public static int countTimestamps(String s)
{
    int count = 0;
    String regex = "(0[1-9]|1[0-2]):[0-5][0-9]\\s*[aApP][mM]";
    Pattern pattern = Pattern.compile(regex);
    Matcher matcher = pattern.matcher(s);
    for(; matcher.find(); )
    {
        count++;
    }
    return count;
}
```

L4.2.c – Pattern-Driven Transformers

In addition to answering the query question "does a pattern exist in a string", regex can also be used to transform a string in two ways:

- **String Tokenization — split**
  Tokenizing a string means to break into pieces (aka tokens) based on some pattern. The split method (in the String class) takes a regex and splits the string on which it is invoked around the matches of that regex. It returns an array of the split pieces.

- **Substring Replacement — replaceAll**
  The replaceAll method (in the String class) takes a regex and replaces all its matches in the string on which it is invoked with a given replacement. It returns the resulting string.

These are *convenience* methods; i.e. you could do without them using the regex template of the previous section, but they come handy in many coding patterns.

As an example of tokenization, suppose you want to find all words in a sentence (perhaps in an analytics or translation application). A word is any sequence of letters. This means a word ends either when followed by a non-letter (such as a space or a digit or punctuation) or when it is at the end of the string. We can therefore describe a word with the following regex:

    [A-Za-z]+

A non-letter can therefore be described by the negation of the above regex:

    [^A-Za-z]+

Based on this, we can extract the words in a string using a fragment like this:

```
String s = "What is >>the area-code<< of: Ottawa?";
String regex = "[^A-Za-z]+"
String[] pieces = s.split(regex);
```

The returned array, pieces, would have 7 elements:

```
0: What
1: is
2: the
3: area
4: code
5: of
6: Ottawa
```

As you can see, the returned array consists of each substring in our string that is terminated by a match the given regex or by the end of the string.

And as an example of replacement, consider the simple implementation of the adage:

i before e except after c

It is intended to remind us how to correctly spell a word like "rec**ei**ve" (rather than rec**ie**ve) and a word like word like "bel**ie**ve" (rather than bel**ei**ve). A spell-checker can detect the mis-spelled pattern using this regex:

```
[c][i][e]
```

and a spell-corrector can fix the mistake using a fragment like this:

```
String s = "I will receive a gift if I believe!";
String regex = "[c][i][e]";
String fixed = s.replaceAll(regex, "cei"));
```

The return string, fixed, would be:

```
I will receive a gift if I believe!
```

Note that the above example is case sensitive; i.e. it will not spell correct "REC**IE**VE". The regex language has an elegant solution for this: simply place (?i) before the pattern and case is ignored. Hence, we can enhance our spell corrector by replacing the second line in the above fragment with:

```
String regex = "(?i)[c][i][e]";
```

or simply:

```
String regex = "(?i)cie";
```

L4.3 – EXERCISES

1. Implement the method shown below which takes a real number and return the sum of the digits in it with any non-digits (such as the sign and decimal point) ignored. For example, `digitSum(-12.25)` should return `10` because the 1+2+2+5 = 10.

    ```
    public int digitSum(double x)
    ```

2. The method `say` takes an `int` and returns a string containing the names of the digits in that integer delimited by a space. For example, the invocation `say(3750)` should return the string: `"THREE SEVEN FIVE ZERO"`. Complete its implementation shown below:

    ```
    public static String say(int n)
    {
      final String WORDS = "ZERO ONE  TWO  THREEFOUR FIVE SIX  SEVENEIGHTNINE ";
      String result = "";
      ...
      return result;
    }
    ```

    You could trivially do this using 10 `if` statements but you are asked to do it without any. Benefit from the provided `WORDS` string which holds the digit names padded (with space) to exactly 5 characters each. Thanks to this padding, a name like `SIX` appears at position 5*6=30. In other words, the position of a name derives from the value of its digit.
    Hint: Extract the digits and use then to extract the name then trim it.

3. Run-length encoding is used to compress images: instead of storing many adjacent pixels that are identical, we store just one along with its repetition count. In this exercise, we simulate this with strings. Complete the method below which takes a string and return it run-length compressed. As an example, the invocation `compress("aaaaaaaaaPPPrrrr")` should return the string: `"8a3P4r "`.

    ```
    public static String compress(String s)
    {
      String result = "";
      ...
      return result;
    }
    ```

4. Implement the method below which validates a given DNA sequence (a string):

    ```
    public boolean isValidDNA(String dna)
    ```

    The sequence is represented by a string of letters each of which represents a nucleotide. To be valid, the sequence must:

    a. be made up exclusively of the capital letters: A, C, G, and T,

    b. start with the amino acid "ATG", and

    c. have a nucleotide count that is divisible by 3.

5. Consider the regex.

    ```
    ^\$(\d{1,3}(\,\d{3})*|(\d+))(\.\d{2})?$
    ```

    Give a few strings of different lengths and structures that match it.

6. Implement the method shown below which takes a string and return a count of the telephone numbers embedded in it. A telephone number consists of a three-digit area code followed by a dash or a space, followed by three digits, followed by a dash or a space, followed by four digits. Note that the two separators need not be the same; i.e. it could be dash/dash, dash/space, space/space, or space/dash.

    ```
    public int telCount(String s)
    ```

7. Implement the method shown below which receives a non-empty string str; extracts the *computing courses* in it; and returns the sum of their credit counts. If the received string has no computing course in it then the method returns 0:

    ```
    public static int totalCredit(String str)
    ```

    A computing course is recognized by the prefix EECS or CSE (in upper or lower case) followed by four digits, followed by one or more period, followed by the credit count, which can optionally be bracketed. The credit count of a course is a single digit. Here are four examples of valid computing courses:

    ```
    EECS1022.3, cse4413..[4], eecs4141....[6], CSE3481..3
    ```

    For example, if str is the string:

    ```
    "Course EECS1022..3 and cse1020.[4] with CSE3421 or CSE6215...8"
    ```

    then the return should be 15.

8. Implement the method below which determines the longest sequence of repeating characters in a given a non-empty string (i.e. consecutive characters that are the same). The return is a string made up of the repeating character and its repetition count delimited by an equal sign.

   If more than one such sequence is found, the return should be about the one that occurs first in the string:

   ```
   public static String longest(String str)
   ```

   For example, if str is the string:

   ```
   "ZZZZAISSDRRIIIIIIIHHHQQQDDDDDDDZZZZZDD"
   ```

   then the return should be the string:

   ```
   "I=7"
   ```

   This is because there are two longest repeating sequences in this string (D and I, each repeating seven times) and the I sequence occurs before the D sequence.

9. Given a non-empty string, this method locates the *Canadian postal code* embedded in it and return the sum of the digits in that postal code.

   If no postal code is found then return –1 and if more than one is found then locate the one that *occurs last* in the string.

   A Canadian postal code consists of a letter-digit-letter sequence followed optionally by one space and then followed by a digit-letter-digit sequence:

   ```
   public static int postalDigitSum(String str)
   ```

   For example, if str is the string:

   ```
   "Try M3J1P3 or m5s 2W8 and m3:9j4"
   ```

   then the return should be the integer:

   ```
   15
   ```

   Note that the letters in the postal code could be in lower, upper, or mixed case (some upper, some lower).

10. Given a non-empty string, this method extracts the timestamp embedded in it, and returns its time expressed as a 4-digit time using the 24-hour clock. The return is thus of the form "hhmm" where hh ranges from "00" to "23" and mm ranges from "00" to "59".

   ```
   public static String get24Time(String str)
   ```

   A timestamp is a substring made up of an integer value between 1 and 12 (representing the hour) followed by : (a colon) followed by a two-digit string between "00" and "59" (representing the minute) followed optionally by some whitespace followed by the string "am" or "pm" in upper, lower, or mixed case.

   You can convert a timestamp to a 24-hour clock by simply adding 12 to the hour if the time is in the afternoon.

   If the entered string has no timestamp embedded in it then return the *empty* string, and if it has more than one then return the one that *occurs last*.

   For example, if str is the string:

   "There was a change from 4:35 to 9:25 Pm tomorrow."

   then the return should be the string

   "2125"

   This is because the relevant timestamp is the second; i.e. "9:25 Pm", and since it is in the afternoon, we add 12 to the hours.

Chapter 5 – Doing

Collections

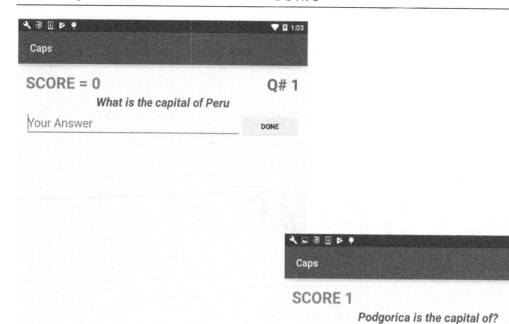

Figure D5.1 Upon launch.

Figure D5.2 After posing the second question.

D5.1 – REQUIREMENT

D5.1.a – The Caps App

This app is a Jeopardy-like game that asks the user questions about countries (the capital of a given country and the country of a given capital—hence the *Caps* name). It also keeps track of the achieved score.

D5.1.b – UI and Behaviour

The visible UI consists of *six* visible widgets (see Fig. D5.1):

- A label in the upper-left corner to show the score.
- A label in the upper-right corner to show the question number.
- A label in the second row in which the question is centred.
- The third row has a textbox with hint "Your Answer".
- The third row also has a button captioned "DONE".
- Below the third row is a big, scrollable label that displays the game's log.

The game's log contains the history of the user's interaction with the app in this session. It lists all the posed questions along with the user's answers and the correct answers.

In the example shown in Fig. D5.1, the game starts by displaying a score of 0 and a question number of 1 and posing the first question (which in this example is about the capital of Peru). The game then waits for the user to enter the answer in the textbox and tapp DONE. The user can type the answer in upper, lower, or mixed case.

Fig. D5.2 shows what happens when DONE is tapped. The app:

- converted the entered answer to uppercase (to become "LIMA").
- evaluated the answer and found it to be correct.
- Incremented the score (making it 1).
- Displayed the new score.
- Appended the game's log.
- Incremented the question number (making it 2) and displayed it.
- Posed the second question (about the capital Padgorica).

Note that game proceeds to the next question automatically; i.e. by tapping DONE, the answer of the current question is evaluated and the next question is posed.

Note also that when the (capitalized) user's answer is evaluated (by comparing it to the correct answer in the game's database) the comparison is case insensitive.

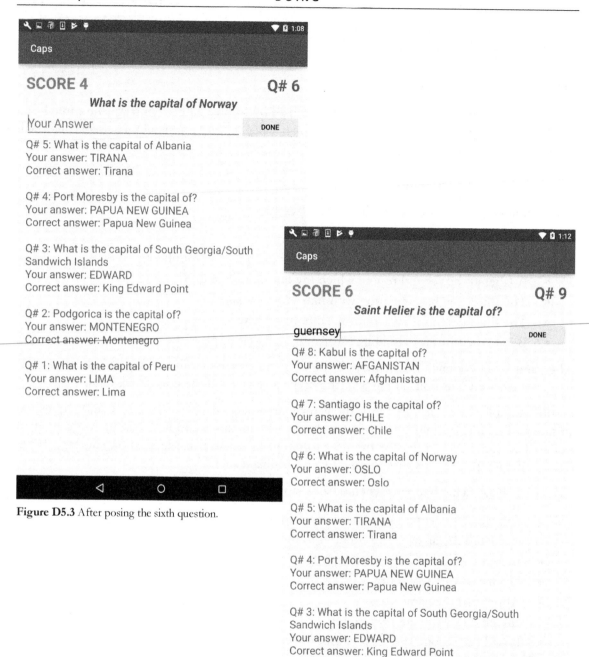

Figure D5.3 After posing the sixth question.

Figure D5.4 After posing the ninth question.

The described behaviour of the app continues in the same manner. For example, Fig. D5.3 shows a screenshot of the device after five questions were asked and answered and the sixth one posed. The score at this stage is 4 out of 5 because the user missed the Q#3. Similarly, Fig. D5.4 shows the status immediately after the 9th question was posed. The score now here is 6 out of 8 because in addition to missing Q#3, the user misspelled the answer to Q#8.

Once DONE is tapped for Q#9, the game should evaluate and log its answer as before, but then the game should end. The maximum score is therefore 9. When the game ends, two things happen as depicted in Fig. D5.5:

- The sentence "Game Over!" appears in the question number label.
- The DONE button becomes disabled.

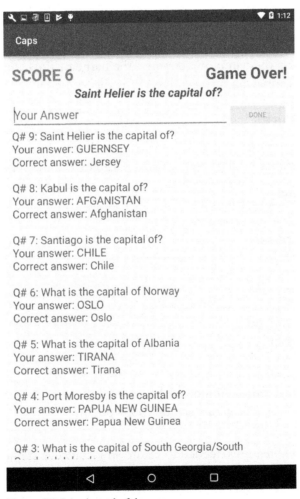

Figure D5.5 At the end of the game.

D5.2 – DESIGN

The textbook's library (i2c.jar) contains two classes whose APIs fulfill some of the needs of the app. The first is Country and the second is CountryDB, and they provide the data from which the app can derive questions and answers. We will therefore incorporate them as part of the app's model (make sure you add the textbook's library to your project's dependencies as shown in Chapter 0).

Our model's architecture will thus consist of *three* classes; the above ready-made ones plus Game which we will write ourselves. The APIs of these three classes are discussed in the following sections.

D5.2.a – The Country API

This class is a simple data wrapper (designed mainly to hold data with minimal behaviour). Each instance of it holds the name of a country, the name of the capital of that country, and the population of that capital (an integer). Its API is shown below.

Country Constructor
`public Country(String n, String c, int p)` Construct an instance having country name n, capital c, and capital population p.
Country Methods
`public String getCapital()` Capital name accessor.
`public String getName()` Country name accessor.
`public int getPop()` Population accessor.
`public String toString()` Construct a textual representation of the instance. Returns the string: "Country{name='name', capital='capital', pop='pop'}"

The API has the minimal features needed to create an instance and query it. The toString method is intended mainly for testing and debugging purposes.

D5.2.b – The CountryDB API

This class holds a database of country-related data. When you create an instance, the database is populated with information about ~250 countries. For each, the database stores the country name, the capital city name, and the population of that capital. The class API allows us to retrieve this data in a number of ways:

CountryDB Constructor
`public CountryDB()` Construct a database instance populated with country-related data derived from the 2015 census.

CountryDB Methods
`public List<String> getCapitals()` Return a list of the names of all capital cities in this database instance.
`public Map<String,Country> getData()` Return a map whose keys are the names of all capital cities in the database and whose values are the corresponding Country instances.

To familiarize ourselves with the API, let us try to retrieve some data. The following fragment explores the usage of the getCapitals method:

```
CountryDB db = new CountryDB();
List<String> capitals = db.getCapitals();
System.out.println(capitals.size());
String c = capitals.get(107);
System.out.println(c);
```

After creating an instance of the database, the fragment invokes getCapitals and holds the returned list of strings in the variable capitals. We can access the information stored in the list through variable. For example, the fragment invokes the size method on it in order to determine how many element are in the list (i.e. how many capitals are available in the database). Afterwards, the fragment picks one of those elements, element number 107, and uses the get method to retrieve the name of the capital stored in that element.

The elements in the list are numbered starting from zero, pretty much like the positions of characters in a string. Hence, if the size of a list (as returned by the size method) happened to be 100 then you can invoke the get method with a parameter value of 0, 1, …, 99. If the value is outside this range then the get method will throw an exception

The second method in the API retrieves far more information than the capital names. Here is a fragment that adds a few lines to the fragment developed earlier:

```
CountryDB db = new CountryDB();
List<String> capitals = db.getCapitals();
System.out.println(capitals.size());
String c = capitals.get(107);
System.out.println(c);

Map<String, Country> data = db.getData();
System.out.println(data.size());
Country ref = data.get(c);
System.out.println(ref.toString());
```

The getData method returns a map, which is a collection of pairs:

```
(c1, ref1)
(c2, ref2)
...
```

Each pair holds a capital city name and a reference to a corresponding Country object. The capital names (c1, c2, ...) are the keys of the map and the references (ref1, ref2, ...) are the values of the map.

The fragment invokes the size method on the map to determine the number of pairs in it. The answer should be the same as the number of elements in the list of capitals because every capital in the list appear as a key in the map.

Next the fragment uses the get method of the map to retrieve the value of the pair whose key is c (the capital that was retrieved earlier from element #107 in the list). This returns an object reference to a Country instance that represents the country whose capital is c.

Here is the complete output of the fragment:

```
241
Ottawa
241
Country{name='Canada', capital='Ottawa', pop=898150}
```

As we expected, both the list and the map have the same number of elements/pairs (241 of them). And apparently, the 107th element in the list is Ottawa. And when we fetched the pair whose key Ottawa, we got a reference to a Country object, and when we printed the return of the toString method invoked on that reference, we got the details of the country Canada whose capital is Ottawa.

D5.2.c – The Game API

This class is the frontend of our model; i.e. the activity talks to it and it talks to the country database. Here is its sought API:

Game Constructor
`public Game()` Construct an instance tied to the `CountryDB` database.
Game Methods
`public String qa()` Randomly pick a country from the database and return a two-line string. The first line contains a question about the country and the second contains the answer.

The constructor must create an instance of `CountryDB` so that the `Game` instance would have access to the `CountryDB` database. The `qa()` method picks a random country from the database and poses a question about it. For example, suppose that the random selection picked the following country:

```
Country{name='Canada', capital='Ottawa', pop=898150}
```

In this case, the method can construct and return either this string:

```
What is the capital of Canada
Ottawa
```

or the string:

```
Ottawa is the capital of?
Canada
```

As you can see the return has a question and its correct answer delimited by the newline character "\n".

The qa method can formulate two types of questions: find the capital given the country, or find the country given the capital, and it randomly chooses between them; i.e. it asks about the country 50% of the times and about the capital 50% of the times.

Java has several methods for generating random numbers. The `random` method of the `Math` class is probably the simplest. It returns a random `double` in $[0,1)$ but can be easily tailored to return an `int` in any range. For example, to generate a random integer in $[0,9)$, you would use it like this (the `int` cast truncates):

```
int n = (int) (9 * Math.random());
```

D5.3 – Implementation

Create a new project with these names: *Project*: Caps, *Activity*: CapsActivity, and *Layout*: caps_layout

D5.3.a – Building the View

As shown in Figure D5.6, you need to insert:

- Two labels in the top row with ids *score* and *qNum* and text as shown.

- One label in the second row with id (and text) *question* and with the text centred.

- A textbox with id answer and a button with id *done* and caption *DONE* in the third row.

- A scroll view under the third row extending across the screen and to the bottom.

- A label with id *log* inside the scroll view in order to hold the history log.

- Set the text size and style to match the shown screen-shots as much as possible.

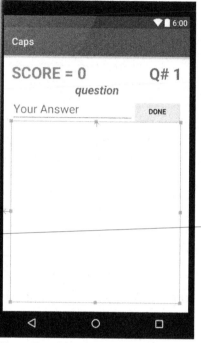

Figure D5.6 The UI elements.

The component tree should thus look as shown in Figure D5.6.

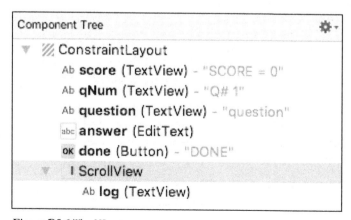

Figure D5.6 The UI component tree.

D5.3.b – The Game Model

The designer's API requires that each instance must be associated with a `CountryDB` instance. This immediately tells us that we must the following attribute in the class:

```
private CountryDB db;
```

The constructor should simply initialize this attribute:

```
public Game()
{
    this.db = new CountryDB();
}
```

The `qa` method requires that we randomly pick a country. Since the map collection does not have an indexed accessor that allows us to retrieve a pair of a given index, we rely on the list of capital names (which does have such an accessor).

The psueodocode for `qa` looks like this:

1. Get a reference to the database's capital city list.
2. Determine the size of this list. Call it `n`.
3. Generate a random number in [0,n). Call it `index`.
4. Invoke `get(index)` on the list to get a random capital city. Call it `c`.
5. Get a reference to the database's data map.
6. Invoke `get(c)` on the map to get a reference to a country. Call it `ref`.

Now that we have a randomly selected country, the only task remaining is to determine the question type. To do that, we generate a second random number and test it like this:

```
if (Math.random() < 0.5)
```

The `if` statement condition will be true 50% of the time. We therefore can generate one type of question in the `if` block and the other type in the `else` block. Composing a question (of either type) is straightforward given `ref` because its accessors:

- `getCountry`
- `getCapital`

provide all the needed ingredients. Remember to embed a newline character between the question and the answer.

Complete the implementation of `Game` and test it.

D5.3.c – Building the Controller

We recommend having the following attributes in the activity class:

- private Game game (to hold the Game instance)
- private String question (to hold the last-posed question)
- private String answer (to hold the answer of the last-posed question)
- private int score (to hold the current score)
- private int qNum (to hold the number of the last-posed question)

These attributes must be properly initialized in the onCreate method.

The controller should have two methods:

- private void ask()
- public void onDone(View v)

The ask method is intended to ask a question and is invoked:

- From onCreate (so a question is asked when the app starts), and
- From onDone (so a question is asked whenever the button is tapped).

Implement ask so that it retrieves a question/answer from the model; sets the attributes of the activity accordingly; and displays the question to the user.

The onDone method is glued to the button via its onClick attribute. Its algorithm should proceed along these lines:

1. If the question number (qNum) is 10 then end the app by invoking finish().
2. Retrieve the user's answer from the view and compare it to the answer attribute.
3. If the two are the same (case insensitive) then update the score attribute.
4. Compose the log entry.
5. Prepend the log entry to the existing log with an empty line in between.
6. Increment the question number, qNum.
7. If qNum has become 10 write Game Over else display the score and qNum.

Complete the implementation of CapsActivity.java.

D5.4 – EXERCISES

1. Add two features to the app:

    a. Clear the textbox once the DONE button is tapped (so the user won't have to do so every time). The cleared answer will still be available in the log.

    b. If the user's answer is ? (a question mark) then assist the user by showing the correct answer plus one other randomly-selected answer. Show these in one toast so as not to disturb the UI.

2. Make the app sound a tone if the answer is correct and a different tone if the answer is wrong. Sound generation is done through the ToneGenerator class. Add an attribute tg of this type to your activity and initialize it in onCreate:

    ```
    this.tg = new ToneGenerator(AudioManager.STREAM_ALARM, 100);
    ```

    To make a sound, use the startTone method, e.g.

    ```
    tg.startTone(ToneGenerator.TONE_CDMA_ALERT_CALL_GUARD, 200);
    ```

    Experiment with various ToneGenerator fields to generate a sound you like.

3. The current app considers the answer correct if it matches the database answer exactly. The only tolerance it applies is case insensitivity. Can you tolerate misspelling?

    Hint:
    Explore dropping all the vowels and comparing only the consonants.

4. Modify the app so that the question number would reset if the device is strongly shaken. Note that this would allow the user to "cheat" by having more than 10 questions and thus achieve a higher score.

5. Add a feature to the app so that it would remember (and display) the highest score that was ever achieved (whether in this session or any prior one).

    Hint:
    Create a file (Section D4.3.d) and update it when a higher score is achieved.

6. Expand the range of possible questions by incorporating the available population data. For example, you can have the app ask:

What is the population of Ottawa?

The answer should be considered correct if it is within 10% of the correct answer.

7. Create a new app named *StockTrader* as shown in Fig. D5.7. The UI consists of four widgets: a textbox (with a hint) to enter the portfolio name; a button captioned ANALYZE next to the text box; a label extending across the screen in the row below (not visible in the figure) for the analysis executive summary, and a scroll view (also not visible and extending across the screen and all the way to the bottom) to hold the analysis details.

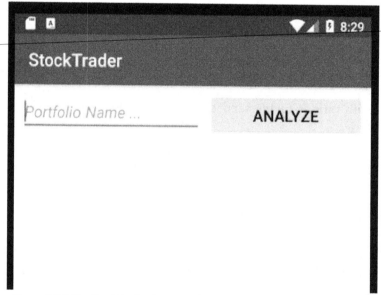

Figure D5.7 The StockTrader App upon launch.

The user is supposed to enter a portfolio name and tap the button. The app analyzes the named portfolio and displays the result as shown in Fig. D5.8. The analysis consists of an executive summary (showing the number of equities in the portfolio, its current market value, and its annualized yield) and a tabulation of all equities in the portfolio (showing the symbol, quantity, book value, date acquired, market value, and yield, of each equity).

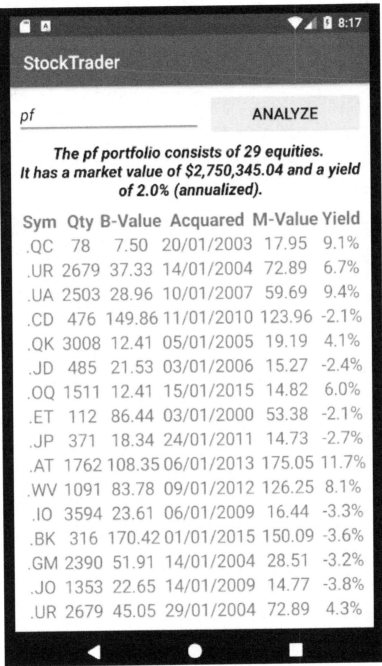

Sym	Qty	B-Value	Acquared	M-Value	Yield
.QC	78	7.50	20/01/2003	17.95	9.1%
.UR	2679	37.33	14/01/2004	72.89	6.7%
.UA	2503	28.96	10/01/2007	59.69	9.4%
.CD	476	149.86	11/01/2010	123.96	-2.1%
.QK	3008	12.41	05/01/2005	19.19	4.1%
.JD	485	21.53	03/01/2006	15.27	-2.4%
.OQ	1511	12.41	15/01/2015	14.82	6.0%
.ET	112	86.44	03/01/2000	53.38	-2.1%
.JP	371	18.34	24/01/2011	14.73	-2.7%
.AT	1762	108.35	06/01/2013	175.05	11.7%
.WV	1091	83.78	09/01/2012	126.25	8.1%
.IO	3594	23.61	06/01/2009	16.44	-3.3%
.BK	316	170.42	01/01/2015	150.09	-3.6%
.GM	2390	51.91	14/01/2004	28.51	-3.2%
.JO	1353	22.65	14/01/2009	14.77	-3.8%
.UR	2679	45.05	29/01/2004	72.89	4.3%

The pf portfolio consists of 29 equities. It has a market value of $2,750,345.04 and a yield of 2.0% (annualized).

Figure D5.8 The StockTrader App upon tapping the ANALYZE button.

A *portfolio* is a collection of equity investments (for background materials and terminology on equities, see Exercise 9 in Section D4.4). The portfolio derives its attributes from those of its underlying equities. Specifically:

- Its book value is the sum (over all its equities) of terms each of which is the product of the quantity and the book value of an equity.

- Its market value is the sum (over all its equities) of terms each of which is the product of the quantity and the market value of an equity.

- Its yield is the weighted average of the yields of its equities with the weights being the book values of the equities times their quantities.

For example, consider the portfolio sc shown in the table below:

Portfolio sc	Symbol	Quantity	Book Value	Acquired	Market Value	Yield
First Equity	.QC	78	7.50	20/02/2003	18.22	9.4%
Second Equity	.UR	2679	37.33	14/09/2004	73.82	7.2%

This portfolio consists of *two* equities and each has a stock symbol, number of shares, a price per share (i.e. a book value), and a purchase date. These four properties are shown in column 2 through 5. When analyzed via the Equity class of Exercise 9, Section D4.4, each equity picks up a market value (the current price per share) and a yield. Based on this, we compute the portfolio properties as follows:

book value = 78 x 7.50 + 2679 x 37.33 = $100,592.07

market value = 78 x 18.22 + 2679 x 73.82 = $199,184.94

yield = (0.094x7.50x78 + 0.072x37.33x2679) / (7.50x78 + 37.33x2679) = 7.2%

In order to store the portfolio, we use the strings.xml file in the values resources of our app. This is similar to what we did earlier to store strings (see for example Exercise 10 in Section D4.4) but we now need to store an **array** of strings rather than simple strings.

For example, to store the data for the sc portfolio analyzed above, we edit the strings.xml file in the res/values tree and insert the following xml fragment in it:

```
<string-array name="sc">
   <item>.QC,78,7.50,20/2/2003</item>
   <item>.UR,2679,37.33,14/9/2004</item>
</string-array>
```

You start with an XML tag that gives a name to the array (so we can fish it out in code). You then add an item tag for each array element. Each item represents an equity and its value is a four-field, comma-delimited string that specifies the four attributes of each equity. You can any number of arrays this way as long as each has a unique name.

To fetch the data of one of the arrays, use a code fragment like this:

```
String p = the entered portfolio name
String[] data;
Resources res = getResources();
data=res.getStringArray(res.getIdentifier(p, "array", this.getPackageName()));
```

Once your activity fetches the data array, you need to convert it to a List<Equity> object.

Hints:

- *Create a class named Portfolio with a List<Equity> attribute.*

- *The constructor takes an array of strings and uses it, together with the Equity class, to set the attribute.*

- *The class must have methods to compute the portfolio properties. In particular, its toString method can return the executive summary that the app displays.*

- *The activity must guard against a non existent array name by using a try-catch block and displaying a toast with an appropriate message if the entered portfolio name does not exist.*

- *To create the UI, create a linear layout in code and add it to the scroll view.*

- *To create the tabulation, create a table layout in code and add it to the linear layout.*

- *To create rows, create a table row object and add it to the table layout.*

- *To populate a row in the table, create text views, one per column, and add it to the table row object.*

8. Refactor the *StockTrader* app of the previous exercise to support the use case in which the user forgot the name of the portfolio. Recall that the `strings.xml` file can hold a number of portfolio arrays, each with a unique name, and that the user must enter the name of the portfolio to be analyzed *exactly* as specified in that file. To make this process friendlier, the refactored app allows the user to enter a question mark in lieu of the name, as shown in Fig. D5.9. When the `ANALYZE` button is tapped in this case, the refactored app must display a list of all the available portfolio names.

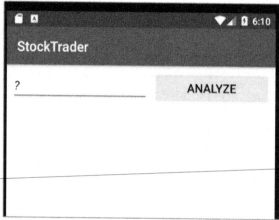

Figure D5.9 The refactored StockTrader App.

There are two challenges in implementing this feature: first, we need an API that allows us to traverse all string arrays defined in `strings.xml` and access their names. Second, we need to display the retrieved names somewhere other than the analysis area that occupies the rest of the screen!

The first challenge is met by an interesting combination of an Android API and a standard Java API. The Android API allows us to write:

`R.array.class`

The class R is automatically created by the Android during build process. It captures all the resources of your app (such as XML layouts and values) so that they can be accessed from a Java program running within the Android platform. The class `R.array.class` is an inner class of R and it captures the array assets in its attributes. To access them, we use Java's reflection API like this:

`Field[] fields = R.array.class.getFields();`

This method returns an array of all the attributes (aka fields) of that inner class and their names are the names of the arrays we seek.

Thanks to these two APIs, we can write a simple loop like the one shown below to browse the names of all arrays defined in `strings.xml`:

```
Field[] fields = R.array.class.getFields();
for (int i = 0; i < fields.length; i++)
{
    String name = fields[i].getName();
    ...
}
```

Moving on to the second challenge, we need to find a place to display those names without affecting the existing UI. One option would be to put them in a toast but this is not scalable approach because:

- Toasts are transient, appearing for only a brief period of time.
- Toasts are small and not scrollable.
- The user cannot interact with a toast (e.g. select an element in it).

A second, more versatile option, would be to put them in a **second activity**. The second activity will be named `ListActivity` and it will come with its own Java file and will have a separate layout (`activity_list.xml`).

To add a new activity to an app, follow these steps:

1. Right-click the `app` tree.
2. Select New…
3. Select Activity.
4. Select Empty Activity.
5. Enter the name `ListActivity`.
6. Accept the suggested layout name and all other defaults.
7. Click Finish.

Populate the new layout with three widgets (see Fig. D5.10):

- A text view centered at the top with the text: *Available Portfolios*.
- A centered button at the bottom with caption: DONE.
- A scroll view with id `sv` in between the above two widgets.

The plan is that when a question mark is entered and the ANALYZE button is tapped, the app transfers control to the second activity as if a hyperlink in an HTML page is clicked. The second activity displays the names, and when its DONE button is tapped it transfers control back to the first activity. The hyperlink action is implement in Android via an **intent**.

In order to transfer the control to the ListActivity when the name is ?, use this pattern:

```
Intent intent = new Intent(this, ListActivity.class);
this.startActivity(intent);
```

When the second activity receives control, its onCreate method is invoked so this is where we need to set up the UI, retrieve the names of the arrays, and then display them. It is recommended that you create a vertical linear layout object:

```
LinearLayout ll = new LinearLayout(this);
ll.setOrientation(LinearLayout.VERTICAL);
```

and insert it in the scroll view sv that you inserted in the linear layout. We then traverse the fields of the array inner class and display the name of each in a dynamically created text view. The fragment below shows the process:

```
Field[] fields = R.array.class.getFields();
for (int i = 0; i < fields.length; i++)
{
    String name = fields[i].getName();
    TextView tv = new TextView(this);
    tv.setGravity(Gravity.CENTER);
    tv.setTextSize(TypedValue.COMPLEX_UNIT_DIP, 20);
    tv.setText(name);
    ll.addView(tv);
}
```

The click handler of the DONE button can return to the original activity using the finish method as shown below:

```
public void onDone(View v)
{
    this.finish();
}
```

We leave it as an exercise for you to enhance this app further by allowing the user to click on the desired portfolio name and have this name transferred back to the first activity so it can be analyzed upon return.

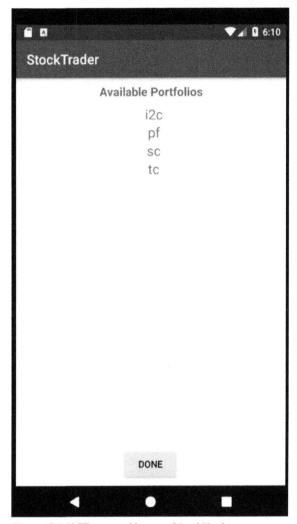

Figure D5.10 The second layout of StockTrader.

CHAPTER 5 – LEARNING

Collections

L5.1 THE COLLECTION FRAMEWORK

L5.2 SELECTED ALGORITHMS

L5.3 EXERCISES

L5.1 – THE COLLECTION FRAMEWORK

L5.1.a – Overview

Many problems in computing require that we store and manipulate a large number of variables, and we have seen in Section L2.1.e that arrays enable us to do that. Working with arrays, however, is quite cumbersome because they are low-level constructs and do not offer any methods. For example, they cannot grow or shrink automatically, so every time we add or remove an element, we would need to move things around in order to maintain the array structure. In other words, building applications with arrays makes you spend more time on the bookkeeping of the array than on the application itself. Because of these reasons, the Java library come with classes that use arrays internally but offer a high-level API that hides the bookkeeping details. These classes are known collectively as the *Java collection framework*.

Using the collection API is not different from using any other APIs—you instantiate, invoke methods, and pass parameters—but there are two subtleties that you should be aware of:

1. Classes are parameterized with **generics**.
2. Declaration is done through **interfaces**.

The first point requires that when we refer to any collection type such as List, that we suffix the type name with the desired type of collection elements surrounded by angle brackets. For example, if you want a list of strings, then write List<String> rather than just List. Similarly write List<Integer> to refer to a list of int elements.

The second point requires that we declare collection references via interfaces and instantiate via classes. Specifically, this textbook deals with the three interfaces and classes shown in the table. So in order to create a list of strings named bag, we would write:

```
List<String> bag;
bag = new ArrayList<String>();
```

The first statement declares the bag variable to be of type List (the interface). The second statement sets the variable using the constructor of the ArrayList class. Note that generics are added to both the interface name and the class name.

INTERFACE	CLASS
List	ArrayList
Set	TreeSet
Map	TreeMap

You could of course combine these two statements into one:

```
List<String> bag = new ArrayList<String>();
```

Aside from these two subtleties you can use the bag object reference just like any other. For example, to put the string "Canada" in the bag collection, you would write:

```
bag.add("Canada");
```

L5.1.b – Working with Lists

A list is a data structure that views its elements as a *sequence*. This means the positional order of the elements is significant (the list [a,b] is not the same as [b,a]) and duplicate elements (as in [a,b,a]) are allowed. (In the same vein, a string as a sequence of characters.)

The List API is powerful and rich. The following table highlights the key methods in it:

Methods (List<E>)
`public boolean add(E e)` Add e at the end of the list.
`public boolean add(int p, E e)` Add e at position p in the list. Exception if p not in [0,size()].
`public boolean contains(E e)` Return true if e is present in the list and false otherwise.
`public boolean get(int p)` Return the element at position p. Exception if p not in [0,size()).
`public boolean remove(E e)` Remove e from the list if present else return false.
`public E remove(int p)` Remove the element at position p. Exception if p not in [0,size()).
`public int size()` Return the number of elements in the list.
`public String toString()` Return the elements of the list bracketed and comma-delimited.

A few remarks about these methods:
- Both add methods are boolean but you can treat them as void.
- The get method allows you to access the list like an array (by index).
- The remove(E e) method removes the *first* occurrence of e.
- The toString method is used mainly for testing and debugging.

These methods enable us to do the typical **CRUD** operations (**C**reate, **R**ead, **U**pdate, **D**elete) associated with databases. How about *traversal* (listing all elements in a list)? This can be done using get in a loop, as shown below.

```
// traverse the elements of list bag of type List<E>:
for (int position = 0; position < bag.size(); position++)
{
    E e = bag.get(position);
    System.out.println(e);
}
```

But since the impetus of moving from arrays to collections is to transcend the positional index and operate at a higher level, there is an alternate way to traverse:

```
// traverse the elements of list bag of type List<E>:
for (E e: bag)
{
    System.out.println(e);
}
```

This is known as the *enhanced for loop* and it works with any collection that has an iterator capable of returning elements one by one.

As a final example, implement the method:

```
public static boolean addIfNew(List<String> bag, String s)
```

It takes a list of strings and a string s. If s is already present in the list then do nothing and return false. Otherwise, add s to the list and return true.

Here is the complete implementation:

```
public static boolean addIfNew(List<String> bag, String s)
{
    boolean result = !bag.contains(s);
    if (result)
    {
        bag.add(s);
    }
    return result;
}
```

We first check if the list already contains the given string. If so, result would be false and the if statement is skipped. Otherwise, result would be true and the string is added.

L5.1.c – Working with Sets

A set is a data structure that views its elements as a *set*. Recall from math that a set does not allow duplicates and treats element order as insignificant (the set [a,b] is the same as [b,a]). You would choose a set over a list if the elements are distinct and you don't care about the order in which they were added.

All the methods in the List API are available as-is in Set except the ones that refer to the position of an element (because sets do not keep track of positions). Here are the highlights:

Methods (Set<E>)
`public boolean add(E e)` Add e to the set.
`public boolean contains(E e)` Return true if e is present in the set and false otherwise.
`public boolean remove(E e)` Remove e from the set if present else return false.
`public int size()` Return the number of elements in the set.
`public String toString()` Return the elements of the set bracketed and comma-delimited.

An important remark here is that the add method is meaningfully boolean. It returns true if and only if the element is added. The element is not added if it already exists.

As an example, suppose we want to implement a method that takes a list of integers, remove all duplicates, and return the resulting distinct integers as a set. This can be done like this:

```
public static Set<Integer> removeDuplicates(List<Integer> list)
{
    Set<integer> result = new TreeSet<Integer>();
    for (Integer i : list)
    {
        result.add(i);
    }
    return result;
}
```

Set traversal is similar to that of lists but can only be done through the enhanced for loop (rather than through an indexed traversal). For example, the fragment below creates a set of strings; adds a few elements to it; and then traverse the set and outputs the visited elements:

```
Set<String> set = new TreeSet<String>();
set.add("Toronto);
set.add("London");
set.add("Seattle");
set.add("Damascus");
for (String city : set)
{
    System.out.println(city);
}
```

One interesting side benefit of the TreeSet class is that it stores elements in sorted order. As such, the traversed elements appear in ascending order. For example, if you execute the fragment above, the generated output would look like this:

```
Damascus
London
Seattle
Toronto
```

As you can see, the elements are sorted even though their insertion order was not.

But how did the TreeSet class know how to sort the elements? In fact, it cannot know how because it doesn't know a priori the type of elements it has—the generics are specified upon instantiation. The secret lies in the String class: the TreeSet class relies on the compareTo method in String to determine the order by which the elements are stored.

In general, element order within a TreeSet depends on the type of elements:

- If numeric, then it is **magnitude** based.
- If strings, then it is **lexicographic**.
- If times or dates, then it is **chronological**.
- Otherwise, order is based on the **compareTo** method if present else an exception.

This algorithm for determining the order relation is known as *natural ordering*.

The toString method is quite handy for checking code correctness and inspecting results. In the above fragment, for example, we could replace the traversal loop with one statement:

```
System.out.println(set.toString());
```

The output would then be: [Damascus, London, Seattle, Toronto].

L5.1.d – Working with Maps

A map is a data structure that views its elements as a *mapping* between a set of *keys* and a list of *values*. Each element in a map is thus a key-value pair. The mapping has to be a function (i.e. one key cannot map to more than one value) but it does not have to be one-to-one (i.e. two keys can map to the same value). Since they keys form a set, they must be distinct.

For example, if you want to store the id numbers and names of students in a course then you store the ids as keys and the names as values. It cannot be the other way around because two students can have the same name (whereas ids are unique by definition).

To create a map in which the key type is K and the value type is V, you would write:

```
Map<K,V> map = new TreeMap<K,V>();
```

The following table highlights the key methods in the Map API:

Methods (Map<K,V>)
`public boolean containsKey(K k)` Return true if the key k is present in the map and false otherwise.
`public V get(K k)` Return the value of the pair with key k if present else return null.
`public Set<K> keySet()` Return the keys of all pairs in the map as a set.
`public V put(K k, V v)` Add the (k,v) pair to the map. If k is already present then v replaces the old value (and in that case, the old value is returned else return is null).
`public boolean remove(K k)` Remove the pair with key k from the map if present and return its value else return null.
`public int size()` Return the number of elements (i.e. pairs) in the map.
`public String toString()` Return the elements of the map as comma-delimited key=value tokens surrounded by braces..

As an example of using maps, consider the fragment:

```
Map<String,String> airport = new TreeMap<String,String>();

airport.add("LHR", "London");
airport.add("YYZ", "Toronto");
airport.add("PEK", "Beijing");
airport.add("DXB", "Dubai");

System.out.println(airport.toString());

airport.remove("LHR");

System.out.println(airport.toString());
```

The fragment starts by creating a map that stores a mapping between an airport code and the city of that airport. It then adds four pairs to the map and outputs it.

Here is the first output

```
{DXB=Dubai, LHR=London, PEK=Beijing, YYZ=Toronto}
```

As in TreeMap, a by-product of using TreeMap is that it stores the keys of the pairs in a sorted manner (based on natural ordering). That is why the output came out in lexicographic order.

After wards, the fragment removes LHR from the map. Since this key is indeed present, its pair gets removed.

Here is the second output

```
{DXB=Dubai, PEK=Beijing, YYZ=Toronto}
```

We used toString in the above fragment as a quick and easy way to trace the logic. But for a formal way to traverse a map, we use the enhanced for loop on the set of keys, which is available to us trough the keySet method. We traverse this set, as we did in the previous section, and then lookup the value of every key as we visit it.

Using this formal map traversal, we can traverse the above airport map as follows:

```
for (String k : airport.keySet())
{
    String v = airport.get(k);
    System.out.println("pair (" + k + "," + v + ")");
}
```

L5.1.e – The Array Bridge

We mentioned earlier that arrays are low-level constructs for aggregation and that we prefer to work instead with the collection framework. There are situations, however, that force us to use arrays so we do need to be comfortable with their syntax and, in particular, to know how to convert an array to a collection and vice versa.

These situations often arise when you use an API and it returns an array (rather than a collection class). For example:

- The split method in the String class breaks a string into pieces based on a regex but it returns the pieces in an array.

- The accelerometer API sends a SensorEvent object when the device moves and it holds the components of the device acceleration in an array field named value.

- The list method in the File class returns the names of all the stored files in the current directory as an array of strings.

In these situations you can either work with the returned array, determining its size via the length field and traversing it via an indexed traversal, or convert it to a list. If you opt for the latter approach, use this method:

Methods (Arrays class)
`public static List<T> asList(T[] array)` Return a list that has the same elements as the given array.

For example, the following fragment creates a new array of strings and places three elements in it. Afterwards, it uses the above method to convert the created array to a list of strings and then outputs the list:

```
String[] names = new String[3];
names[0] = "Adam";
names[1] = "Maya";
names[2] = "Reem";
List<String> list = Arrays.asList(names);
System.out.println(list.toString());
```

Here is the generated output:

```
[Adam, Maya, Reem]
```

L5.2 – SELECTED ALGORITHMS

L5.2.a – Sorting a List

Unlike TreeSet, the ArrayList class does *not* store elements in natural order, as it shouldn't, because lists are supposed to preserve the entry order of their elements. In some applications however, we may need to sort the list elements for presentation purposes, so how can that be achieved? Copying the list elements into a set (implemented by TreeSet) will sort it but all duplicate information will be lost as all elements in a set must be distinct. Fortunately, there is a method in the Collections class that does exactly what we need:

Methods (Collections)
`public static void sort(List<E> list)` Sort the given list (in place) based on natural ordering.

Notice that the method is static so no instantiation is involved. Notice also that it is void so the passed list is itself mutated.

As an example, consider the fragment

```
List<LocalDate> list  = new ArrayList<LocalDate>();
list.add(LocalDate.of(2015, 3, 20));
list.add(LocalDate.of(2020, 10, 31));
list.add(LocalDate.of(2019, 9, 14));
list.add(LocalDate.of(2015, 2, 20));
System.out.println(list.toString());
Collections.sort(list);;
System.out.println(list.toString());
```

It creates a list of dates and then adds four date objects to it. Afterwards, we output the list to see this output:

    [2015-03-20, 2020-10-31, 2019-09-14, 2015-02-20]

As expected, the four objects appear in the order by which they were inserted. Afterwards, the fragment uses the sort method referenced above and then re-output the (now mutated) list. The generated output is:

    [2015-02-20, 2015-03-20, 2019-09-14, 2020-10-31]

As expected, the list is now ordered based on natural order (i.e. based on the compareTo method of the LocalDate class) which, in this case, is chronological.

L5.2.b – Stats with Maps

Maps find many application in statistics because they are well suited to capture the mapping between entities and their attributes. For example, consider the method:

```
public static Map<String,Integer> charStats(String s)
```

It receives a string and returns its letter frequencies in a map whose keys are the characters in s and whose values are the number times those characters appear in the string. For example, if s = "hello there" then the returned map should be (the first key is the space):

```
{ =1, e=3, h=2, l=2, o=1, r=1, t=1}
```

Here is the full implementation:

```
public static Map<String,Integer> charStats(String s)
{
    Map<String,Integer> result = new TreeMap<String,Integer>();
    for (int p = 0; p < s.length(); p++)
    {
        String c = s.substring(p, p+1);
        if (!result.containsKey(c))
        {
            result.put(c, 1);
        }
        else
        {
            int oldFreq = result.get(c);
            int newFreq = oldFreq + 1;
            result.put(c, newFreq);
        }
    }
    return result;
}
```

The method starts by creating an empty map of the desired generics. It then traverses the received string character by character. Whenever a character is visited, we check to see if it has been already encountered and stored in the map. If not, we store it in the map with value 1 to indicate we have encountered it once so far. Otherwise, we retrieve its value from the map to see the old frequency that has been counted so far. We increment the frequency to count the new encounter and store the pair back. Recall that if we store a pair whose key already exists, the new value overwrites the old. The returned map is sorted on its keys.

This solution logic can be tailored to solve several variants of this problem such as ignoring letter case, doing the stats at the word level, and finding the most frequent.

L5.2.c – Inverting a Map

In certain applications, we are required to invert the mapping of a given map; i.e. produce a map whose keys and values are the values and keys of the original maps. At first blush, such a requirement can be met with logic along the lines shown in this example:

```java
public static Map<Integer, String> invert(Map<String, Integer> map)
{
   Map<Integer, String> result = new TreeMap<Integer,String>();
   for (String k : map.keySet())
   {
       int v = map.get(k);
       result.put(v, k);
   }
   return result;
}
```

As a concrete test of this logic, suppose that the original map contains the names of various weather stations and the values hold the current temperatures measured in these stations. We therefore write the following client fragment to test the above method:

```java
Map<String, Integer> map = new TreeMap<String, Integer>();
map.put("BAR", 23);
map.put("YYZ", 23);
map.put("BRM", 20);
map.put("HAM", 24);
map.put("OSH", 23);
map.put("STC", 24);
System.out.println(map);
System.out.println(invert(map));}
```

This generates the following output:

```
{BAR=23, BRM=20, HAM=24, OSH=23, STC=24, YYZ=23}
{20=BRM, 23=YYZ, 24=STC}
```

The output quickly reveals the problem: if two or more values in the original map are equal, only one of their corresponding keys can appear in the inverted map. The problem is *not* in the code but in the question itself: *if a function is not one-to-one, it cannot be inverted.*

Hence, an application that involves reversing a map must indicate what should be done with the keys that have equal values. It could, for example, indicate that only one of them is to be kept (and specify which one) or stipulate that all keys are to be kept (and specify how).

We explore these possibilities below.

Keep the Smaller Key

In this scenario if two (or more) weather stations recorded the same temperature then the inverted map should keep the one whose name is smaller (lexicographically).

Here is the implementation:

```
public static Map<Integer, String> invert_smaller(Map<String, Integer> map)
{
    Map<Integer, String> result = new TreeMap<Integer,String>();
    for (String k : map.keySet())
    {
        int v = map.get(k);
        if (!result.containsKey(v))
        {
            result.put(v, k);
        }
        else
        {
            String existing = result.get(v);
            if (k.compareTo(existing) < 0)
            {
                result.put(v, k);
            }
        }
    }
    return result;
}
```

The logic starts by creating an empty result map and then traversing the given map. When a (k,v) pair in it is visited, there are two possibilities:

1. The temperature v was never encountered before, and hence is not present in result. In that case, simply insert the inverted (v,k) pair in result.

2. The temperature v was encountered before, and hence is present in result. In that case, retrieve the name of the weather station existing in result and compare it with k.

    a. If the name of the station we are currently visiting (i.e. k) is smaller than the name of the existing station in result then insert (v,k) pair in result.

    b. Otherwise, do nothing because the name of the station in result is the smaller.

Based on this code, the resulting map would be this:

```
{20=BRM, 23=BAR, 24=HAM}
```

Keep All Keys

In this scenario if two (or more) weather stations recorded the same temperature then the inverted map should keep all the station names in a collection. Let us keep them in a list.

```
public static Map<Integer, List<String>> invert_all(Map<String, Integer> map)
{
    Map<Integer, List<String>> result = new TreeMap<Integer,List<String>>();
    for (String k : map.keySet())
    {
        int v = map.get(k);
        if (!result.containsKey(v))
        {
            List<String> list = new ArrayList<String>();
            list.add(k);
            result.put(v, list);
        }
        else
        {
            List<String> existing = result.get(v);
            existing.add(k);
        }
    }
    return result;
}
```

The logic starts by creating an empty `result` map and then traversing the given `map`. Note that there is nothing special about having a list inside a map. All collections aggregate objects of any type, so if the type happened to be a collection, we end up with nested collections. In fact, this nesting can extend to an arbitrary number of levels.

When a (k,v) pair in it is visited, there are two possibilities:

1. The temperature v was never encountered before, and hence is not present in `result`. In that case, insert (v,list) in `result` where list is a newly created list that contains k.

2. The temperature v was encountered before, and hence is present in `result`. In that case, retrieve its `list` from `result` and append k to it[1].

Based on this code, the resulting map would be this:

```
{20=[BRM], 23=[BAR, OSH, YYZ], 24=[HAM, STC]}
```

---

[1] There is no need to put (v, list) back in result because it is already there and it points at list in memory, so once we modified the list object in memory, the stored reference would be pointing at the updated object.

L5.3 – EXERCISES

Note that all these exercises involve methods that take references to collections. To minimize logic distraction, assume *as a precondition* that these parameters are not null. This means the passed collection objects do exist. These collections, however, could be empty.

1. Implement the method below which deletes all but the last element from a given list:

    ```
    public static void allButLast(List<String> list)
    ```

    Hint: Be careful when you use remove *in an index-based loop because the removal of an element changes the indices of all its following elements, and changes also the list size.*

2. Implement the method below which returns the largest integer in a given set:

    ```
    public static int largest(Set<Integer> set)
    ```

    To find the largest, you would need to compare every element to some candidate maximum value and update the candidate based on the result of each comparison. When all elements are compared, the final candidate value would be the confirmed maximum.

    Hint:. Do not assume that all elements are positive! For the initial value of the candidate, you can use the first element in the list or the smallest integer field of the Integer class.

3. Implement the method below which returns the largest value in a given map:

    ```
    public static void largestValue(Map<String, Double> map)
    ```

4. Implement the method below which returns true if all the *values* of the given map are distinct, and return false otherwise.

    ```
    public static boolean areDistinct(Map<String,Integer> map)
    ```

    Hint:. The keys of a map are always distinct but the values don't need to be. Traverse the map and store its values in a suitable collection to detect duplication.

5. Implement the method below which takes two sets of integers and returns a set of their common elements (i.e. integers that exist in both):

    ```
    public static Set<String> intersect(Set<String> set1, Set<String> set2)
    ```

    Hint:. Traverse one of the sets. Whenever you visit an element, search for it in the other set to see if it is present, and if so, add it to the result set.

6. **Implement the method below which returns the *median* of the integers in a given set:**

    ```
    public static int median(Set<Integer> set)
    ```

    The median is one of the elements in the set such that the number of elements greater than it, and the number of ones less than it, are equal. You can assume, *as a precondition*, that the set size is odd.

    Hint: If the elements were in a sorted list then the median would be the one in the middle. You can solve the problem using this observation but you should also be able to solve it without any sorting.

7. Implement the method below which returns a *sorted* list of the most occurring integers in a given, *non-empty* list of integers:

    ```
    public static List<Integer> mostOccurring(List<Integer> bag)
    ```

    Example, if bag = [6,12,-5,7,6,2,-12,-5,6,8,-5] then the return should be [-5,6].

8. Given a non-empty list of dates, this method groups them based on the day of the week on which they occurred; selects the earliest one in each group; and return the selected ones. The return is a map whose keys are the short day-of-the-week names and whose values are the selected dates. The map is sorted on its keys:

    ```
    public static Map<String, Date> latestByWeekday(List<Date> list)
    ```

    Example, if list is:

    ```
    [Thu Mar 30 23:30:00 EDT 2017, Sat Dec 31 23:10:00 EST 2016,
    Sat Apr 01 06:00:00 EDT 2017, Thu Aug 11 00:00:00 EDT 2016,
    Sat Dec 31 00:15:00 EST 2016]
    ```

    then the return should be:

    ```
    {Sat=Sat Dec 31 00:15:00 EST 2016, Thu=Thu Aug 11 00:00:00 EDT 2016}
    ```

9. Given a list containing *two or more* integers, this method returns a set containing the two integers in the list that are closest to each other; i.e. the absolute value of the difference between them is minimal. The returned set must be sorted.

    ```
    public static Set<Integer> closest(List<Integer> list)
    ```

    Example, if list = [21, 4, 2, 12, 18, 24, 16, 7, 20, 39, -3, 26] then the return should be [20, 21].

10. Given two maps, this method returns a map whose keys are the common keys between them and whose values are the larger of the two values of the common keys. Note that the returned map must be sorted on its keys:

```
public static Map<String, Integer>
        fuse(Map<String,Integer> map1, Map<String,Integer> map2)
```

For example:

map1 = {May=2, Screen=3, Paper=12, Key=23}

map2 = {May=7, Screen=2, Book=12, File=11}

In this case the return should be

{May=7, Screen=3}

This is because May and Screen are the common keys in the two given maps. The value for key May is 2 in one map and 7 in the other so we pick the larger 7. Similarly, we pick 3 for key Screen.

APPENDIX A

Operators

The table on the next page lists all operators referenced in this book.

When more than one operator appear in an expression, and in the absence of parentheses, the operator with the highest precedence is evaluated first.

The rows of the table are sorted in *descending precedence* order (i.e. the top row has the highest). Operators in the same row have equal precedence.

Two operators of equal precedence are evaluated *left-to-right* or *right-to-left* depending on their associativity.

APPENDIX-A: OPERATORS

CATEGORY	OPERATOR	PRECEDENCE[1]
postfix	. ++ --	(-1) →
prefix	++ -- + - !	(-2) →
creation, cast	new (type)	← (-3)
arithmetic	* / %	(-4) →
arithmetic	+ -	(-5) →
relational	> >= < <= instanceof	(-7) →
relational	== !=	(-8) →
boolean	&&	(-12) →
boolean	||	(-13) →
ternary	? :	← (-14)
assignment	= += -= *= /= %=	← (-15)

[1] **Precedence** is indicated by a parenthesized negative number and an arrow. Operators in the top row have the highest (least negative) precedence. The associativity is indicated by an arrow (left-to-right or right-to-left).

Regular Expressions

These expressions (aka regex) form the language of character patterns. They allow us to describe patterns in a formal, unambiguous fashion.

We use regular expressions to validate user inputs (to determine if they have the format set in the requirement). We also use them to mine strings (to see if a certain pattern occurs in them). In addition, we can transform strings (by splitting them into tokens or by replacing characters in them with others) via a rule driven by a regular expressions.

APPENDIX-B: REGULAR EXPRESSIONS

CHARACTER CLASSES	
[a-m]	One character between a and m, inclusive
[abc]	One character that is a, b, or c
[^abc]	Any one character but not a, b, or c
[a-m[A-M]]	One character between a and m or between A and M
[a-m&&[^ck]]	One character between a and m and not c nor k

SPECIAL SYMBOLS	
^ and $	Designate the beginning and ending positions in the string
X | Y	Either X or Y
(X)	Treat X as a capturing group
(?:X)	Treat X as a non- capturing group
\	Escape the next character
.	Any character
\d	A digit, [0-9]
\s	A whitespace character: [\t\n\x0B\f\r]
\w	A word character: [a-zA-Z_0-9]
\p{Punct}	A punctuation: [!"#$%&'()*+,-./:;<=>?@[\]^_`{|}~]

QUANTIFIERS	
x?	x, once or not at all
x*	x, zero or more times (append ? to make it lazy else greedy)
x+	x, one or more times (append ? to make it lazy else greedy)
x{n}	x, exactly n times
x{n,}	x, n or more times
x{n,m}	x, at least n but no more than m times

APPENDIX C

Character Codes

The simplest way to represent characters is to assign an integer code to each starting from zero. To determine the range of these unsigned integers, one needs to know how many characters there are.

The English-speaking world uses **128** characters (code 0 to 127) in everyday life. This makes up the *Basic Latin Set*. Add other languages and commonly-used symbols and the count quickly reaches **64,000** characters. Add historic languages, scripts, and symbols used in fields like math, science, publishing, and character recognition, and the count exceeds **one million**.

To accommodate all these characters plus any others that will be needed in the future, the International Organization for Standardization (ISO) together with a consortium of industry and research organizations defined a *Universal Character Set* (**UCS**) with room for over **one billion** character. The code table for these characters is known as *ISO-10646* or *Unicode*.

Appendix-C: Character Codes

Even though ISO-10646 assigns a code for every character in UCS, it does *not* define a corresponding encoding. To that end, Unicode defines three different encodings: UTF-8 (which uses a *variable-length* sequence of 1, 2, or 4 bytes), UTF-16 (uses a *variable-length* sequence of 2 or 4 bytes), and UTF-32 (which uses a *fixed-length* sequence of 4 bytes).

The char data type in Java uses two bytes, and hence, can only accommodate 64K characters (the 2 byte sequence of UTF-16). This is adequate for most use cases. For higher code points use the API in the Character and CharSequence classes.

Focusing only on the Basic Latin Set, we find:

- The first 32 (codes 0 to 31) are *control characters*—they are not visible when printable but they actuate an action (such as a carriage return) when printed.

- Five are known as *whitespace characters* and they play an important role in parsing strings. The table below shows their codes in decimal and in hex:

Decimal	Hex	Escape	Character
9	0x0009	\t	HT: horizontal tab
10	0x000a	\n	LF: line feed
12	0x000c	\f	FF: form feed
13	0x000d	\r	CR: carriage return
32	0x0020		SP: space

- While there is no need to memorize any of the codes, it is helpful to keep the following patterns in mind:
  - The code for space is 32
  - Digits start at 48.
  - Uppercase letters start at 65.
  - Lowercase letters start at 97 (i.e. 32 above the uppercase).

- The table below shows the decimal and hex codes for the Basic Latin Set.

Dec	Hex	Char	Dec	Hex	Char	Dec	Hex	Char	Dec	Hex	Char
32	0x0020	SP	56	0x0038	8	80	0x0050	P	104	0x0068	h
33	0x0021	!	57	0x0039	9	81	0x0051	Q	105	0x0069	i
34	0x0022	"	58	0x003a	:	82	0x0052	R	106	0x006a	j
35	0x0023	#	59	0x003b	;	83	0x0053	S	107	0x006b	k
36	0x0024	$	60	0x003c	<	84	0x0054	T	108	0x006c	l
37	0x0025	%	61	0x003d	=	85	0x0055	U	109	0x006d	m
38	0x0026	&	62	0x003e	>	86	0x0056	V	110	0x006e	n
39	0x0027	'	63	0x003f	?	87	0x0057	W	111	0x006f	o
40	0x0028	(	64	0x0040	@	88	0x0058	X	112	0x0070	p
41	0x0029	)	65	0x0041	A	89	0x0059	Y	113	0x0071	q
42	0x002a	*	66	0x0042	B	90	0x005a	Z	114	0x0072	r
43	0x002b	+	67	0x0043	C	91	0x005b	[	115	0x0073	s
44	0x002c	,	68	0x0044	D	92	0x005c	\	116	0x0074	t
45	0x002d	-	69	0x0045	E	93	0x005d	]	117	0x0075	u
46	0x002e	.	70	0x0046	F	94	0x005e	^	118	0x0076	v
47	0x002f	/	71	0x0047	G	95	0x005f	_	119	0x0077	w
48	0x0030	0	72	0x0048	H	96	0x0060	`	120	0x0078	x
49	0x0031	1	73	0x0049	I	97	0x0061	a	121	0x0079	y
50	0x0032	2	74	0x004a	J	98	0x0062	b	122	0x007a	z
51	0x0033	3	75	0x004b	K	99	0x0063	c	123	0x007b	{
52	0x0034	4	76	0x004c	L	100	0x0064	d	124	0x007c	|
53	0x0035	5	77	0x004d	M	101	0x0065	e	125	0x007d	}
54	0x0036	6	78	0x004e	N	102	0x0066	f	126	0x007e	~
55	0x0037	7	79	0x004f	O	103	0x0067	g	127	0x007f	

Given the hex code of any character in the first 64K, you can incorporate it into your strings or outputs by using code as in the following fragment:

```
char arrow = 0x21e8;
System.out.println(arrow + " Toronto");  // output is: ⇨ Toronto
```

For code points above 64K, the char type cannot be used so we go from an int array directly to String as in the following fragment:

```
int[] n = new int[]{0x1f600};
String smiley = new String(n,0,1);
System.out.println(smiley); // output is: 😀
```

APPENDIX D

The

i2c

API

This textbook comes with an *Introduction to Computing* (i2c) library. Section L0.2.c shows you how to fetch its jar file and incorporate it into your apps.

The i2c library was designed as a pedagogic scaffolding tool that sheds light on the more intricate aspects of object oriented programming. It is therefore strongly recommended that you add this library, as a dependency, to all the projects that you build in the Doing parts and in the exercises.

This appendix highlights the library's features and lists its API.

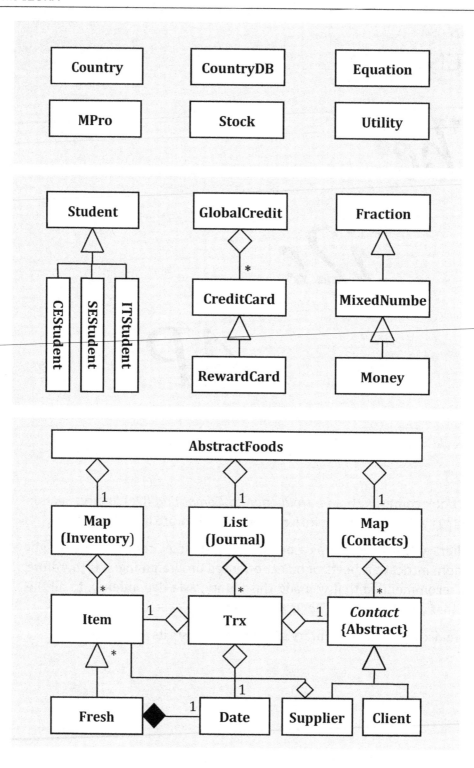

APPENDIX-D: THE I2C API

The diagrams on the opposite page are known as UML (Unified Modelling Language) class diagrams and they show the classes of the i2c library and the relationships amongst them. An arrow from class A to class B implies that A extends (inherits from) B, whereas a line from class A ending with a diamond at class B implies that A is owned by B; i.e. A is a component of B (implying that B aggregates A).

The six classes at the top have no relationships amongst them and are the easiest to use. One of them, Utility, has no public constructor and all its methods are static. Hence, you can invoke its methods simply *on the class*; i.e. you write Utility followed by a dot followed by the method name. The remaining five classes do have public constructors, and hence, you would first need to create an instance of the class and then invoke methods *on the instance*.

The classes in the middle expose inter-class relationships and they come in three families (or hierarchies). The Student class represents a student in the EECS department and keeps track of the student's name, ID number, and transcript (completed courses and grades). Certain students, such as Computer Engineering—CE, Information Technology—IT, and Software Engineering—SE students, are also in EECS, and they require the same services as the rest, except for a few variations, e.g. the ID number must belong to a certain range. Rather than create a self-contained class for each subset (and thus end up with duplicate code), we keep the common services in the Student class and simply extend it. The three "children" of Student contain only the variations that need to be overridden—a case-in-point that exposes the power of inheritance. The Fraction-MixedNumber, Money hierarchy is a second example of inheritance and you are invited to explore it. The third hierarchy in the middle diagram involves inheritance (RewardCard extends CareditCard) as well as aggregation (GlobalCredit aggregates CareditCard).

The classes in the bottom expose a complex, real life hierarchy whose classes are related by inheritance as well as aggregation. This family models a company that sells food items and needs to keep track of its contacts, its inventory, and its accounting. Note that a contact can be a client or a supplier, an example of inheritance. Similarly, an inventory item can be fresh (i.e. it expires) or not, which is another inheritance example. The inventory of the company is represented by an aggregation (a map in this case) of items and similarly for the contacts. The accounting journal is an aggregation of transactions each of which captures a date, a contact, an item, a quantity and an amount, plus a reference number.

Think of i2c as a playground of learning opportunities.

ABSTRACTFOODS

> **Class AbstractFoods**
> **extends Object implements Serializable**

This class encapsulates the inventory and sales business of the Abstract Foods Company. It maintains three collections:

- Inventory: A Map with the item number as key (a String) and the Item object as value.
- Contacts: A Map with the contact number as key (a String) and the Contact object as value.
- Journal: A List of Trx instances each representing a posted sales transaction.

All three collections do not use generics, i.e. their elements are of type Object.

− Constructors:

AbstractFoods

```
public AbstractFoods()
```

Construct a company having empty collections.

AbstractFoods

```
public AbstractFoods(Map<String, Item> inventory,
            Map<String, Contact> contacts,
            List<Trx> journal)
```

Construct a company having the passed collections.

Parameters:

inventory - the inventory map

contacts - the contacts map

journal - the transaction list

− Methods:

getInventory

```
public Map<String,Item> getInventory()
```

Determine the inventory map of this company

Returns:

the inventory map

getContacts

```
public Map<String, Contact> getContacts()
```

Determine the contacts map of this company

Returns:

the contacts map

getJournal

```
public List<Trx> getJournal()
```

Determine the transaction list of this company

Returns:

the transaction list

toString

```
public String toString()
```

Construct a string representation of this company.

Overrides:

toString in class Object

Returns:

the string: "Abstract Foods Company".

getRandom

```
public static AbstractFoods getRandom()
```

Create a randomly chosen Abstract Foods Company. The inventory map consists of about 100 (item number, Item) mappings of which about 25% are for Fresh items. The numbers, names, and prices are randomly chosen but the numbers are 8-character each. The contacts map consists of about 100 (contact number, Contact) mappings of which 50% are Client and 50% are Supplier instances. The numbers, names, ratings (for clients), and catalogues (for suppliers) are randomly chosen but the numbers are formatted as 5-digit each. The journal list consists of about 750 posted Trx transactions spanning approximately 4 months (with the latest occurring in the past 48 hours).

In order to facilitate the testing of front-ends and reports that are based on this randomly-chosen company, it is persisted (serialized) by storing the returned instance on disk in the file data.af.
This method was added for pedagogical reasons.

Returns:

a company with randomly chosen collections.

CESTUDENT

```
                    Class CEstudent
    extends Student implements Serializable, Iterable<String>
```

Provide services to maintain information about a CE (computer engineering) student. The class encapsulates the same information and functionality as Student except for two differences: the ID is auto-assigned serially (starting from 200102001 and ending at 200102999), and there is no 'E' grade. In addition, the return of the toString method is prefixed by "CE".

— Constructors:

CEstudent

```
public CEstudent(String name)
```

Create a CE student having the given name and assigns it a serial 3-digit ID prefixed by "200102" and an empty (fresh) record.
Parameters:

name - the name of the CE student.

— Methods:

setCourseGrade

```
public boolean setCourseGrade(String course,
```

                                String grade)

Update the student's record in exactly the same manner as in the **Student** class except that no 'E' grade is allowed.

Overrides:

setCourseGrade in class Student

Parameters:

course - the course the student took

grade - the achieved grade in that course

Returns:

true if the record was updated as requested and return false otherwise. The record will not be updated if the given course number is not made up of exactly 4 digits or if the given letter grade is not one of the letters (A,B,C,D,E,F) in capital or small-case.

toString

```
public String toString()
```

Return a string representation of this student.

Overrides:

toString in class Student

Returns:

the string "CE student: " followed by the student's name.

CLIENT

```
                        Class Client
  extends Contact implements Serializable, Comparable<Contact>
```

This class encapsulates a client. A client is a contact, but it has a credit rating.

– Constructors:

Client

```
public Client(String name,
              String address,
```

```
            String rating)
```

Construct a client having the given name, address, and credit rating; and assign a unique number to it. Number assignment is handled by the superclass Contact.

Parameters:

name - the name of the contact.

address - the address of the client.

rating - the credit rating of the client.

Throws:

RuntimeException - if any of the parameters is null.

─ Methods:

getRating

```
public String getRating()
```

Determine the credit rating of this client.

Returns:

the credit rating of this client.

setRating

```
public void setRating(String rating)
```

Change the rating of this client.

Parameters:

rating - the new credit rating.

Throws:

RuntimeException - if the parameters is null.

CONTACT

```
            (abstract) Class Contact
extends Object implements Serializable, Comparable<Contact>
```

This class encapsulates a contact. A contact has a name, address, and an auto-generated number.

— Fields

FIRST_NUMBER

```
public static final int FIRST_NUMBER
```

The class generates contact numbers serially starting from this value.

See Also:

Constant Field Values

— Constructors:

Contact

```
public Contact(String name,
               String address)
```

Construct a contact having the given name and address and assign a unique number to it.

The numbers are assigned serially starting from FIRST_NUMBER.

Parameters:

name - the name of the contact.

address - the address of the contact.

Throws:

RuntimeException - if the name or the address is null.

— Methods:

getName

```
public String getName()
```

Determine the name of this contact.

Returns:

the name of this contact.

getAddress

```
public String getAddress()
```

Determine the address of this contact.

Returns:

the address of this contact.

getNumber

```
public int getNumber()
```

Determine the number of this contact.

Returns:

the name of this contact.

setName

```
public void setName(String name)
```

Change the name of this contact.

Parameters:

name - the new name.

Throws:

RuntimeException - if the parameters is null.

setAddress

```
public void setAddress(String address)
```

Change the address of this contact.

Parameters:

address - the new address

Throws:

RuntimeException - if the parameters is null.

getLastContactNumber

```
public static int getLastContactNumber()
```

Determine the number of the last-constructed contact.

Returns:

the the last contact number.

toString

```
public String toString()
```

Construct a string representation of this contact.

Overrides:

toString in class Object

Returns:

the string: "xxx name", where xxx is the contact number and name is its name.

equals

```
public boolean equals(Object other)
```

Test the equality of contacts. An object is considered equal to this contact if it is instantiated from the same class as this one and has the same number.

Overrides:

equals in class Object

Parameters:

other - a reference to the object to test equality with.

Returns:

true if other is not null and it points to an object that is equal (as defined above) to this object. The return is false otherwise.

hashCode

```
public int hashCode()
```

Compute a hash code for this Contact.

Overrides:

hashCode in class Object

Returns:

a hash code value for this object.

compareTo

```
public int compareTo(Contact other)
```

Compares this object with the specified object for order. Returns a negative integer, zero, or a positive integer as this object is less than, equal to, or greater than the specified object.
Specified by:
compareTo in interface Comparable<Contact>
Parameters:
other - the Object to compare to.
Returns:
the same return as that of compareTo(String) in String when invoked on the toString of this item.

COUNTRY

> **Class Country**
> **extends Object**

This class encapsulates a country. Each instance has a name for its country, the name of the country's capital, and the capital's population (an integer).

— Constructors:

Country

```
public Country(String name,
               String capital,
               int pop)
```

Construct an instance having the given parameters.
Parameters:
name - the country name
capital - the capital city name
pop - the population of the capital

− Methods:

getName

```
public String getName()
```

The country name accessor.

Returns:

the country name.

getCapital

```
public String getCapital()
```

The capital name accessor.

Returns:

the capital name.

getPop

```
public int getPop()
```

The population accessor.

Returns:

the capital's population.

toString

```
public String toString()
```

Construct a textual representation of the instance.

Overrides:

toString in class Object

Returns:

"Country {name='name', capital='capital', pop='pop'}"

COUNTRYDB

Class CountryDB
extends Object

This class encapsulates a collection of country data (as of 2015) and provides methods to access it in various forms.

– Constructors:

CountryDB

    public CountryDB()

Construct an instance of the country data collection.

– Methods:

getCapitals

    public List<String> getCapitals()

The capitals accessor.
Returns:
a list of all capitals.

getData

    public Map<String,Country> getData()

The country data accessor.
Returns:
a map whose keys are capitals and whose values are Country instance.

CreditCard

> ## Class CreditCard
> ## extends Object implements Serializable

This class encapsulates a credit card and maintains information about it. Each card is identified by the attributes: card number, holder's name, issue and expiry dates, credit limit, and balance owing. The key methods in the class are charge (used when the holder makes a purchase), pay (used when the holder makes a payment), and credit (when the holder returns a purchase for refund). It also supports standard methods (equals and toString) and a few accessors and mutators.

Note that this class aggregates the issue and expiry dates via a composition.
The card number is 8-character in length and consists of a 6-digit string (set by the user upon construction), a dash, and a MOD-9 check digit. The check digit ensures that the sum of all digits, including it, is a multiple of 9; it is added to detect possible transmission errors. The dash and the check digit are added by the class.

– Fields:

DEFAULT_LIMIT

```
public static final double DEFAULT_LIMIT
```

The default credit limit used by the two-argument constructor.
See Also:
Constant Field Values

MIN_NAME_LENGTH

```
public static final int MIN_NAME_LENGTH
```

The minimum allowed length for the name of the cardholder.
See Also:
Constant Field Values

SEQUENCE_NUMBER_LENGTH

```
public static final int SEQUENCE_NUMBER_LENGTH
```

The number of digits in the serial part of the card number.
See Also:
Constant Field Values

MOD

```
public static final int MOD
```

The sum of the digits in the credit card number must be divisible by this constant. A check digit (possibly zero) is added to the serial card number to meet this requirement.
See Also:
Constant Field Values

– Constructors:

CreditCard

```
public CreditCard(int no,
                  String aName,
                  double aLimit,
                  Date issue)
```

Construct a credit card having the passed number, name, and credit limit; and set its initial balance to zero. The expiry date of the card is set to two years from the given issue date.
Parameters:
no - the credit card number, must be > 0 and ≤ 999999
aName - the name of the holder of this card, must have at
least MIN_NAME_LENGTH characters
aLimit - the credit limit, must be positive
issue - the issue date after which the card becomes valid
Throws:
RuntimeException - if the number is not in the above range, the name has fewer characters than indicated, or credit limit is not positive.

CreditCard

```
public CreditCard(int no,
                  String aName,
                  double aLimit)
```

Construct a credit card having the passed number, holder name, and limit. Invoking this constructor has the same effect as invoking the four-parameter constructor and using today's date for the issue date.

Parameters:

no - the credit card number, must be > 0 and ≤ 999999

aName - the name of the holder of this card, must have at

least MIN_NAME_LENGTH characters

aLimit - the credit limit, must be positive

CreditCard

```
public CreditCard(int no,
                  String aName)
```

Construct a credit card having the passed number and holder name. Invoking this constructor has the same effect as invoking the three-parameter constructor and using DEFAULT_LIMIT for the credit limit.

Parameters:

no - the credit card number, must be > 0 and ≤ 999999

aName - the name of the holder of this card, must have at

least MIN_NAME_LENGTH characters

— Methods:

getBalance

```
public double getBalance()
```

Credit card balance accessor.

Returns:

the balance owing on this credit card.

getNumber

```
public String getNumber()
```

Credit card number accessor.

Returns:

the number of this credit card, a string of 8 characters (see the class description for details).

getName

```
public String getName()
```

Credit card holder accessor.

Returns:

the name of the holder of this credit card.

getLimit

```
public double getLimit()
```

Credit card limit accessor.

Returns:

the credit limit of this credit card.

getIssueDate

```
public Date getIssueDate()
```

Credit card issue date accessor.

Returns:

a copy of the issue date of this credit card.

getExpiryDate

```
public Date getExpiryDate()
```

Credit card expiry date accessor.

Returns:

a copy of the expiry date of this credit card.

setLimit

```
public boolean setLimit(double newLimit)
```

Credit card limit mutator. Attempt to change the credit limit to the passed value. The change is successful only if the passed value is non-negative and not less than the current balance.

Parameters:

newLimit - the new credit limit.

Returns: true if the limit was successfully changed and return false otherwise.

setExpiryDate

```
public boolean setExpiryDate(Date expiry)
```

Credit card expiry date mutator. Attempt to change the expiry date to the passed value. The change is successful only if the passed reference is not null and it occurs at any point of time after the issue date.

Parameters:

expiry - the new expiry date of the card.

Returns:

true if the expiry date was successfully changed and return false otherwise.

credit

```
public void credit(double amount)
```

Credit the credit card (decrease its balance) by the passed amount. This method is used when goods purchased using this card are subsequently returned for refund. An assertion failure occurs if the passed amount is less than 0.

Parameters:

amount - the amount to be credited.

charge

```
public boolean charge(double amount)
```

Attempt to charge the passed amount on the credit card (increase its balance by that amount). If this will lead to a balance greater than the credit limit, the request is denied and false is returned. The request is also denied if the card has expired. Otherwise the balance is increased and true is returned. An assertion failure occurs if the passed amount is less than 0.

Parameters:

amount - the amount (of the purchase) to be charged.

Returns:

true if successful and false if such a charge exceeds the available credit.

pay

```
public void pay(double amount)
```

Make a payment to reduce the balance of this card. If the passed amount is negative, an assertion failure occurs. Otherwise, the balance is reduced by the passed amount (even if it becomes negative). Over-paying (making the balance negative) is a legitimate transaction used in certain circumstances to effectively increase the credit limit

Parameters:

amount - the amount (of payment).

equals

```
public boolean equals(Object other)
```

Test the equality of credit cards. An object is considered equal to this one if it is indeed a credit card object with the same card number as this one.

Overrides:

equals in class Object

Parameters:

other - a reference to the object to test equality with.

Returns:

true if other is not null and it points to an object that is equal (as defined above) to this object, and false otherwise.

hashCode

```
public int hashCode()
```

Compute a hash code for this credit card.

Overrides:

hashCode in class Object

Returns:

a hash code value for this object.

isSimilar

```
public boolean isSimilar(CreditCard other)
```

Test the similarity of two credit cards. A credit card object is considered similar to this one if it has the same balance, to the nearest cent, as this one, regardless of card number. Even if the two cards have different numbers, this method considers them similar as long as the difference between their balances is less than 0.01.

Parameters:

other - a reference to the credit card object to test equality with.

Returns:

true if other is not null and it points to an object that is similar (as defined above) to this object, and false otherwise.

toString

```
public String toString()
```

Return a string representation of this card.

Overrides:

toString in class Object

Returns:

a string like this:

CARD [NO=001005-3, BALANCE=7634.12]

The string starts with CARD and between two brackets, it contains the credit card number (001005-3 in the above example), and balance (rounded to two decimals), formatted as shown.

EQUATION

> ### Class Equation
> ### extends Object implements Serializable

Encapsulates an algebraic equation of the second degree. Each such equation is identified by its three attributes being the coefficients a,b,c in $ax^2 + bx + c = 0$.

The class provides standard methods; accessors and mutators for the coefficients; and accessors for the roots. Root computation takes into account the possibilities of a=0, b=0, and c=0, which lead to several cases and give rise to either two real roots, one real root, no roots, or infinitely many roots.

− **Fields:**

EPSILON

```
public static final double EPSILON
```

This constant is set to a small tolerance value to test equality of real numbers. Two real double's are considered equal if abs(x-y) is less than this constant.

See Also:

Constant Field Values

— Constructors:

Equation

```
public Equation()
```

Construct an equation having all coefficients set to zero.

Equation

```
public Equation(Equation equation)
```

Construct a copy of the passed Equation

Parameters:

equation - the Equation to copy

Equation

```
public Equation(double a,
                double b,
                double c)
```

Construct an equation having the passed coefficients

Parameters:

a - coefficient of x^2

b - coefficient of x

c - the constant term

— Methods:

setCoefficient

```
public void setCoefficient(double a,
                           double b,
```

`double c)`

Set the coefficients of this equation to the passed parameters and re-solve it.

Parameters:

a - coefficient of x^2

b - coefficient of x

c - the constant term

getCoefficient

```
public double getCoefficient(int coefNum)
```

Return the coefficient whose number (0,1,2) is passed.

Parameters:

coefNum - the coefficient number to retrieve. 2 means the coefficient of x^2, 1 is the coefficient of x, and 0 means the constant term.

Returns:

the requested coefficient.

Throws:

RuntimeException - if the passed number is not in the above range.

getRoot

```
public double getRoot(int rootNum)
```

Return the root whose number is passed. The passed root number must be valid in light of the number of roots this equation has (as returned getRootCount())

Parameters:

rootNum - the root number to retrieve. If the equation has one root, rootNum must be set to 1. If the equation has two roots, rootNum can be either 1 or 2, with 1 indicating the smaller of the two roots and 2 the larger.

Returns:

the requested root.

Throws:

RuntimeException - if the passed parameter is not valid.

getRootCount

```
public int getRootCount()
```

Return the number of roots that this equation has.

Returns:

the number of roots, or 0 if there are none, or -1 if there are infinitly many (the equation is an identity).

toString

```
public String toString()
```

Return a string representation of this equation.

Overrides:

toString in class Object

Returns:

the string ax^2 + bx + c = 0", with a,b,c replaced by the actual coefficients and their signs. Note that the equal sign is surrounded by two spaces, and that a blank is inserted between terms.

equals

```
public boolean equals(Object other)
```

Determine if this equation is the same as the passed one. An object is considered equal to this one if it is indeed an Equation object and if the two equations have the same root count (as returned by getRootCount()) and if any present roots are correspondingly equal (within EPSILON).

Overrides:

equals in class Object

Parameters:

other - the equation to compare with this equation.

Returns:

true or false as defined above. The return is false if the passed instance is not an Equation or if the two equations do not share the root count, or if the they both have one root but that root is not the same (within EPSILON), or if they both have two roots but the smaller (larger) root of the first is not equal (within EPSILON) to the smaller (larger) root of the second. The return is true in all other cases.

hashCode

```
public int hashCode()
```

Compute a hash code for this Equation.

Overrides:

hashCode in class Object

Returns:

a hash code value for this object.

FRACTION

```
Class Fraction
extends Object implements Serializable, Comparable<Fraction>
```

This class encapsulates a fraction. It maintains the fraction's state (numerator and denominator) and provides functionality for manipulating fractions. The class ensures that the denominators of all its instances are non-negative at all times by transferring any negative denominator sign to the numerator. Furthermore, the fraction is kept in reduced form at all times, i.e. with no common divisor greater than 1. Note that the numerator and denominator are of the int type, and hence, they maintain closure by wrapping the int range. Note also that a Fraction instance can have a zero denominator either upon creation or after an operation. Such an instance is treated like any other (it can, for example, participate in the operations supported by the class without leading to exceptions) except for two differences: When invoked on such an instance, the toString method returns the literal NaF, which stands for "Not a Fraction". All such instances are considered equal (regardless of their numerator values) and greater than any non-zero denominator fraction. This affects the contracts of compareTo and equals.

− Fields:

separator

```
public char separator
```

A character that separates the numerator denominator pair in the return of the toString() method. The default value is '/'.

(Bad design--should have been kept private. Access would have still been possible via the existing public accessor and mutator.)

isQuoted

```
public static boolean isQuoted
```

A flag that determines if the return of the toProperString() method is surrounded by quotes or not. The default value is true.

(Bad design--should have been kept private. Access would have still been possible via a public static accessor, e.g. isQuoted() and a public static mutator, e.g. setIsQuoted(boolean).)

— Constructors:

Fraction

```
public Fraction()
```

Construct a default fraction with numerator equal to 0, denominator equal to 1, and separator equal to '/'. The rational value of the constructed fraction is, thus, zero.

Fraction

```
public Fraction(int numerator,
                int denominator)
```

Construct a fraction with the passed numerator and denominator and a '/' separator. If the passed denominator is negative, the sign of the numerator is reversed in order to keep the denominator positive.

Parameters:

numerator - the numerator of the fraction to construct.

denominator - the denominator of the fraction to construct.

Fraction

```
public Fraction(Fraction fraction)
```

Construct a copy of the passed Fraction.

Parameters:

fraction - the Fraction to copy.

Throws:

RuntimeException - if fraction = null

Fraction

```
public Fraction(int numerator,
                int denominator,
                char separator)
```

Construct a fraction with the passed numerator, denominator, and separator. If the passed denominator is negative, the sign of the numerator is reversed in order to keep the denominator positive, and if the passed separator is a letter or a digit, it is replaced with '/'.

Parameters:

numerator - the numerator of the fraction to construct.

denominator - the denominator of the fraction to construct.

separator - the separator of the fraction to construct.

– **Methods:**

add

```
public void add(Fraction other)
```

Add the passed fraction to the fraction on which it was called. This method is, in effect, a mutator because it changes the state of the encapsulated object.

Parameters:

other - the fraction to add to this fraction.

subtract

```
public void subtract(Fraction other)
```

Subtract the passed fraction from the fraction on which it was called. This method is, in effect, a mutator because it changes the state of the encapsulated object.

Parameters:

other - the fraction to subtract from this fraction.

multiply

```
public void multiply(Fraction other)
```

Multiply the fraction on which the method was called by the passed fraction. This method is, in effect, a mutator because it changes the state of the encapsulated object.

Parameters:

other - the fraction to multiply this fraction by

divide

```
public void divide(Fraction other)
```

Divide the fraction on which the method was called by the passed fraction. This method is, in effect, a mutator because it changes the state of the encapsulated object.

Parameters:

other - the fraction to divide this fraction by

pow

```
public void pow(int exponent)
```

Raise the fraction on which the method was called to the passed exponent. This method is, in effect, a mutator because it changes the state of the encapsulated object.

Parameters:

exponent - the exponent to raise this fraction to (must be non-negative).

Throws:

RuntimeException - if the exponent is negative.

setNumerator

```
public void setNumerator(int numerator)
```

A mutator of the numerator of this fraction.

Parameters:

numerator - the new numerator.

getNumerator

```
public int getNumerator()
```

An accessor to the numerator of this fraction.

Returns:

the numerator of this fraction.

setDenominator

```
    public void setDenominator(int denominator)
```

A mutator for the denominator of this fraction.

Parameters:

denominator - the new denominator.

getDenominator

```
    public int getDenominator()
```

An accessor to the denominator of this fraction.

Returns:

the denominator of this fraction.

setFraction

```
    public void setFraction(int numerator,
```
                int denominator)

A mutator for this fraction.

Parameters:

numerator - the new numerator of the fraction.

denominator - the new denominator of the fraction.

setFraction

```
    public void setFraction(Fraction other)
```

A mutator for this fraction.

Parameters:

other - the fraction whose numerator and denominator will become those of this fraction.

setSeparator

```
    public boolean setSeparator(char newSeparator)
```

A mutator of the separator of this fraction. The separator must not be a letter or a digit.

Parameters:

newSeparator - the new separator.

Returns:

true if the change was made (i.e. if the passed parameter is neither a letter nor a digit), and return false otherwise.

getSeparator

```
public char getSeparator()
```

An accessor to the separator of this fraction.

Returns:

the separator of this fraction.

toString

```
public String toString()
```

Return a string representation of this fraction. Note that the literal "NaF" (Not A Fraction) is returned if the denominator is zero to indicate that this is not a valid fraction.

Overrides:

toString in class Object.

Returns:

the numerator and denominator of this fraction separated by separator.

toProperString

```
public String toProperString()
```

Return this fraction as a proper fraction. Note that the literal "NaF" (Not A Fraction) is returned if the denominator is zero to indicate that this is not a valid fraction.

Returns:

a string representation of of this fraction in the form:

w n/d

where w is a whole number and n < d. The n/d part and the space that precedes it are not present if the numerator of this fraction is divisible by its denominator. The return is surrounded by double quotes if isQuoted is true.

equals

```
public boolean equals(Object other)
```

Determine if this fraction is the same as the passed one. Two fractions are considered equal if they have the same numerator and denominator (in reduced form).

Overrides:

equals in class Object

Parameters:

other - a reference to the object to test equality with.

Returns:

true if other is not null and points to a fraction that is equal to this one. The return is false otherwise. Note that all zero-denominator fractions are considered equal.

hashCode

```
public int hashCode()
```

Compute a hash code for this Fraction.

Overrides:

hashCode in class Object

Returns:

a hash code value for this object.

resembles

```
public boolean resembles(Fraction other)
```

Determine if this fraction resembles the passed one. Two fractions are said to resemble each other if they have a common denominator.

Parameters:

other - a reference to the object to test resemblance with.

Returns:

true if other is not null and does resemble this object. The return is false otherwise.

getRandom

```
public static Fraction getRandom()
```

Create a random fraction. The numerators and denominators of the created fractions are uniformly distributed in [0,1000) but no zero-denominator fraction is generated.

This method was added for pedagogical reasons.

Returns:

a randomly chosen fraction.

setSeed

```
public static void setSeed(int seed)
```

Change the seed of the random sequence returned by getRandom(). This method is meant to be used by a test harness so that the same sequence can be generated for the app being tested and its oracle.

Parameters:

seed - the initial seed for random number generator.

cloneMe

```
public Fraction cloneMe()
```

Copy the state of this object.

Returns:

a reference to a new Fraction object having exactly the same state as this one.

compareTo

```
public int compareTo(Fraction other)
```

Compare this object with the specified object for order. Return a negative integer, zero, or a positive integer if this object is less than, equal to, or greater than the specified object.

Specified by:

compareTo in interface Comparable<Fraction>

Parameters:

other - the Object to compare to.

Returns:

-1 if this fraction is less than the passed one, +1 if it is greater, and 0 if they are equal. Note that all zero-denominator fractions are considered equal and greater than any other fraction.

FRESH

Class Fresh
extends Item implements Serializable

This class encapsulates a fresh item. It differs from an ordinary item in that it has an expiry date.

– Constructors:

Fresh

```
public Fresh(String number,
             String name,
             double price,
             Date expiry)
```

Construct a fresh inventory item with the given number, name, selling price per unit, and expiry date, and a zero opening stock quantity.

Parameters:

number - the item number.

name - the name of the item.

price - the selling price per unit of the item.

expiry - the date on which the item will expire.

Throws:

RuntimeException - if any of the passed parameters is null.

– Methods:

getExpiry

```
public Date getExpiry()
```

Determine the expiry date of this Item.

Returns:

a copy of the expiry date of this item.

toString

```
public String toString()
```

Construct a string representation of this item.

Overrides:

toString in class Item

Returns:

the string: "Fresh Item# xxxxxx name", where xxxxxx is the item number and name is its name.

equals

```
public boolean equals(Object other)
```

Test the equality of items. An object is considered equal to this item if it is a Fresh object with the same number and expiry date as this one.

Overrides:

equals in class Item

Parameters:

other - a reference to the object to test equality with.

Returns:

true if other is not null and it points to an object that is equal (as defined above) to this object. The return is false otherwise.

GLOBALCREDIT

```
                    Class GlobalCredit
  extends Object implements Serializable, Iterable<CreditCard>
```

This class encapsulates the credit card operations of a Global Credit Centre (GCC), a regional card processing centre of the Global Credit bank. It maintains a collection of credit cards and provides services for traversal and content addressing. You can access the contents of the collection using an iterator.

The collection encapsulated by this class is an example of dynamic allocation; i.e. it can grow and shrink as needed.

– Constructors:

GlobalCredit

```
public GlobalCredit(String name)
```

Construct a GCC having the passed name.

Parameters:

name - the name (typically city name) of this GCC.

GlobalCredit

```
public GlobalCredit()
```

Construct a GCC having the name "NoName".

– Methods:

add

```
public boolean add(CreditCard card)
```

Attempt to add the passed credit card to this GCC. If a card of the same number is already present, no addition is done.

Parameters:

card - a reference to the card to be added.

Returns:

true if the card was added and false if not. The card is not added if a card with the same number has already been added.

Throws:

RuntimeException - if the passed parameter is null.

remove

```
public CreditCard remove(String number)
```

Remove the card whose number is passed from this GCC.

Parameters:

number - the number of the card to remove.

Returns:

the removed credit card or null if there is no card with such a number in the GCC.

get

```
public CreditCard get(String number)
```

Find the card whose number is passed.

Parameters:

number - the number of the card to find.

Returns:

a reference to the card whose number is passed. If the card is not found in the collection, or if the passed number is null, then null is returned.

size

```
public int size()
```

Determine the number of credit cards registered with this GCC.

Returns:

the number of credit cards that were added to this GCC.

toString

```
public String toString()
```

Return a string representation of this GCC.

Overrides:

toString in class Object

Returns:

the string "Global Credit Company [title]: CARDS=xx" , where title is the GCC's name and xx is the actual number of cards in the collection.

iterator

```
public Iterator<CreditCard> iterator()
```

Determine an Iterator over the credit cards in this centre.

Specified by:

iterator in interface Iterable<CreditCard>

Returns:

an Iterator over the credit cards.

getRandom

```
public static GlobalCredit getRandom()
```

Create a randomly chosen GCC. This is a convenience method whose invocation is equivalent to invoking `getRandom(false)`.

Returns:

a randomly generated GCC.

getRandom

```
public static GlobalCredit getRandom(boolean same)
```

Create a randomly chosen GCC. The GCC has no-name and contains anywhere between 2 and 20 credit cards (the count is uniformly distributed between 2 and 20). One of the cards has the number "123456-6"; otherwise, the cards have randomly chosen-numbers, random balances, random expiry dates, and "Random" as the cardholder name. On average, 25% of the cards are reward cards. You should normally invoke this method with a false parameter. The parameter was added to allow a harness to pass the same test cases to an app being tested and to an oracle.

This method was added for pedagogical reasons.

Parameters:

same - a flag that determines if a new GCC is to be generated (when false) or if a reference to the last-generated GCC should be returned (true). You should normally set it to false to get a different GCC per invocation.

Returns:

a GCC that is either randomly generated (if same is false) or is the same as the one last generated by this method. If this method was never invoked before, a random GCC is returned regardless of the passed parameter.

ITSTUDENT

Class ITstudent
extends Student implements Serializable, Iterable<String>

Provide services to maintain information about an IT (information technology) student. The class encapsulates the same information and functionality as Student except for three differences: the ID is auto-assigned serially (starting from 200105001 and ending at 200105999), the return of the toString method is prefixed by "IT", and the GPA is 10-based rather than 5-based; i.e. it is twice that of the Student class.

– Constructors:

ITstudent

```
public ITstudent(String name)
```

Create an IT student having the given name, and assigns it a serial 3-digit ID prefixed by "200105" and an empty (fresh) record.
Parameters:
name - the name of the IT student.

– Methods:

getGpa

```
public double getGpa()
```

Determine the grade-point-average (GPA) of this student. The GPA is computed based on twice the weights attached to grades in the Student class; i.e. they are out of 10, not 5.
Overrides:
getGpa in class Student
Returns:
the base-10 grade-point-average of this student.

toString

```
public String toString()
```

Return a string representation of this student.

Overrides:

toString in class Student

Returns:

the string "IT student: " followed by the student's name.

ITEM

```
                        Class Item
    extends Object implements Serializable, Comparable<Item>
```

This class encapsulates a stock item. Each item is characterized by a unique number, name, and sale price (per unit). The class provides methods for processing purchase and sale transactions and keeps track of their overall quantity and amount.

– Constructors:

Item

```
public Item(String number,
            String name,
            double price)
```

Construct an inventory item with the given number, name, and sale price per unit. The cost price and opening stock quantity are initialized to zero.

Parameters:

number - the item number.

name - the name of the item.

price - the sale price per unit of the item.

Throws:

RuntimeException - if the name or number is null or if the price is negative.

− Methods:

getNumber

```
public String getNumber()
```

Determine the number of this item.
Returns:
the name of this item.

getName

```
public String getName()
```

Determine the name of this item.
Returns:
the name of this item.

getStock

```
public int getStock()
```

Determine the stock quantity of this item.
Returns:
the stock quantity of this item.

getUnitCost

```
public double getUnitCost()
```

Determine the cost per unit of this item. This price is computed by dividing the total purchases amount by the total number of purchased units.
Returns:
the cost per unit of this item.

setUnitPrice

```
public boolean setUnitPrice(double price)
```

Change the posted sale price per unit of this item.
Parameters:

price - the new sale price per unit of the item.

Returns:

true if the price is changed and false otherwise. The price is changed only if the passed parameter is not negative.

getUnitPrice

```
public double getUnitPrice()
```

Determine the sale price per unit of this item.

Returns:

the posted sale price per unit of this item.

getSoldQty

```
public int getSoldQty()
```

Determine the total number of units sold from this item.

Returns:

the total number of units sold from this item.

getSales

```
public double getSales()
```

Determine the overall sales amount of this item.

Returns:

the overall sales amount of this item.

getPurchasedQty

```
public int getPurchasedQty()
```

Determine the total number of units purchased from this item.

Returns:

the total number of units purchased from this item.

getPurchases

```
public double getPurchases()
```

Determine the overall purchases amount of this item.

Returns:

the overall purchases amount of this item.

sell

```
    public boolean sell(int qty)
```

Sell the indicated number of units from this item at the posted sale price. This convenience method has the same effect as invoking the 2-parameter version with getUnitPrice()*qty as amount. The sale request fails if there is not enough quantity in stock.

Parameters:

qty - the sold quantity.

Returns:

true if the sale was processed and false if it failed.

sell

```
    public boolean sell(int qty,
                    double amount)
```

Sell the indicated number of units from this item for the indicated sale amount. The method allows you to specify the total sale amount so that discounts, shipping, and other charges can be incorporated. If the sale is ordinary, i.e. at the posted sale price, use the more convenient one-parameter version of this method. The sale request fails if there is not enough quantity in stock.

Parameters:

qty - the sold quantity.

amount - the sale amount for the entire quantity qty.

Returns:

true if the sale was processed and false if it failed.

purchase

```
    public void purchase(int qty,
                        double amount)
```

Purchase the indicated number of units from this item for the indicated purchase amount.

Parameters:

qty - the purchased quantity.

amount - the purchase amount for the entire quantity qty.

toString

```
public String toString()
```

Construct a string representation of this item.

Overrides:

toString in class Object

Returns:

the string: "Item# xxx name", where xxx is the item number and name is its name.

equals

```
public boolean equals(Object other)
```

Test the equality of items. An object is considered equal to this item if it is an Item object with the same number as this one.

Overrides:

equals in class Object

Parameters:

other - a reference to the object to test equality with.

Returns:

true if other is not null and it points to an object that is equal (as defined above) to this object. The return is false otherwise.

hashCode

```
public int hashCode()
```

Compute a hash code for this Item.

Overrides:

hashCode in class Object

Returns:

a hash code value for this object.

compareTo

```
public int compareTo(Item other)
```

Compares this object with the specified object for order. Returns a negative integer, zero, or a positive integer as this object is less than, equal to, or greater than the specified object.

Specified by:

compareTo in interface Comparable<Item>

Parameters:

other - the Object to compare to.

Returns:

the same return as that of compareTo(String) in String when invoked on the toString of this item.

MPRO

```
Class MPro
extends Object
```

This class encapsulates a mortgage. An instance of this class is characterized by a principle amount, an amortization period measured in years, and an annual interest rate expressed as a percent. The state of any instance has a positive principle, an amortization period in [AMORT_MIN,AMORT_MAX], and an interest rate percent in [0, INTEREST_MAX].

– Fields:

AMORT_MIN

```
public static final int AMORT_MIN
```

The minimum amortization period allowed.

See Also:

Constant Field Values

AMORT_MAX

```
public static final int AMORT_MAX
```

The maximum amortization period allowed.

See Also:

Constant Field Values

INTEREST_MAX

    public static final int INTEREST_MAX

The maximum interest rate percent allowed.

See Also:

Constant Field Values

EPSILON

    public static final double EPSILON

A small number that sets the resolution in this class such that any real number less than it in absolute value is deemed to be zero.

See Also:

Constant Field Values

— Constructors:

MPro

    public MPro(String p,
                String a,
                String i)

Construct an instance having the given principle, amortization, and interest.

Parameters:

p - the principle amount

a - the amortization period

i - the rate

Throws:

RuntimeException - if the parameters are not numeric, if p is not positive, a is not in [AMORT_MIN,AMORT_MAX], or i is not in [0, INTEREST_MAX].

MPro

    public MPro(String p,
                String i)

Construct an instance having the given principle and interest and a default amortization as set in AMORT_MAX

Parameters:

p - the principle amount

i - the rate

Throws:

RuntimeException - if the parameters are not numeric or if p is not positive or i is not in [0, INTEREST_MAX].

MPro

```
public MPro()
```

Construct an instance having zero principle, AMORT_MIN amortization, and zero interest.

─ Methods:

getPrinciple

```
public String getPrinciple()
```

The principle accessor.

Returns:

the principle amount.

getAmortization

```
public String getAmortization()
```

The amortization accessor.

Returns:

the amortization period.

getInterest

```
public String getInterest()
```

The interest accessor.

Returns:

the interest rate percent.

setPrinciple

```
public void setPrinciple(String p)
```

The principle mutator.

Parameters:

p - the principle amount

Throws:

RuntimeException - if p is not numeric or not positive.

setAmortization

```
public void setAmortization(String a)
```

The amortization mutator.

Parameters:

a - the amortization period.

Throws:

RuntimeException - if a is not numeric or not in [AMORT_MIN,AMORT_MAX].

setInterest

```
public void setInterest(String i)
```

The interest mutator.

Parameters:

i - the rate

Throws:

RuntimeException - if i is not numeric or not in [0, INTEREST_MAX].

computePayment

```
public String computePayment(String format)
```

Compute the monthly payment.

Parameters:

format - the format specifier.

Returns:

the computed monthly payment formatted as per the given specifier.

outstandingAfter

```
public String outstandingAfter(int years,
                                    String format)
```

Compute the balance that is still outstanding after the given number of years.

Parameters:

years - the number of years since the mortgage started.

format - the format specifier.

Returns:

the computed balance formatted as per the given specifier.

toString

```
public String toString()
```

Return a textual representation of this instance.

Overrides:

toString in class Object

Returns:

the string "MPro instance with principle=..., amortization=..., interest=...";

equals

```
public boolean equals(MPro other)
```

Determine if this instance is equal to the given instance. Two instances are deemed equal if they have the same amortization period and their principles and interest rates differ in magnitude by less than EPSILON.

Parameters:

other - the given instance

Returns:

true if the state of this instance is the equal to the given one and return false otherwise.

MixedNumber

> ## Class MixedNumber
> ## extends Fraction implements Serializable, Comparable<Fraction>

This class encapsulates a mixed number. A mixed number created by this class has four attributes: a sign s, a whole part w, a proper numerator n, and a proper denominator d; where s is +1 or -1; w, n, d are *unsigned* integers; and n<d (i.e. the fraction is *proper*). The corresponding rational value of the mixed number is s*(w+n/d) or the fraction s*(wd+n)/d.

The class derives all its features from its superclass, Fraction, because any mixed number is a (possibly improper) fraction. The case of zero denominator is handled the same as in Fraction (see its API for details). In particular, if a string representation of a zero-denominator mixed number is requested, the literal NaMN (Not a Mixed Number) is returned.

– Constructors:

MixedNumber

```
public MixedNumber()
```

Construct a default mixed number with sign +1, whole part equal to 0, numerator equal to zero, and denominator equal to 1. The rational value of the constructed mixed number is, thus, zero.

MixedNumber

```
public MixedNumber(MixedNumber mixed)
```

Construct a copy of the passed mixed number.

Parameters:

mixed - the mixed number to copy.

MixedNumber

```
public MixedNumber(int s,
                   int w,
                   int n,
                   int d)
```

Construct a mixed number having the passed sign, whole part proper numerator, and proper denominator.

Parameters:

s - the sign of the mixed number. Must be +1 or -1.

w - the whole part of the mixed number. Must be non-negative.

n - the proper numerator of the mixed number to construct. Must be non-negative.

d - the proper denominator of the mixed number to construct. Must be non-negative.

Throws:

RuntimeException - if any of the passed parameters is not valid as specified above.

— Methods:

getSign

```
public int getSign()
```

Determine and return the sign of this mixed number.

Returns:

the sign of this mixed number. The return is +1 is the mixed number is positive or zero, and -1 if the mixed number is negative.

getWhole

```
public int getWhole()
```

An accessor to the whole part of this mixed number.

Returns:

the whole part of this mixed number. The return is always non-negative.

getProperNumerator

```
public int getProperNumerator()
```

An accessor to the proper numerator of this mixed number.

Returns:

the numerator of this mixed number. The return is always non-negative.

getProperDenominator

```
public int getProperDenominator()
```

An accessor to the proper denominator of this mixed number.

Returns:

the denominator of this mixed number. The return is always non-negative.

toString

```
public String toString()
```

Determine and return a string representation of this mixed number.

Overrides:

toString in class Fraction

Returns:

the string "+" or "-" depending on the sign of this mixed number, followed by a space, followed by its whole part, followed by a space, followed by the proper numerator and poper denominator separated by a slash. Note however that if the proper denominator is zero, the literal NaMN is returned.

resembles

```
public boolean resembles(MixedNumber other)
```

Determine if this mixed number resembles the passed one. Two mixed numbers are said to resemble each other if they have the same whole part.

Parameters:

other - a reference to the object to test resemblance with.

Returns:

true if other is not null and does resemble this object. The return is false otherwise.

getRandom

```
public static Fraction getRandom()
```

Create a random mixed number with a randomly selected sign and with a whole part, proper numerator, and denominator uniformly distributed in [0,1000) (but no zero-denominator mixed number is generated). The return is a MixedNumber instance 50% of the times. In the remaining 50%, the return is supplied by the getRandom method of the Fraction superclass.

This method was added for pedagogical reasons.

Returns:

a randomly chosen fraction.

MONEY

> ### Class Money
> ### extends MixedNumber implements Serializable, Comparable<Fraction>

This class encapsulates an amount of money. The amount has three attributes: an overall sign and a dollar / cent amounts (both are unsigned integers).

The class derives all its features from its superclass, MixedNumber, because any amount of money is a mixed number having the same sign, a whole part equal to the dollar amount, a proper numerator equal to the cent amount, and a proper denominator of 100. The case of division by zero is handled the same as in the superclass. In particular, if a string representation of an amount with a zero-denominator is requested, the literal NaM (*Not a Money*) is returned.

– Constructors:

Money

```
public Money()
```
Construct a default money amount of +1 dollar and zero cents.

Money

```
public Money(Money money)
```
Construct a copy of the passed Money object.
Parameters:
money - the Money object to copy.

Money

```
public Money(double m)
```

Construct a money amount having the passed real number value. The passed value is rounded to two decimals using IO.format(String, String) and the dollar and cent parts are then extracted.

Parameters:

m - the real value of the money amount to construct.

Money

```
public Money(int s,
             int d,
             int c)
```

Construct a money amount having the passed sign, dollar amount, and cent amount.

Parameters:

s - the sign of the money amount. Must be +1 or -1.

d - the dollar amount. Must be non-negative.

c - the cent amount. Must be non-negative.

Throws:

RuntimeException - if any of the passed parameters is not valid as specified above.

– Methods:

getDollar

```
public int getDollar()
```

An accessor to the dollar amount of this money amount.

Returns:

the dollar amount of this money amount.

getCent

```
public int getCent()
```

An accessor to the cent amount of this money amount.

Returns:

the cent amount of this money amount.

toString

```
public String toString()
```

Determine and return a string representation of this money amount.

Overrides:

toString in class MixedNumber

Returns:

the amount expressed as the following string: If the amount is negative, the string begins with "(minus) $", otherwise it begins with "$". This is followed by the dollar amount (with thousand separators) followed by " dollars and ", and then the cent amount followed by " cents.". Note however that if the amount involves division by zero, the literal NaM is returned.

resembles

```
public boolean resembles(Money other)
```

Determine if this money object resembles the passed one. Two money objects are said to resemble each other if their cent amounts can be expressed using the same number of quarters (25-cent coin). In other words, the quotient of dividing the cent amount by 25 should be the same for both.

Parameters:

other - a reference to the object to test resemblance with.

Returns:

true if other is not null and does resemble this object. The return is false otherwise.

getRandom

```
public static Fraction getRandom()
```

Create a random fraction. The return is a Money instance 50% of the times. In the remaining 50%, the return is supplied by the getRandom method of the MixedNumber superclass; i.e. the return is an instance of Money with a probability of 0.5, of MixedNumberwith a probability of 0.25, and of Fraction with a probability of 0.25. The Money instances are uniformly distributed in [1000,3000).

This method was added for pedagogical reasons.

Returns:

a randomly chosen fraction.

REWARDCARD

> ### Class RewardCard
> ### extends CreditCard implements Serializable

This class encapsulates a special kind of credit card that is similar to CreditCard except it offers reward points. In addition to the dollar balance of an ordinary credit card, this card has a point balance such that whenever a purchase is charged to the card, a certain number of reward points is added to the point balance. Similarly, if the holder returned a purchase for refund, the point balance would be reduced by the same rate. The accumulated points can be redeemed for free merchandise.

− Fields:

DEFAULT_LIMIT

`public static final double DEFAULT_LIMIT`

The default credit limit used by the two-argument constructor.

See Also:

Constant Field Values

REWARD_RATE

`public static final int REWARD_RATE`

The rate used to compute the number of reward points. When a purchase is charged, one reward point is given for every REWARD_RATE dollars spent. And when a return is made, one reward point is taken back for every REWARD_RATE dollars returned.

See Also:

Constant Field Values

– Constructors:

RewardCard

```
public RewardCard(int no,
                  String aName,
                  double aLimit)
```

Construct a reward credit card having the passed number, holder name and credit limit and set its initial dollar and point balances to zero. See the corresponding superclass constructor for precondition details.

Parameters:

no - the credit card number, must be > 0 and ≤ 999999

aName - the name of the holder of this card, must have at least CreditCard.MIN_NAME_LENGTH characters

aLimit - the credit limit, must be positive

RewardCard

```
public RewardCard(int no,
                  String aName)
```

Construct a reward card having the passed number and holder name, and set its initial dollar and point balances to zero. Invoking this constructor has the same effect as invoking the three-parameter constructor but using CreditCard.DEFAULT_LIMIT for the credit limit.

Parameters:

no - the credit card number, must be > 0 and ≤ 999999

aName - the name of the holder of this card, must have at least CreditCard.MIN_NAME_LENGTH characters

– Methods:

getPointBalance

```
public int getPointBalance()
```

Return the number of reward points accumulated on this reward card.

Returns:

the point balance of this reward card.

charge

```
public boolean charge(double amount)
```

Attempt to charge this card. Same behavior as the overridden method except the point balance is increased (if the charge succeeded) at the rate of 1 point per REWARD_RATE.
Overrides:
charge in class CreditCard
Parameters:
amount - the charge amount
Returns:
true if successful and false if such a charge exceeds the available credit.

credit

```
public void credit(double amount)
```

Credit the credit card (decrease its dollar balance) by the passed amount. Same behavior as the overridden method except the point balance is decreased (possibly making it negative) at the rate of 1 point per REWARD_RATE.
Overrides:
credit in class CreditCard
Parameters:
amount - the amount to be credited.

redeem

```
public void redeem(int point)
```

Redeem the passed number of points and reduce the point balance accordingly. This method is invoked when the card holder exchanges reward points for free merchandise.
Parameters:
point - the number of reward points to redeem.
Throws:
RuntimeException - if point is negative or more than the point balance.

toString

    public String toString()

Return a string representation of this card.

Overrides:

toString in class CreditCard

Returns:

the same string as the overridden method except the prefix "CARD" is replaced by "RWRD", and the reward point balance is shown; e.g.

RWRD [NO=001005-3, BALANCE=7634.12, POINTS=500]

isSimilar

    public boolean isSimilar(RewardCard other)

Test the similarity of two reward cards. A reward card object is considered similar to this one if it has the same dollar balance (to the nearest cent) and the same point balance as this one, regardless of card number. Even if the two cards have different numbers, this method considers them similar as long as the difference between their dollar balances is less than 0.01 and the difference between their point balances is zero.

Parameters:

other - a reference to the credit card object to test equality with.

Returns:

true if other is not null and it points to an object that is similar (as defined above) to is similar (as defined above) to this object, and false otherwise.

SESTUDENT

Class SEstudent
extends Student implements Serializable, Iterable<String>

Provide services to maintain information about a SE (software engineering) student. The class encapsulates the same information and functionality as Student except for two differences: the ID is auto-assigned serially (starting from 200107001 and ending at 200107999), and the return of the toString method is prefixed by "SE".

– Constructors:

SEstudent

```
public SEstudent(String name)
```

Create a SE student having the given name, and assigns it a serial 3-digit ID prefixed by "200107" and an empty (fresh) record.

Parameters:

name - the name of the SE student.

– Methods:

toString

```
public String toString()
```

Return a string representation of this student.

Overrides:

toString in class Student

Returns:

the string "SE student: " followed by the student's name.

STOCK

```
Class Stock
extends Object implements Serializable
```

This class encapsulates a stock. It holds attributes relevant to a stock; such as its symbol, name, and last-traded price; and refreshes them on demand. In addition to standard methods (toString and equals), the class provides accessors for all, and mutators for some, of its attributes. The stock price is updated automatically when the stock is first created or when the symbol is mutated; and it can also be updated manually via the refresh() method.

The class simulates two kinds of stock exchanges:

- A simple exchange made up of 26 static stocks with symbols HR.L, where L is any letter in the alphabet. The class assigns fixed names and prices to these stocks, which makes this exchange suitable for conducting reproducible tests.

- A realistic exchange made up of 676 dynamic stocks with symbols .LL (a dot followed by two letters). The class assigns fixed names to these stocks and prices that are functions of real time.

– Fields:

name

```
public String name
```

The name of this stock as listed on the exchange. If no such stock exists, the name is set to null.

(Bad design --this field should not be made public.)

delimiter

```
public char delimiter
```

This field determines what character is inserted between the stock symbol and its name in the return of the toString() method (assuming the symbol exists). The default is space.

(Bad design --should have been kept private. Access would have still been possible via the existing public accessor and mutator.)

titleCaseName

```
public static boolean titleCaseName
```

This field controls the format of the stock name as returned by the getName() method. If set to false (default), the name is returned exactly as listed on the exchange. Otherwise, it is returned in title case (1st letter of each word capitalized).

– Constructors:

Stock

```
    public Stock()
```
Construct a default Stock having a null symbol. This convenience constructor has the same effect as passing null to the 1-parameter, overloaded constructor.

Stock

```
    public Stock(String symbol)
```
Construct a Stock having the (capitalized) passed symbol. All of the stock attributes will be set as per the refresh() method.
Parameters:
symbol - the (ticker) symbol of the stock to construct.

Stock

```
    public Stock(Stock stock)
```
Construct a copy of the passed Stock.
Parameters:
stock - the Stock to copy.
Throws:
RuntimeException - if stock = null

– Methods:

getName

```
    public String getName()
```
Determine the name of this Stock as listed on the exchange. The letter case is as indicated in the titleCaseName field.
Returns:
the name of this Stock. If no such stock exists, null is returned.

getSymbol

```
    public String getSymbol()
```
Determine the symbol of this Stock.
Returns:

the symbol of this Stock.

getPrice

```
public double getPrice()
```

Determine the price of this Stock.

Returns:

the price of this Stock as last obtained from the exchange.

getDelimiter

```
public char getDelimiter()
```

Determine the delimiter of this Stock.

Returns:

the delimiter of this Stock.

setDelimiter

```
public boolean setDelimiter(char myDelimiter)
```

Mutator to change the delimiter of this stock to the passed one. No change is made, however, if the passed delimiter is a letter or a digit.

Parameters:

myDelimiter - the new delimiter character

Returns:

true if the change was made (i.e. if the passed parameter is neither a letter nor a digit), and return false otherwise.

setSymbol

```
public void setSymbol(String symbol)
```

Mutator to change the symbol of this stock to the (capitalized) passed symbol. The stock attributes are re-set as per the refresh() method.

Parameters:

symbol - the symbol to change to.

toString

```
public String toString()
```

Construct a string representation of this Stock.

Overrides:

toString in class Object

Returns:

the stock's symbol (capitalized), followed by the delimiter character, followed by the stock's name. However if the symbol doesn't exist, the string "No such stock!" is returned.

equals

```
public boolean equals(Object other)
```

Test the equality of stock objects. An object is considered equal to this one if it is a stock object with the same symbol as this one.

Overrides:

equals in class Object

Parameters:

other - a reference to the object to test equality with.

Returns:

true if other is not null and it points to an object that is equal (as defined above) to this object. The return is false otherwise.

hashCode

```
public int hashCode()
```

Compute a hash code for this Stock.

Overrides:

hashCode in class Object

Returns:

a hash code value for this object.

refresh

```
public void refresh()
```

Connect to the exchange and obtain the name and price of this stock and update its attributes accordingly. If the symbol is null or is not listed on the exchange, the name is set to null and its price to 0.

cloneMe

```
public Stock cloneMe()
```

Copy the state of this object.

Returns:

a reference to a new Stock object having exactly the state as this one.

STUDENT

```
                    Class Student
    extends Object implements Serializable, Iterable<String>
```

Provide services to maintain information about an electrical engineering and computer science (EECS) student and his or her academic record. The record is very concise consisting of the course number (4 digits) of each EECS course the student has taken and the letter grade (A,B,C,D,E,F) that was obtained in it. The record does not include non-EECS courses, does not keep track of when the course was taken, and keeps only the last grade if a course is taken more than once; i.e. there is only one grade per course.

‒ Constructors:

Student

```
public Student(String id,
               String name)
```

Create an EECS student having the given ID and name, and an empty (fresh) record.

Parameters:

id - a 9-digit ID# of the student

name - the name of the student.

Throws:

RuntimeException - if the given ID is not a 9-digit string.

– Methods:

getID

```
public String getID()
```

Determine the ID of this student.

Returns:

the ID of this student.

getName

```
public String getName()
```

Determine the name of this student.

Returns:

the name of this student.

iterator

```
public Iterator<String> iterator()
```

Determine an Iterator over the course numbers in the record of this student. The iterator does not support the remove operation.

Specified by:

iterator in interface Iterable<String>

Returns:

an Iterator over the courses.

getCourseGrade

```
public String getCourseGrade(String course)
```

Determine the grade of this student in the given course.

Parameters:

course - the given 4-digit course number.

Returns:

the grade that this student has achieved in the given course. If the given course does not appear in the student's record, null is returned.

setCourseGrade

```
public boolean setCourseGrade(String course,
                              String grade)
```

Update the student's record by indicating in it that the student has obtained the given grade in the given course. Note that if the given course number is already present in the student's record then the given grade overwrites the existing one, thereby keeping only the grade of the latest attempt. In either case, the given letter grade is converted to upper case before updating the record.

Parameters:

course - the given 4-digit course number.

grade - the given 1-letter grade.

Returns:

true if the record was updated as requested and return false otherwise. The record will not be updated if the given course number is not made up of exactly 4 digits or if the given letter grade is not one of the letters (A,B,C,D,E,F) in capital or small-case.

equals

```
public boolean equals(Object other)
```

Test the equality of students. An object is considered equal to this one if it is indeed a student object with the same ID number as this one.

Overrides:

equals in class Object

Parameters:

other - a reference to the object to test equality with.

Returns:

true if other is not null and it points to an object that is equal (as defined above) to this object, and false otherwise.

hashCode

```
public int hashCode()
```

Compute a hash code for this student.

Overrides:

hashCode in class Object

Returns:

a hash code value for this object.

getGpa

```
public double getGpa()
```

Determine the grade-point-average (GPA) of this student. The GPA is computed assuming all courses have equal weights and that A has 5 points and F has zero.

Returns:

the grade-point-average of this student.

toString

```
public String toString()
```

Return a string representation of this student.

Overrides:

toString in class Object

Returns:

the string "EECS student: " followed by the student's name.

getRandom

```
public static Student getRandom()
```

Create a randomly chosen student. This is a convenience method whose invocation is equivalent to invoking getRandom(false).

Returns:

a randomly chosen student.

getRandom

```
public static Student getRandom(boolean same)
```

Create a random student having a random ID, a randomly chosen four-letter name, and a random academic record. The record consists of at least one and at most 25 courses having random course numbers and random letter grades.

The returned student is an **EECS** student (class Student) 40% of the times, a computer engineering student (class **CEstudent**) 20% of the times, a software engineering student (class **SEstudent**) 20% of the times, and an information technology student (class **ITstudent**)

20% of the times.

This method was added for pedagogical reasons.

Parameters:

same - a flag that determines if a new student is to be generated (if false) or if a reference to the last-generated student is to be returned (if true). You should normally set it to false to get a different student per invocation.

Returns:

a randomly chosen student.

setSeed

```
public static void setSeed(long seed)
```

Change the seed of the random sequence returned by getRandom(). This method is meant to be used by a test harness so that the same sequence can be generated for the app being tested and its oracle.

Parameters:

seed - the initial seed for random number generator.

SUPPLIER

```
Class Supplier
extends Contact implements Serializable, Comparable<Contact>
```

This class encapsulates a supplier. A supplier is a contact with a catalog listing all items it supplies and their prices.

This class aggregates the catalog map via a regular aggregation, not a composition.

– Constructors:

Supplier

```
public Supplier(String name,
                String address)
```

Construct a supplier having the indicated name and address, and assign a unique number and an empty catalog of type HashMap to it. Number assignment is handled by the superclass Contact.

Parameters:

name - the name of the supplier.

address - the address of the supplier.

Throws:

RuntimeException - if either parameter is null.

Supplier

```
public Supplier(String name,
                String address,
                Map<Item,Double> catalog)
```

Construct a supplier having the indicated name, address, and catalog, and assign a unique number to it.

Parameters:

name - the name of the supplier.

address - the address of the supplier.

catalog - the catalog of the supplier. A map containing an Item reference as key and its price as value.

Throws:

RuntimeException - if any of the parameters is null.

– Methods:

getCatalog

```
public Map<Item,Double> getCatalog()
```

Determine the catalog this supplier.

Returns:

the catalog of this supplier.

setCatalog

```
public void setCatalog(Map<Item,Double> catalog)
```

Set the catalog of this supplier to the passed one.

Parameters:

catalog - the catalog to mutate the state to.

TRX

```
                    Class Trx
    extends Object implements Serializable
```

This class encapsulates a transaction. A transaction has a date, a code, a reference number, a Contact, an Item, a quantity, and an amount.

This class aggregates Date, Contact, and Item via a regular aggregation, not a composition.

– Constructors:

Trx

```
public Trx(Date date,
           String code,
           String ref,
           Contact contact,
           Item item,
           int qty,
           double amount)
```

Construct a transaction having the passed parameters.

Parameters:

date - transaction date.

code - transaction code.

ref - transaction reference.

contact - transaction contact.

item - transaction item.

qty - transaction quantity.

amount - transaction amount.

− **Methods:**

getDate

    `public Date getDate()`

Determine the date of this transaction

Returns:

the date of this transaction.

getCode

    `public String getCode()`

Determine the code of this transaction

Returns:

the code of this transaction.

getRef

    `public String getRef()`

Determine the reference of this transaction

Returns:

the reference of this transaction.

getContact

    `public Contact getContact()`

Determine the contact of this transaction

Returns:

the contact of this transaction.

getItem

    `public Item getItem()`

Determine the item of this transaction

Returns:

the item of this transaction.

getQty

```
public int getQty()
```

Determine the quantity of this transaction

Returns:

the quantity of this transaction.

getAmount

```
public double getAmount()
```

Determine the amount of this transaction

Returns:

the amount of this transaction.

toString

```
public String toString()
```

Construct a string representation of this transaction.

Overrides:

toString in class Object

Returns:

the string: "TRX code=xxx, date=ddd", where xxx is the transaction code and ddd is its date.

UTILITY

```
                        Class Utility
                        extends Object
```

This class contains various utilities—all methods are static.

Refer to the Prof Roumani's textbooks for details.

− **Methods:**

crash

```
public static void crash(boolean condition,
                              String msg)
```

Test the passed condition and throw an exception if it is true. Otherwise do nothing. This is a convenience method to be used in lieu of an if and a throw statements.

Parameters:

condition - to test.

msg - a custom exception message.

Throws:

RuntimeException - (with the passed message)

repeat

```
public static String repeat(int count,
                                   char c)
```

Create a string containing the passed character repeated as many times as specified. If count is less than 1, a zero-length string is returned.

Parameters:

count - the number of repetitions.

c - the character to be repeated.

Returns:

a string containing count repetitions of c.

mortgagePayment

```
public static double mortgagePayment(double amount,
                                   double rate,
                                   int period)
```

Compute the monthly payment on a mortgage assuming constant payments and constant interest rate.

Parameters:

amount - the present value

rate - the interest rate as an annualized percent, i.e. pass 4.5 for 4.5%

period - the amortization period in years

Returns:

the monthly payment

Throws:

RuntimeException - if amount < 0, rate ≤ 0, or rate ≥ 100

getBMI

```
public static double getBMI(double weight,
                              String height)
```

Compute the body mass index.

Parameters:

weight - the weight in pounds. To be valid, weight must be positive.

height - the height in feet'inches. To be valid, height must have a feet component (a positive integer) optionally followed by an inches component (a non-negative integer less than 12). And if both components are present then they must be separated by a single quote.

Returns:

the body mass index (BMI) for the given weight and height

Throws:

RuntimeException - if either weight or height is not valid as defined above.

factorial

```
public static double factorial(int n)
```

Determine the factorial of the passed integer.

Parameters:

n - a non-negative integer

Returns:

the factorial of n, n!.

Throws:

RuntimeException - if n is negative.

gcd

```
public static int gcd(int a,
                        int b)
```

Determine the GCD (Greatest Common Divisor) of the two passed integers.

Parameters:

a - a positive integer.

b - a positive integer.

Returns:

GCD(a,b).

Throws:

RuntimeException - if either integer is not positive.

gf

```
public static int gf(int x)
```

Determine the Greatest Factor (GF) of the passed integer. A factor of a positive integer x is an integer in [1,x) that divides x evenly.

Parameters:

x - the positive integer to factor.

Returns:

the greatest factor of x.

Throws:

RuntimeException - if $x \leq 0$.

m2FtInch

```
public static String m2FtInch(double h)
```

Convert from meters to feet and inches.

Parameters:

h - the meter amount to be converted.

Returns:

the same amount in the format F'I" where F and I are the corresponding feet and inches. The inches are rounded to the nearest inch.

mark

```
public static double mark()
```

Mark the current time and determine the elapsed time since the last invocation.

Returns: the number of milliseconds that have elapsed since this method was called last.

INDEX